Richmond City, Virginia

Hustings Deed Book

1782–1790

Ruth and Sam Sparacio

HERITAGE BOOKS
2022

HERITAGE BOOKS
AN IMPRINT OF HERITAGE BOOKS, INC.

Books, CDs, and more—Worldwide

For our listing of thousands of titles see our website
at
www.HeritageBooks.com

Published 2022 by
HERITAGE BOOKS, INC.
Publishing Division
5810 Ruatan Street
Berwyn Heights, Md. 20740

International Standard Book Number
Paperbound: 978-1-68034-517-9

RICHMOND CITY, VIRGINIA
HUSTINGS DEEDS No. 1
1782-1792

p.   (On margin: RICHARDSON's Bond)

1   KNOW ALL MEN by these presents that we GEORGE RICHARDSON, WILLIAM RICHARDSON & ZACHARIAH ROWLAND are held and firmly bound unto WILLIAM FOUSHEE Mayor, WILLIAM HAY Recorder, JACQUELIN AMBLER, JOHN BECKLEY, ROBERT MITCHER (?) and JAMES HUNTER JR., Gent., Aldermen, And ISAAC YOUNG, Husband, RICHARD ADAMS, JAMES BUCHANAN, SAMUEL SHERER, ROBERT BOYD (?) & JOHN McKEAND, Common Councilmen of the City of Richmond in the sum of One thousand pounds to the payment whereof well and truly to be made to said Mayor, Recorder, Aldermen and Common Counmcilmen & their Successors we bind ourselves and each of us firmly by these presents; Sealed with our Seals this fifteenth day of July 1782 in the seventh year of the Commonwealth

THE CONDITION of the above Obligation is such that Whereas the above bound GEORGE RICHARDSON hath been appointed SERJEANT of the said City of Richmond, If therefore he shall truly and faithfully perform the duties of his Office according to Law & in all respects demean himself as a good Officer, then the above Obligation to be void otherwise to remain in full force and virtue

Sealed & Delivered in the presence of   GEO: RICHARDSON
      The Court   W: RICHARDSON
                                     ZACH: ROWLAND

At a Court held for the City of Richmond held at the Courthouse in the said City the 15th day of July 1782 This Bond was acknowledged by the Obligors & ordered to be recorded   Teste ADAM CRAIG C. C.

pp.   (On margin: WILLIAMS to BARR)

1-   THIS INDENTURE WITNESSETH that RICHARD WILLIAMS of the City of Richmond
2   hath put and by these presents doth put his Son, ISAAC WILLIAMS, of said City, an Apprentice to RICHARD BARR, Shoemaker, of the same place, to learn his art, trade and mistery, And after the manner of an Apprentice to serve RICHARD BARR from the day of the date hereof during the full term of seven years during all which time the said Apprentice his said Master faithfully shall serve and in all things behave himself as a faithfull Apprentice ought to do, And the said Master shall teach or cause to be taught or instructed the said Apprentice in the trade or mistery of Shoemaker and provide for him sufficient meat drink cloths washing and lodging fitting for an Apprentice and the Master shall also give the Apprentice one years Schooling and after the expiration of his apprenticeship shall furnish him a good and decent suit of new cloths. And for the true performance of all the covenants and agreements aforesaid, the parties bind themselves each unto the other firmly by these presents; In Witness whereof the parties have interchangeably set their hands & seals hereunto dated the (blank) day of (blank) in the year of our Lord one thousand seven hundred and Eighty three

Sealed and Delivered in the presence of
    (no witnesses recorded)   RICHARD WILLIAMS
                                  RICHARD BARR

At a Court of Hustings for the City of Richmond held at the Courthouse in the said City
the 16th day of June 1783   This Indenture was acknowledged by the parties & ordered
to be recorded   Teste ADAM CRAIG, C.C.

pp.   (On margin: BRAXTON to LOVE)
2-   TO ALL PERSONS to whom this present writing shall come, KNOW YE that I
4   CARTER BRAXTON of County of KING WILLIAM in the Commonwealth of Virginia,
         Merchant, for divers good causes and considerations me thereunto moving, & in
consideration of a large quantity of Tobacco which I owe & the (   ) of which in the City
of LONDON, It is my will and desire to make and secure ALEXANDER LOVE of the aforesaid
Commonwealth, Merchant, by these presents do make and appoint ALEXANDER LOVE to
be my true and lawful Attorney within the City of LONDON, in the Kingdom of Great
Britain irrevocable untill after the debt shall have been satisfied and paid off conformable to the terms of an agreement and entered into between me and the sd. ALEXAN-
DER now in my possession and bearing date the twenty eighth day of June last past to
ask require demand and receive to his own use from JACK POWER of LONDON Esquire all
sums of money as may be in the hands of said JACK POWER to me belonging or to which
I may have any manner of right and for the said money received, to sign seal and execute the said JACK or his Executors full and sufficient acquittance or discharge. I also
give and grant my Attorney full and absolute power and authority to sell and dispose of
all my (   ) of that Estate in the City of LONDON held by me as Tenant in Common with
MARY CLAIBORNE in fee simple or on such terms and conditions as to my Attorney shall
seem meet and convenient (there appears to be five more lines at the bottom of page 2 blurred
by what appears to be tape); And CARTER BRAXTON do by these presents bind myself my
heirs to ALEXANDER LOVE his Exors. in the sum of Three thousand pounds Sterling
money to be forfeited to be paid to the said ALEXANDER his Executors in case I shall or
do revoke this present Letter of Attorney or any authority therein given; In Witness
whereof I have hereunto set my hand and seal at the City of Richmond in Virginia this
first day of July Anno Dom; one thousand seven hundred and eighty three
Signed Sealed & Delivered in presence of
         ROBERT KING JR., JOHN STEWART,   CARTER BRAXTON
         NATHL· HERON, FLEMING JORDAN,
         ROBERT BAYNE
     MEMORANDUM: It is meant and intended by CARTER BRAXTON & so admitted and under-
stood by ALEXANDER LOVE that the Powers and authority by the annexed Letter of Attorney granted to said ALEXANDER shall not supercede or suspend those formerly granted
to JACK POWER Esqr. by said CARTER by Letter of Attorney impowering JACK POWER
Esqr. to sell the Estate in the annexed Deed mentioned
     Virginia 1st July 1793
Teste ROBERT KING JR. JOHN STEWART,   ALEXANR: LOVE
         NATHL. HERON, FLEMING JORDAN,   CARTER BRAXTON
         ROBERT BAINE
     At a Court of Hustings for the City of Richmond held at the Courthouse in the sd. City
the 21st day of July 1783. This Power of Attorney with the Memorandum thereon
endorsed was proved by the Oaths of NATHANIEL HERON & FLEMING JORDAN, two of the
witnesses thereto & ordered to be recorded
                         Teste ADAM CRAIG, C.C.

pp.   (On margin: HARRISON to DAVIS)
4-   TO ALL whom these presents may concern, I BENJAMIN HARRISON of BERKLEY
5   in CHARLES CITY County, Esquire, send Greeting; Whereas about forty years ago
        or upwards a certain JOHN COLES & NICHOLAS DAVIES agreed to purchase on
then joint account and for their joint benefit from WILLIAM BYRD Esqr., Father of the
late Honourable WILLIAM BYRD, Esquire, deceased, twelve acres of land in HENRICO
County and contiguous to the Town of Richmond, which purchase was accordingly
made by sd. JOHN COLES on the joint account of himself and the said NICHOLAS DAVIS
and the whole thereof conveyed by WILLIAM BYRD Esqr. to said JOHN COLES, who
afterwards made partition of said land between himself and said DAVIES by allotting six
acres thereof to said DAVIS as his sole property in fee simple and soon after died without having executed a Conveyance thereof to said DAVIES & Whereas the said DAVIES in
consequence of the purchase and partition entered upon and took possession of said six
acres of land allotted to him and afterwards sold one half acre thereof to my late Father,
BENJAMIN HARRISON of BERKLEY, Esquire, now deceased, and put him in possession
thereof by metes & bounds for a valuable consideration to him paid by said BENJAMIN
for the same, who on or about the year one thousand seven hundred and Forty five died
possessed of said half acre of land, whereby his equitable right thereto descended upon
and became vested in me, his Eldest Son and Heir at Law, and possession thereof by me
retained without disturbance untill a certain ROBERT BROWN of the City of Richmond
under pretence of a Deed for the same to him granted by the heirs and devisee of the
aforesaid JOHN COLES, has usurped a title to the said half acre of land; NOW KNOW YE
that for preventing all future litigation and controversy which might at any time
hereafter arise between me, the said BENJAMIN HARRISON, and said NICHOLAS DAVIS,
and between all persons claiming or to claim by through or under either of us
touching the said half acre of land so as aforesaid sold to my said Father, deceased, by
NICHOLAS DAVIS, I said BENJAMIN HARRISON in consideration of One shillings current
money of Virginia to me in hand paid by NICHOLAS DAVIS of BEDFORD County do by
these presents acquit discharge and release NICHOLAS DAVIS his heirs from all suits
actions at Law or in Equity which I or my heirs might at any time hereafter be in any
wise entitled to have against said NICHOLAS his heirs; In Witness whereof I have
herunto set my hand & seal at the City of Richmond this twenty first day of July in the
year of our Lord one thousand seven hundred and eighty three
Signed Sealed and Acknowledged before
        THOS. MERIWETHER,   BENJAMIN HARRISON
        ANDREW RONALD, JOHN CONNOR
    At a Court of Hustings for the City of Richmond held at the Courthouse in the said City
the 21st day of July 1783   This Indenture of Release was proved by the Oaths of THO-
MAS MERIWETHER, ANDREW RONALD & JOHN CONNOR, the witnesses thereto, & ordered
to be recorded   Teste ADAM CRAIG, C.C.

pp.   (On margin: SCHERER & Ux. to PADLEY)
5-   THIS INDENTURE made this eighteenth day of October in the year of our Lord
6   one thousand seven hundred and Eighty three Between SAMUEL SCHERER &
        HANNAH his Wife of City of Richmond of one part and THOMAS PADLEY of the
same place of the other part; Witnesseth that in consideration of the sum of Thirty five
pounds current money of Virginia by said THOMAS to said SAMUEL in hand paid by
these presents do bargain sell and confirm unto THOMAS PADLEY his heirs a certain
part of a lot of land lying in City of Richmond situate on the Main Street of said City and
running upon the South side thereof sixteen feet in front & back, from thence in a

direct line sixteen feet square which part of a lot of land lies between the Corner of said PADLEY's House and the Corner of a Store, the property of said SCHERER; at present in the occupation of MARCUS ELSON, and is used by said PADLEY as a Common entry into his lot lately purchased of JACOB THOMAS. And all houses gardens profits and appurtenances to the same belonging, and the rents issues and profits thereof; To have and to hold the premises with appurtenances unto THOMAS PADLEY his heirs; And SAMUEL SCHERER & his heirs the premises unto THOMAS PADLEY his heirs against the lawful claims and demands of all persons will warrant & forever defend by these presents; In Witness whereof the parties to these presents have hereunto interchangeably set their hands & affixed their seals the day & year first above written
Sealed & Delivered in the presence of

WILLIAM BARKER,   SAML: SCHERER
BERRY his mark X ROUNTREE   HANNAH SCHERER

At a Court of Hustings for the City of Richmond held at the Courthouse in the said City ye 20th day of Octr: 1783   This Indenture was acknowledged by SAMUEL SCHERER, one of the parties thereto & ordered to be recorded

Teste ADAM CRAIG, C.C.

pp.   (On margin: BYRD's Trustees to LYONS)
7-   THIS INDENTURE made this fifth day of May in the year of our Lord one thou-
8   sand seven hundred and Eighty three Between CHARLES CARTER of SHIRLEY in County of CHARLES CITY Esq., Surviving Trustee of the Honourable WILLIAM BYRD Esquire deceased, of one part and PETER LYONS of County of HANOVER of other part; Whereas the said WILLIAM BYRD did by his Deed of Record in the General Court convey certain lands & tenements unto the said CHARLES CARTER and others in Trust for the uses and purposes therein declared as by the said Deed may more fully appear; And Whereas the said WILLIAM BYRD and his Trustees did afterwards dispose of part of the land mentioned in said Deed by way of Lottery in which Lottery said PETER LYONS was an Adventurer and drew a Prize of one lot or half acre of land lying in Town of Richmond in County of HENRICO and distinguished in the plot of said Lottery Land by the number Six hundred and Fifty four; And CHARLES CARTER Esquire is by a late Act of Assembly impowered to convey the said Prize Lands & Lots to the persons intitled to them under said Lottery; NOW THEREFORE THIS INDENTURE Witnesseth that CHARLES CARTER, the Surviving Trustee of WILLIAM BYRD, by virtue of said Act of Assembly as well in consideration of the money paid by PETER LYONS for the Tickets he bought in said Lottery as for the sum of Five shillings to him said CHARLES CARTER in hand paid by PETER LYONS, by these presents doth bargain & sell unto PETER LYONS all that lot or half acre of land lying in Town of Richmond in County of HENRICO drawn by him as a Prize in said Lottery and distinguished by the number Six hundred and Fifty four with all buildings trees profits & appurtenances; To have and to hold the lot or half acre of land with the appurtenances unto PETER LYONS his heirs; In Witness whereof the parties to these presents have hereunto interchangeably set their hands and affixed their seals the day and year first above written
Sealed & Delivered in presence of

JAMES BUCHANAN,   CHAS: CARTER
ALEXR: BUCHANAN, JNO: McKEAND

Received of PETER LYONS the sum of Five shillings being the consideration money within mentioned to be by him paid to me this fifth day of May one thousand seven hundred and eighty three

Witness JAMES BUCHANAN. ALEXR. BUCHANAN,   CHARLES CARTER
SAMUEL WILLIAMSON, JOHN McKEAND

At a Court of Hustings for the City of Richmond held at the Courthouse in the said City the 19th day of August 1783.   This Indenture with the Receipt thereon endorsed was proved by the Oaths of JAMES BUCHANAN and ALEXANDER BUCHANAN, witnesses thereto: And at another Court of Hustings held for said City the 20th day of October following, the said Indenture & Receipt were further proved by the Oath of JOHN McKEAND, the other witness thereto, & ordered to be recorded
                    Teste ADAM CRAIG, C.C.

pp.   (On margin: BYRD's Trustees to ROBINSON's Admors.)
8-   THIS INDENTURE made this fifth day of May in the year of our Lord one thou-
9   sand seven hundred and eighty three Between CHARLES CARTER of SHIRLEY
         in the County of CHARLES CITY Esquire, Surviving Trustee of WILLIAM BYRD
Esquire, deceased, of one part & EDMUND PENDLETON & PETER LYONS, Esquires, Surviving Administrators of JOHN ROBINSON Esquire, deceased, of the other part; Whereas
WILLIAM BYRD did by his Deed of Record in the General Court convey certain lands and
tenements unto CHARLES CARTER & others in Trust for certain uses and purposes therein declared as by said Deed may more fully appear; And Whereas WILLIAM BYRD and
his Trustees did afterwards dispose of part of the land mentioned in the said Deed by
Lottery in which Lottery BERNARD MOORE Esquire, since deceased, was an Adventurer,
and having purchased a Ticket number Three thousand five hundred and fifty did draw
a prize of an Island distinguished in the plot of the Lottery Land by the number Three
hundred and Twenty one, which Ticket and Prize he assigned to EDMUND PENDLETON &
PETER LYONS, as Administrators of JOHN ROBINSON, to be by them sold for & towards discharging a Debt due from BERNARD MOORE to the Estate of said JOHN ROBINSON and delivered them the Ticket for the purpose aforesaid; And said CHARLES CARTER Esquire by a
late Act of Assembly impowered to convey the said Prize Lands, lots and Island to the
persons entitled to the same under the said Lottery, THIS INDENTURE THEREFORE WIT-
NESSETH that CHARLES CARTER as Surviving Trustee of said WILLIAM BYRD by virtue of
the said Act of Assembly in consideration of the premises & of the sum of Five shillings
to him in hand paid by EDMUND PENDLETON and PETER LYONS, by these presents doth
bargain sell and confirm unto EDMUND PENDLETON and PETER LYONS all that Island so
drawn by said BERNARD MOORE as a Prize in the Lottery aforesaid, lying in JAMES
RIVER within the Town of Richmond in the County of HENRICO, distinguished by the
number Three hundred and Twenty one, with all buildings trees profits and appurtenances of any sort thereto belonging; To have and to hold the Island & premises unto
EDMUND PENDLETON and PETER LYONS and the Survivor of them & his heirs to the uses
and purposes herein before mentioned; In Witness whereof the parties to these presents have hereunto interchangeably set their hands and affixed their seals the day
and year first above written
Sealed & Delivered in presence of
        JAMES BUCHANAN, ALEXR. BUCHANAN,   CHAS: CARTER
        SAMUEL WILLIAMSON,   JOHN McKEAND
  Received of EDMUND PENDLETON & PETER LYONS the sum of five shillings being the
consideration money within mentioned to be by them paid to me this fifth day of May
one thousand seven hundred and eighty three
Witness: JAMES BUCHANAN, ALEXR. BUCHANAN,   CHARLES CARTER
        SAMUEL WILLIAMSON.   JOHN McKEAND
  At a Court of Hustings for the City of Richmond held at the Courthouse in the said City
the 19th day of August 1783   This Indenture with the Receipt thereon endorsed were
proved by the Oaths of JAMES BUCHANAN. ALEXR: BUCHANAN, witnesses thereto; And at

a Court of Hustings held for the said City the 20th day of October following, the said Indenture and Receipt were further proved by the Oath of JOHN McKEAND another witness thereto & ordered to be recorded   Teste ADAM CRAIG, C. C.

pp.   (On margin: BYRD &c., to MATTHEWS &c.)
10-   THIS INDENTURE made this eighteenth day of July in the year of our Lord one
12   thousand seven hundred and Seventy three Between WILLIAM BYRD, PEYTON
             RANDOLPH, JOHN PAGE, CHARLES CARTER & CHARLES TURNBULL, Esquires, of
one part & SAMPSON MATTHEWS, GEORGE MATTHEWS and PATRICK LOCKHART of the
other part; Witnesseth that in consideration of the sum of Ten pounds current money of
Virginia to said WILLIAM BYRD, PEYTON RANDOLPH, JOHN PAGE, CHARLES CARTER and
CHARLES TURNBULL in hand paid by SAMPSON MATTHEWS, GEORGE MATTHEWS and
PATRICK LOCKHART by these presents do bargain sell and confirm unto SAMPSON
MATTHEWS, GEORGE MATTHEWS & PATRICK LOCKHART and their heirs one lot or half
acre of land lying in the Town of MANCHESTER in County of CHESTERFIELD, denoted in
the plan of a Lottery called BYRDs LOTTERY by the figures One hundred and Two on the
South side of the Main Street and fronting the same, And all houses orchrds profits and
appurtenances to said premises belonging; To have and to hold the lands hereby conveyed and premises with appurtenances unto SAMPSON MATTHEWS, GEORGE MAT-
THEWS and PATRICK LOCKHART and heirs free and clear from all incumbrances whatsoever, (the Quitrents hereafter to grow due for and in respect of the premises only
excepted and foreprized); And (the Grantors) to the (Grantees) against WILLIAM BYRD his
heirs shall warrant and forever defend by these presents; In Witness whereof the said
parties hath hereunto set their hands and seals the day and year first above written
Sealed & Delivered in presence of
          W. DANDRIDGE, JR. as to Col: Byrd,   W. BYRD
          RD. CRUMP to Colo: Byrd   CHAS. CARTER
          BERD: MARKHAM for Colo. Byrd,
          DAVID PATTERSON for Colo. Byrd,
          JAMES BUCHANAN for C. C.
          ALEXR. BUCHANAN for C. C.
          SAML. WILLIAMSON,   JOHN McKEAND
   At a Court of Hustings for the City of Richmond held at the Courthouse in the said City
the 19th day of August 1783   This Indenture was proved by the Oaths of JAMES
BUCHANAN and ALEXANDER BUCHANAN, witnesses thereto, And at another Court of
Hustings held for the said City the 20th day of October following, the said Indenture was
further proved by the Oath of JOHN McKEAND, another witness thereto, and ordered to
be recorded   Teste ADAM CRAIG, C. C.

pp.   (On margin: BRICE & Ux. to RONALD. Examined & delivered A. RONALD)
12-   THIS INDENTURE made this Eighteenth day of October in the year of our Lord
13   one thousand seven hundred & Eighty three Between ARCHIBALD BRICE of
             County of GOOCHLAND & MARY his Wife of one part and ANDREW RONALD of City
of Richmond & County of HENRICO of other part; Witnesseth that said ARCHIBALD &
MARY in consideration of the sum of One hundred and fifty pounds current money of
Virginia to them in hand paid by said ANDREW, by these presents do bargain sell and
confirm unto said ANDREW his heirs one lot of land in City of Richmond containing
half an acre or thereabouts, lying on West side of the Street leading to SHOKOE WARE-
HOUSES and distinguished in the Original Plan of said City by the number 348, Three
hundred & Forty eight, together with all priviledges & appurtenances, as also all the

right title or demand of said ARCHIBALD and MARY or either of them in the premises;
To have and to hold the granted premises unto said ANDREW his heirs, And the said
ARCHIBALD for himself and his heirs doth covenant that said ARCHIBALD and his heirs
the granted premises unto said ANDREW his heirs against all persons shall warrant and
by these presents forever defend; In Witness whereof the said parties have hereunto
set their hands & seals the day & year first in these presents mentioned
Signed Sealed and Delivered in presence of
    (no witnesses recorded)   ARCHD: BRYCE
                                         MARY BRYCE

    Received 18th October 1783, from ANDREW RONALD one hundred and Fifty pounds
being the consideration money within mentioned   L. 150.
                                         ARCHD: BRYCE

    At a Court of Hustings for the City of Richmond held at the Courthouse on Monday the
20th of October 1783   This Indenture with the Receipt endorsed were acknowledged by
ARCHIBALD BRYCE, one of the parties thereto, & ordered to be recorded
                         Teste ADAM CRAIG, C. C.

p.   (On margin: BRYCE & Ux. to McKEAND. Delivered to McKEAND)
13   THIS INDENTURE made this Eighteenth day of October in the year of our Lord
      one thousand seven hundred & Eighty three Between ARCHIBALD BRYCE of
County of GOOCHLAND & MARY his Wife of one part and JOHN McKEAND of City of Richmond of other part; Witnesseth that ARCHIBALD BRYCE & MARY his Wife in consideration of the sum of One thousand Five hundred pounds current money of Virginia to
them in hand paid by JOHN McKEAND, by these presents do bargain & sell unto JOHN
McKEAND his heirs two lotts with their appurtenances lying in City of Richmond and
marked with their Boundaries in the plan of said City No. 354 (Three hundred & Fifty
four) and 349 (Three hundred and Forty nine) except on that side of the lots that adjoins
DOCTOR JAMES CURRIE, where the line has been varied by mutual consent & is now
established by the new pailing lately erected on that part of the tenement by Mr. JAMES
HUNTER; To have and to hold the said lots with their appurtenances to JOHN McKEAND
and his heirs against the claim of said ARCHIBALD & MARY or any other person; In
Witness whereof the said parties have hereunto set their hands and seals the day & year
first in these presents mentioned
Signed Sealed & Delivered in presence of
    (no witnesses recorded)   ARCHD: BRYCE
                                         MARY BRYCE

    Received 16th October 1783. from JOHN McKEAND One thousand five hundred pounds
being the consideration money within mentioned. L. 1500.
                                         ARCHD; BRYCE

    At a Court of Hustings for the City of Richmond held at the Courthouse the 20th of
October 1783.   This Indenture with the Receipt endorsed was acknowledged by ARCHI-
BALD BRYCE one of the parties thereto & ordered to be recorded
                         Teste ADAM CRAIG, C. C.

pp.   (On margin: RAWLINGS & Ux. to SINCLAIR.)
14-   THIS INDENTURE made this third day of November in the year of our Lord one
15   thousand seven hundred and eighty three Between ROBERT RAWLINGS and
      SARAH his Wife of City of Richmond of one part and ALEXANDER SINCLAIR of
the Town of STAUNTON, Merchant, of other part; Witnesseth that ROBERT RAWLINGS in
consideration of the sum of fifteen hundred pounds current money of Virginia by said

ALEXANDER to said ROBERT in hand paid; said ROBERT RAWLINGS and SARAH his Wife by
these presents do bargain sell and confirm unto ALEXANDER SINCLAIR his heirs all that
lot or half acre of land lying in City of Richmond on the North side of the Main Street
measuring sixty six feet in front and one hundred and sixty five feet at the back of said
lot and bounded on the East by the Lot of ANTHONY GEOGHAGIN, on the West by a Cross
Street, on the North by a lot the property of GABRIEL GALT and on the South by the
Main Street; which lot or half acre of land was a part of the lot now occupied by said
ANTHONY GEOGHAGIN and conveyed to ROBERT RAWLINGS by Indenture from the said
GEOGHAGIN bearing date the first day of October in the year aforesaid; and recorded in
the County Court of HENRICO, reference being thereunto had will more fully appear;
And all houses gardens profits and appurtenances to the same belonging; To have and
to hold the premises with the appurtenances unto ALEXANDER SINCLAIR his heirs, And
ROBERT RAWLINGS for himself his heirs unto ALEXANDER SINCLAIR and his heirs will
warrant and forever defend by these presents; In Witness whereof the parties to these
presents have hereunto interchangeably set their hands and affixed their seals the day
and year first above written
Sealed and Delivered in presence of
    (no witnesses recorded)   ROBERT RAWLINGS
                            SARAH RAWLINGS

   At a Court of Hustings for the City of Richmond held at the Courthouse on Monday the
14 of December 1783.   This Indenture was acknowledged by ROBERT RAWLINGS and
SARAH his Wife parties hereto, the said SARAH having been first privily examined as
the Law directed and ordered to be recorded
              Teste ADAM CRAIG, C.C.

pp   (On margin: THOMAS & Ux. to PEDLEY)
15-   THIS INDENTURE made this eighteenth day of October in the year of our Lord
16   one thousand seven hundred and eighty three Between JACOB THOMAS and
       ANNE his Wife of City of Richmond of one part and THOMAS PEDLEY of the same
place of other part; Witnesseth that in consideration of the sum of One hundred and
seventy pounds current money of Virginia by said THOMAS to said JACOB in hand paid
by these presents do bargain sell and confirm unto THOMAS PEDLEY his heirs a certain
parcel or half acre of a lot of land lying in City of Richmond situate on the Main Street
of said City and running upon the South side thereof twenty two feet in front and back,
from thence eighty five feet in length and twenty five feet in the rear and adjoins on
the right the House and lot of said JACOB THOMAS which fronts the Store of Messrs.
COHEN, ISAACS and COMPANY, and on the left the lot of SAMUEL SHERER which part or
half of a lot of land was a part of & belonging to the lot of land formerly the property of
FREDERICK THOMAS (Father of said JACOB) and given by him to said JACOB THOMAS (his
Son) by Deed duly recorded in County Court of HENRICO, reference being thereunto had
will more fully appear; And all houses yards ways, profits and appurtenances to the
same belonging; To have and to hold the premises with the appurtenances unto THOMAS
PEDLEY his heirs; And JACOB THOMAS and his heirs the premises unto THOMAS PEDLEY
his heirs against the lawful claim and demand of all persons will warrant and forever
defend by these presents; In Witness whereof the parties to these presents have hereunto interchangeably set their hands and affixed their seals the day and year first
above written
Sealed and Delivered in presence of
    SAMUEL SHERER,   JACOB THOMAS
    GEORGE RICHARDSON   NANCY her mark + THOMAS

At a Court of Hustings for the City of Richmond continued & held at the Courthouse on Tuesday the 15th day of December 1783   This Indenture was acknowledged by JACOB THOMAS, one of the parties thereto, and ordered to be recorded
Teste ADAM CRAIG, C.C.

pp   (On margin: SMITH to REILLY & CO.)
16-   EXCHANGE for 1300 Spanish Milled Dollars.
17   ST. THOMAS April the 19th 1783
        At fifteen days sight pay this my second of Exchange, (first, third and fourth of same Tenor and date not paid) to Messrs. PHILIP REILLY & CO., with thirteen hundred Spanish Milled Dollars, value received and place the same to account of
To Messrs. WILLIAM PENNOCK & CO.   Gentlemen your Obt. Servt.
Virginia   M. SMITH JR.
PHILIP REILLY & CO. MICHAEL FALVEY
  Pay the contents to Mr. CHARLES IRVIN value in Account
JOHN WARDROP

City of Richmond, in Virginia Sct.
  I WILLIAM DANDRIDGE, Attorney at Law (no Notary Public in this City being) on application made to me by Mr. ROBERT BAINE in behalf of Mr. CHARLES IRVIN, do hereby certify - declare and make known to all to whom these presents may come or in any wise concern, that on the thirtieth day of May in the year of our Lrod one thousand seven hundred and Eighty three, in the Application aforesaid made, exhibited the Original Bill, a true copy whereof is above written, to Mr. WILLIAM PENNOCK the person to whom the said Bill is directed and demands payment thereof, which he refused and anwered that he had noted & meaned to protest the same;
  Whereupon, the said ROBERT BAINE desires me to make protest thereof. Therefore, I the said WILLIAM DANDRIDGE at the request of the said ROBERT BAINE have and by these presents do in the most solemn manner protest against the drawers and endorsers of said Bill and all others therein concerned for all damages costs and interest suffered or which shall or may be suffered for want of payment of said Bill.
  Thus done and protested in the presence of JAMES BUCHANAN and JOHN McKEAND, two reputable witnesses, inhabitants of the said City called on for this purpose agreeable to the Mercantile Law in such cases used and approved of;
  In Testimony whereof I have hereunto subscribed my name and obtained the Seal of this City to be affixed hereto the same thirtieth day of May in the year of our Lord one thousand seven hundred and eighty three
WM: DANDRIDGE
  This day, to wit, the thirty first day of May in the year of our Lord 1783, came the above said WILLIAM DANDRIDGE, Attorney at Law, before me, WILLIAM FOUSHEE, Mayor of the City aforesaid, and made Oath to the truth of his demand of payment of the Bill aforesaid in manner aforesaid and of the denial of payment of the same in manner above discribed. Given under my hand and Seal of the Corporation the day & year aforesaid
SEAL   W. FOUSHEE
At a Court of Hustings for the City of Richmond held at the Courthouse on Monday the 15th day of March 1784   This Bill of Exchange was presented in Court and together with the protest & Certificate thereunder written, are ordered to be recorded
Teste ADAM CRAIG C.C.

pp. (On margin: SMITH to REILLY & CO.)
17- EXCHANGE for 1283 Spanish Milled Dollars.　　ST. THOMAS April 19th 1783
18 At twenty days sight pay this my second of Exchange (first, third and fourth of same tenor and date not paid) to the Order of Messrs. PHILIP REILLY & CO.,
twelve hundred and eighty three Spanish Milled Dollars value received of Mr. WILLIAM BARROW in Account, and place the same to account of
To Messrs. WILLIAM PENNOCK & CO.　　　　　Gentlemen Your Obedt. Servt.
　　　　　Virginia　　　　　　　　　　　　　　　　M. SMITH JR.
Endorsed PHILLIP REILLEY & CO. MICHAEL FALVEY
Pay the Contents to Mr. CHARLES IRVING value in Account
　　　　　　　JOHN WARDROP
CITY of RICHMOND in Virginia Sct.
I WILLIAM DANDRIDGE, Attorney at Law, on application to me made (no Notary Public in this City being) on application to me made by Mr. ROBERT BAINE on behalf of Mr. CHARLES IRVING, do hereby certify declare and make known to all to whom these presents shall come or in any wise concern; That on the thirtieth day of May in the year of our Lord one thousand seven hundred and eighty three, I on the application aforesaid made did exhibit the Original Bill, a true copy whereof is above written, to Mr. WILLIAM PENNOCK, the person to whom the said Bill is directed and demanded payment thereof, which he refused and answered that he had noted and meaned to protest the same;
　Whereupon, the said ROBERT BAINE desired me to make protest thereof; Therefore I the said WILLIAM DANDRIDGE at the request of said ROBERT BAINE have and by these presents do in the most solemn manner protest against the drawer and endorsers of the said Bill and all others concerned therein for all costs damages and Intrest suffered or which shall or may be suffered for want of payment of the said Bill;
　Thus done and protested in the presence of JAMES BUCHANAN and JOHN McKEAND, two reputable witnesses, inhabitants of the said City called on for this purpose agreeable to the Mercantile Law in such cases used and approved of
　IN TESTIMONY whereof I have hereunto subscribed my name and obtained the Seal of the City to be affixed thereto the same thirtieth day of May in the year of our Lord one thousand seven hundred and eighty three
　　　　　　　WM: DANDRIDGE JR.
　This day to wit the thirty first day of May in the year of our Lord 1783 came the above said WILLIAM DANDRIDGE, Attorney at Law, before me, WILLIAM FOUSHEE, Mayor of the City aforesaid and made Oath to the truth of his demand of payment of the Bill aforesaid in manner aforesaid and of the denial of payment of the same in manner above described; Given under my hand and the Seal of the Corporation the day & year aforesaid　　　　　WILLIAM FOUSHEE
　At a Court of Hustings for the City of Richmond held at the Courthouse on Monday the 15th day of March 1784.　This Bill of Exchange was presented in Court & together with the protest & certificate thereunder written are ordered to be recorded
　　　　　　　Test ADAM CRAIG. C. C.

p. (On margin: JOHNSTON to BUCHANAN &c.)
19 KNOW ALL MEN by these presents that I WILLIAM JOHNSTON of DOWNPK. County of Down and Kingdom of IRELAND, by these presents do make and appoint JAMES BUCHANAN Esqr. and HENRY SADLER, Mercht., both of Richmond in Virginia, my true & lawfull Attorney for me and in my name to ask demand sue for and receive all such sums of money dues or demands now owing unto me in America for recovery thereof and to compound and agree for the same & acquittances or discharges for me to make

seal and deliver, and to do all other acts and things in the premises, and to sell and dispose of any goods or effects belonging to me, allowing and confirming what my said
Attorney or either of them severally shall do in virtue of these presents as fully as if I
were personally present. In Witness whereof I have hereunto sett my hand and seal
the Eight day of August 1783
Signed Sealed & Delivered in presence of
(being first duly stamped)
      THOS· KEOUN,   WM: JOHNSTON
      JAMES CHAMBERS
  At a Court of Hustings for the City of Richmond held at the Courthouse the 10th day of
April 1784   This Power of Attorney was proved by the Oath of THOMAS KEOUN one of
the witnesses and ordered to be recorded
             Teste ADAM CRAIG, C. C.

pp.   (On margin: STEWART's Bond Vendue Master)
19-   KNOW ALL MEN by these presents that we JOHN STEWART, ISAAC YOUNGHUS-
20   BAND and WILLIAM PENNOCK of the City of Richmond are held and firmly bound
      unto the Mayor, Recorder & Aldermen of said City & their Successors in the sum
of five thousand pounds, to which payment well and truly to be made we bind ourselves
our heirs firmly by these presents; Witness our hands and seals this Seventeenth day
of May in the year of our Lord one thousand seven hundred & eighty four
  THE CONDITION of the above obligation is such that whereas the above bound JOHN
STEWART hath been this day appointed VENDUE MASTER of the City of Richmond, Now
if the said JOHN STEWART shall duly & faithfully execute the said Office of Vendue
Master and shall well & truly demean himself therein, then the above obligation to be
void, otherwise to remain in full force and virtue
Sealed and Delivered in the presence of
      The Court   JOHN STEWART
                         JESSE YOUNGHUSBAND
                         WM: PENNOCK
  At a Court of Hustings for the City of Richmond held at the Courthouse the 17th day of
May 1784   This Bond was acknowledged by the Obligors and ordered to be recorded
            Test ADAM CRAIG, C. C.

p.   (On margin: CAMPBELL to CLARK)
20   PHILDELPHIA. the 27th May 1784 for L. 300 English
      At sixty days date pay this first of Exchange to the Order of JAMES KINGSTON
Esqr Three hundred pounds English with the Exchange as p Endorsement
  Value of Messrs. CAMPBELL & KINGSTON which place to account as advised
To Capn JOHN CLARK in DUBLIN or else where   JOHN CAMPBELL
      Virginia   Accepted

                           JOHN CLARK June 11th 1784.
  At a Court of Hustings for the City of Richmond held at the Courthouse in the said City
the 20th day of June 1784   This Bill of Exchange was presented in Court by RT.
MITCHEL Gent., & together with the acceptance thereunto written are ordered to be
recorded   Teste ADAM CRAIG, C. C.

pp.   (On margin: M MOODY's Bond as Serjeant)
20-   KNOW ALL MEN by these presents that we MATHEW MOODY, SAML. SCHERER &
21   ANTHONY GEOGHEGAN of City of Richmond are held and firmly bound unto the
      Mayor, Recorder Aldermen & Common Council of said City in the sum of One

thousand pounds current money to which payment well & truly to be made we bind
ourselves our heirs firmly by these presents; Witness our hands and seals this 19th day
of July one thousand seven hundred & eighty four and in the 9th year of the Commonwealth

THE CONDITION of the above obligation is such that whereas the above bound MATHEW
MOODY hath been appointed SERJEANT of the City of Richmond, Now if the said MATHEW
MOODY shall duly & faithfully execute the duties of his said Office according to Law &
shall well and truly demean himself therein, Then this obligation to be void, otherwise
to remain in full force & virtue
Sealed & Delivered in presence of
   The Court   MATHW: MOODY
                  SAML: SCHERER
                  ANTHONY GEOGHEGAN
At a Court of Hustings for the City of Richmond held at the Courthouse the 19th day of
July 1784   This Bond was acknowledged by the Obligors and ordered to be recorded
        Test ADAM CRAIG, C. C.

pp.   (On margin: BYRD's Trustees to AMBLER. Delivered April 1807. S. Craig.)
21-   THIS INDENTURE made this 15th day of August in the year of our Lord one thou-
22   sand seven hundred and eighty four Between CHARLES CARTER Esqr., of SHIR-
     LEY in County of CHARLES CITY, Surviving Trustee of the Honble: WILLIAM
BYRD Esqr., deceased, of one part and JACQUELIN AMBLER of City of Richmond of other
part, Witnesseth Whereas the said WILLIAM BYRD did by his Deed of Record in the
General Court convey certain lands and tenements unto CHARLES CARTER and others in
Trust for the use and purposes therein declared as by said Deed may more fully appear;
And Whereas said WILLIAM BIRD and his Trustees did afterwards dispose of part of the
land mentioned in the said Deed by way of Lottery, in which Lottery the Ticket number
(757) seventeen hundred and Fifty seven came up a Prize of half an acre or one lot of
land lying in City of Richmond in County of HENRICO, & distinguished in the plot of said
City by the number (480), Four hundred and Eighty, which Ticket the said JAQUELIN
AMBLER purchased of the REVEREND JAMES MAURY FOUNTAINE of GLOCESTER County;
And Whereas said CHARLES CARTER is by a late Act of Assembly empowered to convey
the said Prize, lands & lots to the persons entitled to them under the said Lottery, Now
Therefore this INDENTURE WITNESSETH that CHARLES CARTER the Surviving Trustee of
said WILLIAM BYRD by virtue of said Act of Assembly as well in consideration of the
money paid by JAQUELIN AMBLER for the Ticket bought of said JAMES MAURY FON-
TAINE as for the sum of Five shillings to him the said CHARLES CARTER in hand paid by
these presents doth bargain & sell unto JAQUELIN AMBLER all that lot or half acre of
land lying in City of Richmond distinguished by the number (480), Four hundred and
Eighty with the appurtenances belonging; To have & to hold the lot or half acre of land
with the appurtenances unto JAQUELIN AMBLER his heirs; In Witness whereof the
parties to these presents have hereunto set their hands and affixed their seals the day &
year first above written
Sealed & delivered in presence of
   JAMES BUCHANAN,   CHARLES CARTER
   ALEXANDER BUCHANAN, JOHN McKEAND
At a Court of Hustings for the City of Richmond held at the Courthouse the 16th day of
August 1784.   This Indenture was proved by the Oaths of JAMES BUCHANAN, ALEXAN-
DER BUCHANAN & JOHN McKEAND, the witnesses thereto, and ordered to be recorded
        Test ADAM CRAIG C. C.

pp.   (On margin: PICKETT to RICHARDSON &c.)
22-   TO ALL TO WHOM these presents shall come, Greeting. Know ye that I GEORGE
23   PICKETT of City of Richmond in consideration of the sum of One hundred and
         Twenty pounds to me in hand paid by WILLIAM RICHARDSON and GEORGE
RICHARDSON of same City, by these presents do bargain sell and confirm unto WILLIAM
RICHARDSON and GEORGE RICHARDSON their heirs three Negro women slaves named
Jenny, Hanah & Suckey, together with their future increase, which three Negro
women slaves with their future increase I do hereby warrant and defend unto them the
said WILLIAM and GEORGE RICHARDSON their heirs against me the said GEORGE PICKET
my heirs and against the title claim and demand of all persons, In Witness whereof I
have hereunto set my hand & affixed my seal this twenty third day of April in the year
of our Lord one thousand seven hundred & eighty four
Sealed and Delivered in presence of
      ISHAM WILLIAMS,   GEO: PICKETT
      JOHN PICKETT
   At a Court of Hustings for the City of Richmond held at the Courthouse the 16th day of
August 1784   This Bill of Sale was proved by the Oath of JOHN PICKETT, a witness
thereto and ordered to be recorded   Teste ADAM CRAIG, C. C.

pp.   (On margin: BRICE & Ux. to RONALD)
23-   The Commonwealth of Virginia to STEPHEN SAMPSON & WILLIAM MILLER, Gent.
24   Greeting. Whereas ARCHIBALD BRICE & MARY his Wife by their certain Inden-
         ture of Bargain & Sale bearing date the Eighteenth day of October 1783, have
sold & conveyed unto ANDREW RONALD one half acre lot of land with the appurtenances
lying in City of Richmond, And whereass the said MARY cannot conveniently travel to
our Court of Hustings for the said City to make acknowledgment of the said Conveyance, Therefore we give unto you or any two or more of you power to receive the acknowledgment which the said MARY shall be willing to make before you (the Commission
for the privy examination of MARY, the Wife of ARCHIBALD BRICE); Witness ADAM CRAIG Clerk
of our said Court of Hustings the sixteenth day of February 1784 in the eighth year of
the Commonwealth   ADAM CRAIG, C. C.
   GOOCHLAND County Ss. In Obedience to the within Dedimus Potestatem to us directed,
we the Subscribers, Justices of the Peace for the County of GOOCHLAND went this day to
the Dwelling House of ARCHIBALD BRICE in the Indenture of Bargain & Sale hereunto
annexed named in said County of GOOCHLAND and then & there examined MARY, the
Wife of the said ARCHIBALD, privily and apart from her said Husband; (the return of the
execution of the privy examination of MARY BRICE); Given under our hands & seals at the
County aforesaid this 1st day of May 1784   STEPHEN SAMPSON
                                                    WM: H. MILLER
   At a Court of Hustings for the City of Richmond held at the Courthouse in the said City
on Monday the 21st day of September 1784   This Commission with the Certificate of
the execution thereof endorsed, was this day returned & ordered to be recorded
                     Teste ADAM CRAIG, C. C.

pp.   (On margin: BRICE & Ux. to McKEAND)
25-   The Commonwealth of Virginia to STEPHEN SAMPSON & WILLIAM MILLER Gent.
26   Greeting, Whereas ARCHIBALD BRICE & MARY his Wife by their certain Inden-
         ture of Bargain & Sale bearing date the 18th day of October 1783 have sold and
conveyed unto JOHN McKEAND two certains lots of land with the appurtenances lying
in City of Richmond, And Whereas the said MARY cannot conveniently travel to our

Court of Hustings for the said City to make acknowledgment of the said conveyance;
Therefore we do give unto you or any two or more of you power to receive the acknow-
ledgement which the said MARY shall be willing to make (the Commission for the privy
examination of MARY, the Wife of ARCHIBALD BRICE); Witness ADAM CRAIG, Clerk of our said
Court of Hustings the sixteenth day of February 1784 and in the eighth year of the
Commonwealth   ADAM CRAIG, C. C.
   GOOCHLAND County Sct. In Obedience to the within Dedimus Potestatem to us directed,
we the Subscribers, Justices of the Peace for the aforesaid, went this day to the Dwelling
House of ARCHIBALD BRYCE in the Indenture of Bargain & Sale hereunto annexed
named & then & there examined MARY, the Wife of the said ARCHIBALD privately &
apart from her said Husband; (the return of the execution of the privy examination of MARY
BRICE). Given under our hands & seals at the County aforesaid this 1st day of May 1784
                                             STEPHEN SAMPSON
                                             WM: H. MILLER
   At a Court of Hustings for the City of Richmond held at the Courthouse of the said City
on Monday the 21st of September 1784   This Commission with the Certificate of the
execution thereof endorsed was this day returned & are ordered to be recorded
                         Teste ADAM CRAIG, C. C.

pp.   (On margin: TURPIN to COHEN & ISAACS)
26-   THIS INDENTURE made this second day of August in the year of our Lord one
27   thousand seven hundred and Eighty four Between THOMAS TURPIN of County of
         POWHATAN, Gentleman, of one part and JACOB COHEN and ISAIAH ISAACS of City
of Richmond, Merchants and Partners, of other part; Witnesseth that in consideration
of Thirty two thousand five hundred pounds of Crop Tobacco by said JACOB COHEN &
ISAIAH ISAACS to THOMAS TURPIN in hand paid, said THOMAS by these presents doth
bargain sell and confirm unto JACOB COHEN & ISAIAH ISAACS and to their heirs one lot
or parcel of land lying in City of Richmond known in the plan thereof by the number
Seven hundred & fifty (750); laid off for & containing about one half acre with the
rents issues & profits thereof; To have and to hold the lot of land and all other the bargained premises unto JACOB COHEN & ISAIAH ISAACS their heirs as Tenants in Common
and THOMAS TURPIN and his heirs the granted lot of land and premises unto JACOB
COHEN & ISAIAH ISAACS & to their heirs against all persons shall warrant & defend; In
Witness whereof the said THOMAS TURPIN hath hereunto set his hand & seal the day
and year first above written
Signed Sealed & Delivered in the presence of
         JOSEPH MORDECAI,   THOS: TURPIN
         JOSEPH DARMSDA, MOSES A MYERS
   August 2d. 1784. Received from JACOB COHEN & ISAIAH ISAACS the full quantity of
Thirty two thousand five hundred pounds of Crop Tobacco, being the consideration for
the within mentioned lot of land
Teste JOSEPH MORDECAI,   THOS: TURPIN
         JOSEPH DARMSDA, MOSES A. MYERS
   At a Court of Hustings for the City of Richmond held at the Courthouse of the said City
on Monday the 15th of November 1784   This Indenture with the Receipt thereon en-
dorsed was proved by the Oaths of JOSEPH MORDECAI, JOSEPH DARMSDA & MOSES A.
MYERS, the witnesses thereto & are ordered to be recorded
                         Teste ADAM CRAIG, C. C.

pp   (On margin: CLARK to WEBB)
28-   KNOW ALL MEN by these presents that I DANIEL CLARKE of PENSYLVANIA by
29   these presents do make and appoint FOSTER WEBB Esqr., to be my true certain &
            lawful Attorney for me and in my name to demand levy sue for recover &
receive by all lawful ways from all persons whom it doth or may concern all sums of
money debts dues goods & things which now are or hereafter shall grow due owing
payable or belonging to me said DANIEL CLARKE, particularly from the Government of
Virginia upon or by virtue of any Bond, Bill book or upon account of trading or dealing
by these presents granting my Attorney full power and authority in the premises and
generally to do act & perform all matters requisite as fully as I might or could do were I
personally present. In Witness whereof I have hereunto set my hand and seal this
Twenty third day of April one thousand seven hundred and eighty four
Sealed and Delivered in the presence of
    FRANCIS GRAVES.   DANIEL CLARK
    GEO: WEBB JR.
  At a Court of Hustings for the City of Richmond held at the Courthouse in the said City
on Monday the 20th of December 1784   This Power of Attorney was proved by the Oath
of FRANCIS GRAVES one of the witnesses thereto, & ordered to be recorded
                Teste ADAM CRAIG, C.C.

pp.   (On margin: AMBLER to MARSHALL. Deed. Delivered FISHER April 1807)
29-   THIS INDENTURE made the fifteenth day of March in the year of our Lord one
30   thousand seven hundred and Eighty five Between JACQUELIN AMBLER of City of
            Richmond of one part and JOHN MARSHALL of said City of other part; Witnes-
seth that JAQUELIN AMBLER in consideration of the sum of Ten pounds current money
to him in hand paid by JOHN MARSHALL, said JAQUELIN AMBLER by these presents doth
bargain and sell unto JOHN MARSHALL his heirs one half acre Lot in the City of Richmond on SHOCKOE HILL known in the plan of said City by the number 480 (Four hundred and eighty) and also all lands trees profits and appurtenances; To have and to hold
the premises unto JOHN MARSHALL his heirs; And JAQUELIN AMBLER for him and his
heirs the lot and premises against every person to JOHN MARSHALL his heirs shall
warrant and forever defend by these presents; In Witness whereof the parties to these
presents have hereunto set their hands & seals the day and year above written
                              J. AMBLER
  City of Richmond. At a Hustings Court held the 21st day of March 1785; This Indenture
was acknowledged by JAQUELIN AMBLER Esqr., one of the parties thereto & ordered to
be recorded   Teste ADAM CRAIG, C.C.

pp.   (On margin: BOYD to BOYD)
30-   KNOW ALL MEN by these presents that I the REVEREND MR. WILLIAM BOYD,
33   Minister of the Gospel in the Parish of PENNINGHAME in County of WIGTOWN
            North Britain, Whereas Mr. WALTER BOYD, late Merchant in Virginia, my
younger Brother, and lawful Children of the deceased Reverend Mr. ANDREW BOYDE
some time Minister of TWINSDALE in the Stewartay of Kirkenbright North Britain died
some years ago in Virginia leaving considerable heritable and moveable subjects to
some of what I as heir at Law have undoubted right and as JOHN BOYD my Eldest lawful
Son is about to set out for Virginia, I am desirous to invest him with full powers to act
for me as my Attorney in collecting and managing the Estates real and personal left by
the said WALTER and ROBERT BOYD or either of them so far as I have right thereto.
Therefore will ye me to have made and appointed said JOHN BOYD to enter into and take

possession of all heritable and Real Estate and subjects which belonged to my said
deceased Brothers WALTER and ROBERT BOYD, or either of them in Virginia or else-
where in North America and not specially devised or conveyed away and particularly a
piece of ground purchased by ROBERT BOYD after having executed a Deed of Settlement
or Latter Will to commence and carry on all actions and suits either in my name or his
own as my Attorney that shall be necessary for obtaining right to and possession of the
said Estates and particularly my said Son and Attorney shall have power to call to
account and receive from the acting Trustees and Executors of said WALTER and ROBERT
BOYD my just and legal share of any sums of money goods or effects of any kind to
which I have right by their latter Wills and Testaments or by the Latter Will and
Testament of JOHN GILLIAM, Father in Law of said Mr. ROBERT BOYD, to make sign seal
and deliver all discharges necessary and to perform every things which I myself might
do if personally present In Witness whereof I have hereunto set my Hand & seal this
Third day of June in the year of our Lord one thousand seven hundred and Eighty four
and of his Majestys Reign the Twenty fourth year
Signed Sealed & Delivered (being first duly stamped)
In presence of WILL: McCONNELL.   WILL: BOYD
        JOHN DABZIEL
(Certifications and Testaments as to the validity of the Power of Attorney follow.)
City of Richmond. At a Hustings Court held the 18th day of April 1794
This Power of Attorney was presented in Court & with the Certificates thereon endorsed
was ordered to be recorded   Teste ADAM CRAIG, Cl C.

pp.   (On margin: BANKS to GOLSTON)
34-   THIS INDENTURE made this sixteenth day of October in the year of our Lord one
36   thousand seven hundred and eighty four Between HENRY BANKS of City of Rich-
         mond of one part and RAWLEIGH COLSTON of the same place of the other part,
Witnesseth that HENRY BANKS in order to secure to RAWLEIGH COLSTON the payment of
the sum of One thousand four hundred and sixty two pounds, Fourteen shillings and
eleven pence three farthings with lawful Interest on the same from the seventh day of
January one thousand seven hundred and eighty four till paid, as also in consideration
of the sum of Five shillings to him in hand paid said HENRY BANKS by these presents
doth bargain sell and confirm unto RAWLEIGH COLSTON his heirs the following lots and
tenements (with all houses and improvements which are at present or may hereafter
be placed thereon by said HENRY BANKS) lying in City of Richmond, vizt. one lot of
piece of ground which HENRY BANKS purchased of the Commissioners for the Sale of
Public Lands in City of Richmond situate on the North side of the Street leading by the
buildings at present occupied as the Capitol containing in front on said Street sixteen
feet and running back in parallel lines seventy one feet, bounded by the lot or tenement lately purchased by said COLSTON of the aforesaid Commissioners on the one side &
by the tenement at present in the occupation of said HENRY BANKS on the other side;
Also one other lot or piece of ground situated on the same Street below the Public Buildings at present called the Capitol running on the said Street on the North side thereof
(blank) feet and extending back to the Street lately established by said Commissioners
being a lot lately sold by the Commissioners to HENRY BANKS. Also one other lot of
ground situate on South side of the Street or Road leading to SHOCKOE WAREHOUSES adjoining the tenement of Mr. WILLIAM BURTON and running on the said Street or Road
sixty four feet where it joins the land of CLARK, being the land or lot lately the property of HUNTER BANKS & CO. and purchased at Vendue by the said HENRY BANKS of HUN-
TER BANKS & CO. and extending back from the said Street or Road forty feet; To have

and to hold the lands lots and tenements together with all such buildings and improvements as now are or may hereafter be placed on the same to RAWLEIGH COLSTON his
heirs and HENRY BANKS will warrant and forever defend the granted lands and premises with every of their appurtenances unto RAWLEIGH COLSTON his heirs against the
demand of all persons; IN TRUST NEVERTHELESS that HENRY BANKS his heirs shall well
and truly pay said RAWLEIGH COLSTON or assigns the sum of One thousand four hundred
& sixty two pounds, fourteen shillings and eleven pence three farthings with lawful
Interest thereon from the seventh day of January one thousand seven hundred and
eighty four till paid on or before the first day of January next in which case the lands
lots or tenements and premises to stand discharged and released unto HENRY BANKS his
heirs as if this Indenture had never been made; In Witness whereof the said HENRY
BANKS hath hereunto set his hand and seal the day and year above written
Sealed and Delivered in presence of
        MATTHEW WRIGHT,   HENRY BANKS
        CUTHBERT BANKS, JOHN BEALE
 City of Richmond. At a Hustings Court held the 16th day of May 1785.
This Indenture of Mortgage was proved by the Oaths of MATTHEW WRIGHT, CUTHBERT
BANKS & JOHN BEALE, the witnesses thereto, and ordered to be recorded
               Teste ADAM CRAIG, C.C.

pp.   (On margin: WM. CARSON's Will)
37-   IN THE NAME OF GOD Amen. the Twenty first of October in the year of our Lord
38   God 1782. I WILLIAM CARSON being sick in body but of good and perfect memo-
         ry thanks be to Almighty God, and calling to remembrance the uncertain estate
of this Transitory Life and that all flesh yield unto death when it shall please God to call
do make constitute ordain and declare this my Last Will & Testament in manner and
form following, revoking and annuling by these presents all and every Testament and
Testaments, Will & Wills, heretofore by me made and declared, either by word or writing
and this is to be taken only for my Last Will and Testament and none other, And first
being penitent and sorrow from the bottom of my heart for my Sins past, most humbly
desiring forgiveness for the same, I give and commit my Soul unto Almighty God my
Saviour & Redeemer in whom and by the merits of Jesus Christ I trust and believe sure-
ly to be saved and to have full remission and forgiveness of all my Sins, and that my
Soul with my body at the General Day of Resurrection shall rise again with Joy and
through the merits of Christs death and passion possess and inherit the Kingdom of
Heaven prepared for his Elect and Chosen, and my body to be buried and inter'd decent-
ly as becomes a Christian and that by the side of my Brother in HANOVER County.
  And now for the Settling of my temporal Estate and such goods chattles and debts as it
hath pleased God far above my desert to bestow upon me, I do order give and dispose the
same in manner and form following, that is to say, First I will that all those debts and
dues as I owe in right or Conscience to any manner of persons shall be well and truly
contented and paid or ordained to be paid within convenient time after my decease by
my Executrix hereafter named. I give and bequeath unto my beloved ELIZABETH CAR-
SON all my personal Estate in goods chattles implements of household and commodities
whatsoever to the aforesaid ELIZABETH CARSON my sole Executrix of all my goods &
chattles, without any manner of challenge claim or demand whatsoever. I give and
bequeath unto my Nephew. WILLIAM CARSON, all my wearing apparel, a pair Silver
knee buckles and my hand buckles of Silver, and a Silver based buckle and all my books
whatsoever, I do give to my Nephew without any challenge claim or demand whatsoever. In Witness hereof being in good and sound memory, I attest this to be my Last
Will & Testament in presence of

Test JNO. CREAGH,   WILLIAM CARSON
    SIMON MURRAY

At a Court of Hustings for the City of Richmond held at the Courthouse in the said City the 17th day of February 1783   This Will was proved by the Oath of SAMUEL MURRAY, a witness thereto, who also deposed that he saw JOHN CREAGH the other sub-scribing witness attest the same; Whereupon the said Will is ordered to be recorded. And at another Court held for the said City at the Courthouse aforesaid the 21st day of July following, On the motion of ELIZABETH CARSON, the Executrix named in the said Will, who made Oath thereto, and together with ISAAC YOUNGHUSBAND her Security entered into and acknowledged their Bond in the penalty of fifty pounds, conditioned as the Law directs, a Certificate is granted her for obtaining a Probat thereof in due form
                                  Teste ADAM CRAIG, C. C.

pp.   (On margin: RICHARD WINSTON's Appt.)
39-   Agreeable to an Order of the Court of Hustings in HENRICO, being appointed to
40   appraise the Estate of RICHARD WINSTON deced., being sworn, vizt., November
         16th 1784   One great Coat, one close body Coat, Fur waistcoats, 6 pair breeches, overalls and drawers, 10 shirts, 8 handkerchiefs and remnant of linnen, 2 pair shoes, 4 pair stockings, gloves & garters, 2 snuff boxes and 2 can sets, Remnant of gold and Silver Lace, stock and buckle, one hat, one blanket, sheep sheares, five carving knives and four forks, seven razors, 2 pen knives, spectacles, combs and the movements of a watch, one dressing glass, one pair old saddle bags, one fan, one strap case & two razors, one chest, 8 handkerchiefs, one powder puff, one small old trunk, one pair knee buckles, sundry crockery ware, six flasks in case, 18 black bottles
Total: L. 19...7 ..4   SAMUEL COUCH
                                           ISAIAH ISAACS
                                           SMITH BLAKEY
HENRICO Sct. SMITH BLAKEY, SAMUEL COUCH & ISAIAH ISAACS sworn to before
                                           ISAAC YOUNGHUSBAND
    July 18th 1785. Returned into Court of Hustings for the City of Richmond the 21st day of February 1785. & ordered to be recorded.
                        Teste ADAM CRAIG, C. C.

pp.   (On margin: JAMES MAYBORNE's Appt.)
40-   In Obedience to an Order of the Court of Hustings for the City of Richmond
41   hereunto annexed, we have appraised the Personal Estate of JAMES MAYBORNE
         deced. as follows;   1 waistcoat and breeches, 3 pair silk stockings, one case raZors &c. shaving boxes, 1 bag & puff, 1 warming plate, 1 new blue broad cloth coat, 1 blue ditto, 1 grate ditto. 2 Regimentals ditto, 2 new shirts, pair red legings, 6 stocks, one pair shoe boots, 3 pair mens shoes, saddle & bridle, pair shoe buckles, pair ditto (knee), one stock buckle and sleeve buttons, gold broach, 1 purse, 3 shirts, 5 ditto, 7 pair stockings, 2 pair breeches, 1 pr. old ditto, 2 pair gloves, 1 flesh brush, 1 Ink pot, 2 pen-cils, 2 small brushes and trash bag, 2 pair overalls, 5 waistcoats, 2 old ditto, 1 pair drawers, 3 silk handkerchiefs, 2 old ditto, 2 napkins & 1 Crevat, 1 portmantua and cover, 1 apron & bricklaying tools, case and bottles, old hat, 4 brushes, 9 old Books, 2 doz. S. coat buttons, old lancet, 1 jugg, 2 combs & 1 cork skrew, one chest, one grey horse;
Total 49 .19.. 8.   DABNEY MILLER
                                           SAMUEL TROWER
                                           JOHN SMITH
    Returned into the Court of Hustings for the City of Richmond the 21st day of February 1785 & ordered to be recorded   Teste ADAM CRAIG, C. C.

pp.   (On margin: RALPH MACNAIR's Will)
41-   BE IT KNOWN that I RALPH MACNAIR, late of ORANGE County in NORTH CARO-
43   LINA, Attorney at Law, being in perfect health of body and sound of mind but
         for divers good causes do make publish & declare this my Last Will and Testa-
ment hereby revoking and making void all Wills by me heretofore made. First it is my
desire that all debts due and owing by me whether on my own account or as Partner
with my Brother, EBENEZERMACNAIR, may be discharged out of the first money arising
from the sales of my effects or from the collection of Debts due to me. Secondly, I hereby direct and ordain that all the Real Estate I may be possessed of in NORTH or SOUTH
CAROLINA at my decease be sold at two years credit and all my personal Estate every
where at twelve months credit. Thirdly, I desire that all the residue of my Estate after
paying all just demands shall be equally divided between my Wife, DOLLY MACNAIR,
and my Children, each one to share alike, the Childrens part to be lent out to Interest or
proper securities till they severally arrive at full age. Fifthly, it is my will and desire,
if my said Wife shall think fit to marry again, that the Children shall be then taken out
of her care with all that is their's and that she shall be required to advance as much as
shall appear to be equivalent to one third part of their maintenance and education till
they are of age so as that allowance shall not reduce her share below the sum of Two
hundred and fifty pounds Sterling money of Great Brittain. Lastly, I hereby make and
appoint my Brothers, JOHN MACNAIR and EBENEZER MACNAIR, late of ORANGE County
aforesaid, and my Brother in Law, EDWARD HALL, of County of EDGECOMBE (all of whom
both by nature and inclination I think the fittest and best Guardians and protectors of
my said Wife and Children) and every of them Executors of this my Last Will & Testament, and do hereby allow them a Commission of Six p: centum on all the money they
may receive and apply to the discharge of my debts aforesaid, And for the first one
thousand pounds Sterling money for my said Wife and Children and Ten p:centum on all
sums over that, to be received by him or them respectively, who shall do the business,
and I hope they will consider this the only mark I can give them of my esteem and
regard in the present uncertain state of my affairs;
Signed Sealed & Published and declared in presence of
         JAS. ANDERSON, WILL: BURGES,   RALPH MACNAIR
         JNO· TELFAIR, GEO: MILLER
    At a Court of Hustings for the City of Richmond held at the Courthouse in the said City
on Monday the 19th of September 1785   This Will was presented in Court by EBENEZER
MACNAIR one of the Executors therein named, And thereupon WILLIAM HAY and
JAMES REID, being sworn severally deposed that they are well acquainted with the
Testators hand writing and verily believe that the said Will and the name thereto subscribed are all of the said Testators proper hand writing, Whereupon the said Will is
ordered to be recorded. And on the motion of the said Executor, who made Oath thereto,
and together with WILLIAM HAY & DAVID LAMBERT his Securites, entered into and
acknowledged their Bond in the penalty of Two thousand pounds, conditioned as the
Law directs. Certificate is granted him for obtaining a Probat thereof in due form,
Liberty being reserved to the other Executors named in the said Will to join in the
Probat when they shall think fit
                    Teste ADAM CRAIG, C C

pp.   (On margin: TURPIN to MONROE)
43-   THIS INDENTURE made this fifteenth day of October in the year of our Lord one
44   thousand seven hundred and Eighty five Between PHILIP TURPIN of the County
         of POWHATAN of one part and JAMES MONROE of the County of (blank) of other

part; Witnesseth that PHILIP TURPIN in consideration of the sum of One hundred and
sixty pounds current money of Virginia to him in hand paid by JAMES MONROE, by
these presents doth bargain & sell unto JAMES MONROE a certain tract of land lying in
City of Richmond in County of HENRICO being Lots No. 781 & 782, in the plan of said City,
being part of a tract of land call'd WATSONS TENEMENT, with all the profits and advantages thereunto belonging; and the rents issues and profits thereof; To have and to hold
the lots and premises with the appurtenances unto JAMES MONROE his heirs; And
PHILIP TURPIN the parcel of land and premises with the appurtenances unto JAMES
MONROE his heirs against all persons whatsoever shall warrant and forever defend by
these presents; In Witness whereof the said PHILIP TURPIN hath to these presents set
his hand and affix'd his seal the day and year above written
Sealed and Delivered in presence of
     JAMES LYLE,   PHILIP TURPIN
     RICHD: BOOKER,   ALEX: BANKS
  At a Court of Hustings for the City of Richmond held at the Vendue Office in the said
City on Monday the 21st of November 1785   This Indenture was acknowledged by
PHILIP TURPIN, party thereto, and ordered to be recorded
             Teste ADAM CRAIG, C. C.

pp   (On margin: CONAND to LeCANUT)
43-   THIS INDENTURE made the Nineteenth day of December in the year of our Lord
47   one thousand seven hundred and Eighty five Between JAMES FRANCIS CONAND
       of City of Richmond and State of Virginia of one part and Capt. CHARLES Le
CANUT of the City & State aforesaid of other part; Witnesseth that JAMES FRANCIS
CONAND in order to secure to the said CHARLES Le CANUT the payment of One hundred
and sixty one pounds, Seventeen shillings and eleven pence specie, current money of
Virginia, with legal Interest thereon from the fifteenth day of August next until paid,
as also in consideration of the sum of Five shillings to him in hand paid, said JAMES
FRANCIS CONAND by these presents doth bargain sell and confirm to CHARLES Le CANUT
his heirs all the right title land Interest to that parcel of ground lying on West side of
SHOCKOE CREEK in City aforesaid, which granted premises were conveyed by DIDIER
COLIN unto said CONAND by Lease bearing date the first day of July in the year one
thousand seven hundred and Eighty five,together with all buildings and improvements
profits commodities and appurtenances to the same belonging; And also sundry articles
in the Shop as per Invoice, that is to say, Sixty one gallons of Rum, twelve gallons of
Brandy, two hundred pounds of Tallow, sixteen bottles of Snuff, nine bottles of Oil,
twenty eight bottles of Liquors, twenty bottles of Aniseed, eleven bottles of Coffee
Water, one hundred and ten bottles (empty), half a pound of sewing Silk, two pounds of
white thread, eighteen yards silk, two marble mortars, two small and one large mugs,
three tobacco sifts, twenty six candle forms, two wooden dishes, one tea kettle, two small
bedsteads, two tables and an half pound of cloves; To have and to hold the granted premises with their appurtenances unto CHARLES Le CANUT his heirs and JAMES FRANCIS
CONAND doth for himself his heirs agree with CHARLES Le CANUT his heirs that he will
warrant and forever defend the granted land or piece of a lot of ground against the
claim or demand of every person; IN TRUST Nevertheless that JAMES FRANCIS CONAND
his heirs shall well and truly pay and satisfy unto CHARLES Le CANUT or assigns the
said sum with lawful Interest in which case the before granted lot of ground and premises & other articles as before mentioned to stand discharged and released unto JAMES
FRANCIS CONAND his heirs in like manner as if this Indenture had never been made;
In Witness whereof the said JAMES FRANCIS CONAND hath hereunto set his hand &
affixed his seal the day and year first above written

Signed Sealed and Delivered in the presence of
    (no witnesses recorded)   CONAND
  At a Court of Hustings for the City of Richmond held at the Courthouse in the said City on Monday the 19th day of December 1785   This Indenture was acknowledged by JAMES FRANCIS CONAND, party thereto and ordered to be recorded
          Teste ADAM CRAIG C. C.

pp   (On margin: LIGGON to GILBERT)
47-   MEMORANDUM of an AGREEMENT made this fifth day of June 1785 Between
48   JOHN LIGGON of City of Richmond of one part and ROBERT GILBERT of the same
       place of other part; to wit, the said LIGGON doth Lease to said GILBERT for five years commencing on the first day of January last, his tenement situate on the back street in the said City and adjoining the Lot of MRS. ALLEGRE, running back (blank) feet and in width as now inclosed for the yearly rent of L. 100, to be paid quarterly and in case of failure of payment for 4 successive quarters, the Lease to be void; And whereas said GILBERT hath made considerable additions and improvements to said Tenement, it is agreed that from the aforesaid yearly rent the sum of L. 30...0...0 pr. annum is to be deducted by said GILBERT until the amount of the improvements shall be reimbursed, and shou'd any overplus of the said improvements be remaining in favor of said GILBERT at the expiration of the Lease, he is to keep possession of said Tenement at the aforesaid Rent of L 100 per annum until the whole shall be reimbursed to him; for the due performance and compliance with the within the parties bind themselves their heirs each to the other firmly by these presents; As Witness our hands and seals the day and year aforesaid
Witness ADAM CRAIG,   JOHN LIGGON
    W. WHITLOCK, JAMES CRAIG   ROBT. GILBERT
  At a Court of Hustings for the City of Richmond held at the Courthouse in the said City on Monday the 16th January 1786   This Memorandum of Lease and Agreement was proved by the Oaths of ADAM CRAIG, WILLIAM WHITLOCK and JAMES CRAIG, witnesses thereto and ordered to be recorded Teste ADAM CRAIG, C. C.

pp.   (On margin: BUCHANAN to HOLLOWAYs. Original Deed Deld. DAVD. HOLLOWAY)
49-   THIS INDENTURE made this Seventeenth day of March in the year of our Lord
50   one thousand seven hundred and Eighty six Between JAMES BUCHANAN of one
       part and NATHANIEL HOLLOWAY and DAVID HOLLOWAY of the other part; Witnesseth that JAMES BUCHANAN in consideration of the sum of Five shillings current money of Virginia to him in hand paid, by these presents doth bargain sell and confirm unto NATHANIEL HOLLOWAY and DAVID HOLLOWAY their heirs, as Tenants in Common, the Westermost half of Lot No. 704 (Seven hundred and four) adjoining Lot No. 723, and the Westermost half of Lot No. 703 (Seven hundred and three) adjoining Lot No. 771, both lying in City of Richmond; To have and to hold the houses improvements and appurtenances thereunto belonging to NATHANIEL HOLLOWAY and DAVID HOLLOWAY their heirs as Tenants in Common; And JAMES BUCHANAN against all persons claiming the said lots to said NATHANIEL HOLLOWAY and DAVID HOLLOWAY their heirs by these presents shall warrant and forever defend; In Witness whereof the said JAMES BUCHANAN hath hereunto set his hand and affixed his seal the day and year above written
Signed Sealed and deliver'd in presence of
    (no witnesses recorded)   JAMES BUCHANAN

At a Court of Hustings for the City of Richmond held at the Courthouse in the said City, Monday the 21st March 1786   This Indenture was acknowledged by JAMES BUCHANAN party thereto and ordered to be recorded

Teste ADAM CRAIG, C. C.

pp.   (On margin: WILLIAM LUDEMAN's Will)
50-   IN THE NAME OF THE HOLY TRINITY Amen. I WILLIAM LUDEMAN of the City of
52   Richmond and State of Virginia being weak and infirm in body but of sound and perfect memory, do make and declare this my Last Will and Testament. After all my just debts and funeral charges are paid, I give and bequeath unto my loving Sisters, CHRISTINA SOPHIA and CATHARINA JULIANA, sixteen hundred dollars Certificates and Sixteen hundred sixty six and two thirds acres of land which are to be located on Scots,. It is my wish and desire that sixty dollars specie shou'd be sent for mourning cloath with the first letters. In case my Sisters should be dead, her share goes to her Children and shou'd CATHARINA JULIANA have died, unmarried, her share falls to her Sister and Children. I give and bequeath unto Miss SALLY STEWART and my God Daughter, Miss KITTY ROWLAND (not only on account of the love and attachment I have for the little girls but also for the high esteem and friendship I feel for their amiable Mothers) one thousand acres of land which is located in CUMBERLAND, shou'd any of these young Misses die, their share shall go to the eldest Daughter in the family, if there is none, it goes to their Mothers. I could wish that the land might not be turned into money till the young ladies are at least ten or twelve years of age, unless a very good bargain cou'd be made, else my good intention will not have the desired effect. Item. I give and bequeath unto my Friend, JOHN STEWART, my much beloved Sword and War companion after it is properly repaired. I give and bequeath unto NANCY LYLES near WINCHES-TER from Nine to Fifteen pounds specie for a mourning Ring on account of the great Friendship and esteem which has subsisted between us for these five years. I likewise give and bequeath to my much respected acquaintances, Miss NANCY (HA--) and Miss PEGGY RICHARDSON,from three to five pounds each for a Mourning Ring. Whatever money shall remain after all expences &c. are duly discharged shall go to the Executors of this my Last Will. The Friendship which I have experienced from Mr. WILLIAM RICHARDSON and Mr. HARRY HETH induces me to leave them as a small mark of my Friendship and Gratitulde, the remainder of my Certificates, Six hundred and sixty four dollars. I make do doubt they will leave them untouched till they come of value.when the sight of them perhaps after years will call their departed friend to their remembrance. It is my will and desire that Mr. WILLIAM RICHARDSON and Mr. HARRY HETH be Executors Administrators &c. of this my Last Will & Testament. In Witness whereof I have set my hand and affixed my seal this first day of March in the year of our Lord one thousand seven hundred and Eighty six.

WM: LUDEMAN

At a Court of Hustings for the City of Richmond held at the Courthouse in the said City on Monday the 20th March 1786.   This Will was presented in Court by WILLIAM RICHARDSON & HARRY HETH,the Executors therein named, and there being no witnesses to the said Will; ALEXANDER W. ROBERTS and JOHN GUNN being sworn severally deposed that they are well acquainted with the Testators hand writing & verily believe that the said Will and the name thereto subscribed are all of the Testators proper hand writing. Whereupon the said Will is ordered to be recorded; And on the motion of the said Executors who made Oath according to Law, and JOHN GUNN their Security entered into and acknowledged their Bond in the penalty of five hundred pounds conditioned as the Law directs., Certificate is granted them for obtaining a Probat thereof in due form

Teste ADAM CRAIG, C. C.

pp.   (On margin: JAS: McCLANE's Appraisment)
52-   INVENTORY of sundry articles taken at the House of Mr. SAMUEL ARCHIBALD
55   belonging to the Estate of JAMES McCLANE deced., October 24th 1785.

Three pairs shoes and buckles, one pair knee buckles, 3 coats, 3 waistcoats, 3 pair breeches, 6 pair stockings, 5 shirts, 2 hatts, 1 Silver watch, 1 Memorandum Book & pencil, 1 Pocket Bible, 1 great Coat, 2 hand saws, 1 tenant saw, 1 sash ditto, 2 duftil ditto, 6 augers, 1 cove and bed ditto, 2 ditto grooving ditto, 2 ditto rabbit ditto, 4 ditto beads, 1 ditto astical, 3 ditto Jams of round and hollow, 1 ditto quarter round, 1 ditto side rabbitt, 1 ditto filester, 1 ditto fore, 2 jack ditto, 2 ditto smothing, whipsaw handle, 2 squares,1 bevil, 9 mortar chizels, 8 hamers, 3 ditto socket, 9 gouges, 2 socket ditto, 4 screw drivers, 9 rasps, flat and files, 5 hammers, stringling hatchet, broad ax. addze, 4 augers, 3 spike gimblets, 1 bed rench, drawing knife, doz: of pullys, 3 moving gages, 2 spok hawes, pair nippers, turkey stone, brace & 3 bitts, 4 plow bitts, pair nippers, 6 whip saws, 6 saw files, 14 files, box screws, 11 gimblets; hand vice, pair pincers; Cash 0...7...10.
Total 22...12...10.

We the Subscribers being first sworn have appraised the Estate of JAMES McCLANE deced. as within. Given under our hands this 24th day of October 1785

                                        A. W. ROBERT
                                        JOHN HAGUE

Returned into Court of Hustings for the City of Richmond the 20th March 1786 & ordered to be recorded   Teste ADAM CRAIG, C.C.

pp.   (On margin: BURTON & Ux. to COUCH)
55-   THIS INDENTURE made the twenty eighth day of March in the year of our Lord
58   one thousand seven hundred and Eighty six Between JOHN BURTON and FRANCES ANN BURTON his Wife of City of Richmond of one part and SAMUEL COUCH of the same City of other part; Witnesseth that in consideration of the sum of Two hundred pounds current money of Virginia to JOHN BURTON in hand paid by SAMUEL COUCH, said JOHN BURTON and FRANCES ANN BURTON his wife by these presents do bargain sell and confirm unto SAMUEL COUCH his heirs one half acre lott or tenement of land in the City of Richmond adjoining the WAREHOUSES of the TOBACCO INSPECTION at ROCKITTS LANDING. and marked and numbered in the plan of said (No. 169) being the same lot or tenement of ground which is conveyed in fee simple by Deed of Bargain & Sale bearing date the twenty third day of this present month of March from GILLY LEWIS to said JOHN BURTON. together with all houses gardens and other improvements thereunto belonging: To have and to hold the half acre lot with appurtenances unto SAMUEL COUCH his heirs freely and clearly discharged from all incumbrances, And JOHN BURTON and FRANCES ANN BURTON his Wife will forever warrant and defend the right title and possession of the same unto SAMUEL COUCH his heirs against the demand of every person: In Witness whereof the said JOHN BURTON and FRANCES ANN BURTON his Wife have hereunto set their hands and affixed their seals the day and year above written
Sealed and Delivered in the presence of

ZENAS TAIT, ELIJAH FRANKLIN   JOHN BURTON
WM: VAUGHAN, ALEXR. MONTGOMERY,   FRANCES ANN her mark ⌐ BURTON
PLEASANT JORDAN, JOHN STEWART,
JOHN GUNN

The Commonwealth of Virginia to WILLIAM PENNOCK, GABRIEL GALT, FOSTER WEBB & ROBERT BOYD. Gentlemen. Justices of our Court of Hustings for the City of Richmond, Greeting. Whereas (The Commission for the privy examination of FRANCES ANN, the Wife of JOHN BURTON): Witness ADAM CRAIG, Clerk of our said Court the 28th day of March 1786, in the 10th year of the Commonwealth   ADAM CRAIG C.C.

Richmond 29th March 1786

By virtue of the within Commission to us directed, we have privily examined the within named FRANCES ANN BURTON seperate and apart from her Husband and received her acknowledgment of the conveyance thereto subjoined (the return of the execution of the privy examination of FRANCES ANN BURTON); Given under our hands & seals the day and year above written   G. GALT

                                        ROBT. BOYD

At a Court of Hustings for the City of Richmond held at the Public Buildings in the said City on Monday the 17th of April 1786   This Indenture was proved by the Oaths of ZENAS TAIT, ALEXANDER MONTGOMERY and PLEASANT JORDAN, witnesses thereto, and together with the Commission annexed and the Certificate of the execution thereof are ordered to be recorded   Teste ADAM CRAIG, C. C.

pp.   (On margin: ROPER to WILSON)

58-   THIS INDENTURE made and entered into this twenty eighth day of February one

59   thousand seven hundred and Eighty six Between JESSE ROPER of City of Richmond of one part and JOHN WILSON of the same City of other part, as followeth: The said JESSE ROPER doth bargain and sell unto JOHN WILSON in fee simple a certain parcel of ground situate on the Main Street in the City aforesaid, now in the occupation of Mr. WILLIAM RICHARDSON, adjoining the House of Mr. MOSES AUSTIN to contain ten feet in front and sixty feet in depth and no more; Together with a House thereon as the same now stands of the dimensions of thirty four feet by ten and it is understood between the parties that JOHN WILSON shall be forever limitted to the said ten feet in front as well in the Cellar as in the ground floor but is permitted the privilege to extend a room on the second floor to the dimensions of twelve feet in front and no more & farther that the partitions which unite two other shops or stores belonging to said JESSE ROPER under the same roof with that now sold to JOHN WILSON shall remain as they now are, not interfering with the privilege here granted to JOHN WILSON, In consideration whereof JOHN WILSON doth agree to pay JESSE ROPER the sum of Two hundred and twenty five pounds specie in the following manner, to wit, the sum of One hundred pounds at the sealing and delivery hereof, the sum of Twenty five pounds on the tenth day of April next and the sum of One hundred pounds on the first day of March one thousand seven hundred and Eighty seven; on which day last mentioned the said JESSE ROPER doth oblige himself to convey the above granted premises by good and sufficient Deed in the Law unto JOHN WILSON and his heirs in fee simple and for the full performance of this Agreement JESSE ROPER and JOHN WILSON respectively bind themselves their heirs each to the other in the penalty of Four hundred pounds specie; In Witness whereof the said JESSE ROPER and JOHN WILSON have hereunto set their hands and affixed their seals the day and year first above written

Sealed & Acknowledged in presence of

       JOHN BECKLEY,   JESSE ROPER

       CHARLES HAY   JNO: WILSON

At a Court of Hustings for the City of Richmond held at the Public Buildings Monday the 17th of April 1786   This Agreement was proved by the Oaths of JOHN BECKLEY & CHARLES HAY, the witnesses thereto, & ordered to be recorded

                      Teste ADAM CRAIG, C. C.

pp.   (On margin: BYRD's Trustees to ELLIOTT)

60-   THIS INDENTURE made this fifteenth day of March in the year of our Lord one

61   thousand seven hundred and Eighty six Between CHARLES CARTER, the only Surviving Trustee of the Honble. WILLIAM BYRD Esquire deceased of one part

and THOMAS ELLIOTT of the other part; Witnesseth that CHARLES CARTER pursuant to
the power vested in him by Act of Assembly as the only Surviving Trustee of the said
WILLIAM BYRD deced., and in consideration of the sum of Five shillings current money
of Virginia to him in hand paid, by these presents do bargain sell and confirm unto
THOMAS ELLIOTT his heirs a certain half acre lot lying and being in the City of Richmond and known in the plan of said City by the number (624) Six hundred and Twenty
four p. Ticket No. (3692); To have and to hold the half acre lot with all the houses improvements and appurtenances belonging to THOMAS ELLIOTT his heirs; And CHARLES
CARTER by virtue of the trust in him reposed against all persons claiming under him
the half acre lot and its appurtenances to THOMAS ELLIOTT his heirs by these presents
shall warrant and forever defend; In Witness whereof the said CHARLES CARTER the
only Surviving Trustee of WILLIAM BYRD Esqr. hath hereunto set his hand and affixed
his seal the day and year above written
Signed Sealed and delivered in presence of
     ANDW. RONALD, F. WEBB JUNR.   CHAS. CHARTER
     GEO: NICOLSON, JAMES CURRIE
At a Court of Hustings for the City of Richmond held at the Courthouse in the said City
on Monday the 20th March 1786   This Indenture was proved by the Oaths of ANDREW
RONALD & GEORGE NICOLSON, two of the witnesses thereto, And at another Court held for
the said City the Seventeenth day of April following, the same was further proved by
the Oath of FOSTER WEBB JR., another witness thereto, and ordered to be recorded
           Teste ADAM CRAIG, C. C.

pp.   (On margin: BYRD's Trustee to MINOR)
61-   THIS INDENTURE made this 15th day of March in the year of our Lord one thou-
62   sand seven hundred and Eighty six Between CHARLES CARTER, the only Survi-
     ving Trustee of the Honorable WILLIAM BYRD Esqr., deceased, of the one part
and DABNEY MINOR of the other part; Witnesseth that CHARLES CARTER, pursuant to
the Power vested in him by an Act of the General Assembly as the only Surviving Trustee of the said WILLIAM BYRD deceased and in consideration of the sum of Five shillings current money of Virginia to him in hand paid by these presents doth bargain
sell and confirm unto DABNEY MINOR his heirs a certain half acre lot lying in the City
of Richmond number Six hundred and five, as laid down in the plan of said City; To
have and to hold the half acre lot with all houses improvements and appurtenances
belonging to DABNEY MINOR his heirs, And CHARLES CARTER by virtue of the Trust in
him reposed against himself his heirs and all persons claiming under him the half acre
lott and its appurtenances to DABNEY MINOR his heirs by these presents shall warrant
and forever defend; In Witness whereof said CHARLES CARTER, the only Surviving
Trustee of WILLIAM BYRD Esqr., hath hereunto set his hand and affixed his seal the day
and year above written
Signed Sealed and delivered in presence of
     ANDRW: RONALD, F. WEBB JR.,   CHAS: CARTER
     GEO: NICOLSON, JAMES CURRIE
At a Court of Hustings for the City of Richmond held at the Courthouse of the said City
on Monday the 20th March 1786   This Indenture was proved by the Oaths of ANDREW
RONALD and GEORGE NICOLSON, two of the witnesses thereto, And at another Court held
for the said City the Seventeenth day of April following, the same was further proved
by the Oath of FOSTER WEBB JUNR. another witness thereto, and ordered to be recorded
           Teste ADAM CRAIG, C. C.

p.   (On margin: EGE &c. to BENN (a Negro slave)
63   KNOW ALL MEN by these presents that we DOROTHEA EGE, SAMUEL EGE, JACOB
        EGE, ANN EGE, DAVID LAMBERT and GABRIEL GALT, all of the City of Richmond
and County of HENRICO, in consideration of the sum of Twenty pounds to us in hand paid
or secured to be paid by a Negro man slave named Ben, belonging to us, have and do
emancipate and set Free the said Negro man slave Ben by hereby relinquishing and
forever quiting claim to all estate right title or property which we our heirs have or
might and could have had if these presents had never been made, granting him all
rights priviledges and advantages which free Negroes are by Law intitled to and forever warranting to him the said Ben his heirs the peaceable possession of the Freedom
and Emancipation aforesaid against the title claim or demand of every person claiming
under us our heirs: As Witness we have hereunto set our hands and seals this Sixth day
of April 1786
Witness JOHN CLARK.   DOROTHEA EGE
        DAVID EAST   SAMUEL EGE
                                             JACOB EGE
                                             ANN EGE
                                             D. LAMBERT
                                             G. GALT
    At a Court of Hustings for the City of Richmond held at the Public Buildings in the said
City on Monday the 17th April 1786   This Deed of Emancipation was proved by the
Oaths of JOHN CLARK and DAVID EAST, the witnesses thereto and ordered to be recorded
                        Teste ADAM CRAIG, C.C.

pp.   (On margin: LEWIS to BURTON)
64-   THIS INDENTURE made the twenty third day of March in the year of our Lord
65   one thousand seven hundred and Eighty six between GILLY LEWIS of County of
        HENRICO of the one part and JOHN BURTON of City of Richmond of the other part:
Witnesseth that in consideration of the sum of Five shillings to him in hand paid by
JOHN BURTON, he the said GILLY LEWIS by these presents doth bargain sell and confirm unto JOHN BURTON his heirs one half acre lot or tenement of land in City of Richmond adjoining the WAREHOUSES of the TOBACCO INSPECTION at ROCKITTS LANDING and
marked and numbered in the plan of said City (No. 169); Together with all houses gardens and other improvements belonging; To have and to hold the half acre lott or tenement of land with all appurtenances unto JOHN BURTON his heirs And GILLY LEWIS will
forever warrant and defend the right title and possession of the same unto JOHN BUR-
TON his heirs against the demand of all persons; In Witness whereof the said GILLY
LEWIS hath hereunto set his hand and affixed his seal the day and year above written
Sealed and delivered in presence of
        JOHN ROPER, JOHN STEWART,   GILLEY LEWIS
        JOHN GUNN, JACOB THOMAS
    At a Court of Hustings for the City of Richmond held at the Publick Buildings in the
said City on Monday the 17th April 1786
This Indenture was proved by the oaths of JOHN ROPER and JACOB THOMAS, two of the
witnesses thereto, And at a Court continued and held for the said City on Tuesday following, the same was further proved by the Oath of JOHN GUNN, another witness thereto and ordered to be recorded   Teste ADAM CRAIG, C.C.

pp.   (On margin: JOHN BRYAN's Will)
65-   IN THE NAME OF GOD Amen. I JOHN BRYAN of the City of Richmond being sick
67   and weak of body but of sound mind and perfect sense and memory do make and
         ordain this my last Will and Testament, in manner and form following. Vizt.,
first I recommend my Soul into the hands of Almighty God and my body to the ground to
be buried at the discretion of my Executors herein after named; in sure and certain
hope of the resurrection from death.

Item. I give and bequeath unto my five Children, Vizt. JOHN BRYAN, SIMKIN BRYAN,
PRISCILLA BRYAN, BENJAMIN BRYAN, WILSON BRYAN and to my two Grand Children,
JOHN SIMMONER MAUZEY and WILLIAM MURPHY, the two half acre lots on which I now
live (directing that my Son, SIMKIN BRYAN, may have a right of Choice to that part
where the Store now stands in lieu of any other part if he chuses) to be equally divided
amongst them to them and their heirs forever;

Item. I give unto my Daughter, MARY MAUZEY one Silver Table Spoon and a pair of
Silver Tea tongs to her and her heirs forever;

Item. I give unto my Daughter, PRISCILLA BRYAN, one Cow and Calf, two Candle
Moulds, two Silver Tea Spoons, a horse of Ten pounds value, a saddle and bridle of the
price of four pounds, also a Negro girl named Pall, and her increase, to her and her
heirs forever; but if she shou'd die before she becomes of age or without leaving lawful
issue then and in that case my desire is that what is given to her may be sold and the
money arising from such sale to be equally divided amongst my other four children
named above and the Children of my Daughter, MARY MAUZEY & SARAH MURPHEY, to
them and their heirs forever.

Item. I give unto my Daughter, SARAH MURPHEY, one Cow and Calf and two candle
Moulds to her and her heirs forever;

Item. I give unto my Wife, OBEDIENCE BRYAN, my Negro girl Sarah, and her increase,
also all my household and kitchen furniture not already bequeathed for and during the
term of her natural life & at her death my order and desire is that the said Negroe girl
and her increasse, if any, also the household and kitchen furniture be sold and the
money arising from such sale to be divided in the same manner as is directed in case
my Daughter, PRISCILLA BRYAN, dies before she arives at age or without lawful issue.
My desire is that my Wife may have her thirds of the Lots where she now lives during
her life.

Item. My desire and order is that the Rent of that part of my lotts which may fall to my
two grand Children, JOHN SIMMONER MAUZEY and WILLIAM MURPHEY, may be equally
divided between them and ELIZABETH MAUZEY and JOHN MURPHEY JUNR. until the said
JOHN SIMMONER MAUZEY and WILLIAM MURPHEY shall arive to the aGe of twenty one
years;

Item. I appoint my Sons, JOHN BRYAN, SIMKIN BRYAN, my Son in Law, PETER MAUZEY
and my Friend, JOHN BROOKE, Executors of this my Last Will and Testament, herEby revoking all former Wills by me made. In Witness whereof I have hereunto set my hand
& seal this Ninth day of December one thousand seven hundred and eighty five
Signed Sealed and delivered in presence of
         HENRY ANDERSON, DAVID HOLLOWAY   JOHN BRYAN
         JAMES BISSET, JOHN COURTNEY
At a Court of Hustings for the City of Richmond continued and held at the Public Buildings in the said City on Tuesday the 18th of April 1786
This Will was proved by the Oaths of JAMES BISSETT and JOHN COURTNEY, two of the witnesses thereto and ordered to be recorded. And on the motion of JOHN BRYAN, one of
the Exors named in the said Will, who made Oath thereto, and together with SIMKIN

BRYAN & JAMES BISSET, his securities, entered into and acknowledged their Bond in the penalty of Two hundred pounds, conditioned as the Law directs, Certificate is granted him for obtaining a Probat thereof in due form; Liberty being reserved to the other Executors therein named to join in the said Probat when they shall think fit
Teste ADAM CRAIG, C.C.

pp.   (On margin: WILLIAM LUDEMAN's Appraismt.)
68-   1 1/2 yds. Cloth, 1 blue great coat, 1 blue close bodied ditto, 1 green ditto, 1 pea
70   green ditto, 1 light blue ditto, 1 white O. waistcoat & breeches, 2 pair black
         breeches. 1 waistcoat, 2 pair velvet breeches, 3 waistcoast and one pair drawers
flannel. 1 silk & cotton waistcoat pattern, 1 1/2 yds. Cambrick, 8 yds. linnen, a mourning gown, 6 stocks, 5 cravats, 11 shirts, 2 pair drawers linnen,3 purses, 12 handkerchiefs, 2 black silk waist and breeches, 1 silk stok. wt. pattern, 1 cotton ditto, 2 straw
col· silk wt., 1 silk waistcoat, 3 waistcoats, 3 pair breeches dimity, 3 pr. nankeen
breeches and 1 waistcoat, 1 gingham waistcoat, 9 pair silk stockings, 7 pair cotton and
thread ditto. 1 pair worsted ditto, 7 pair gloves; 6 tassels, 1 razor case, 1 sword, box contg.
a pair paste knee buckles, 1 paste stock buckle, 1 Silver ditto, 2 pair plated knee ditto; 1
pair Gold sleve buttons, 1 Gold Ring & Broach, 3 pair black tin shoe buckles, 1 pair
plated spurrs, 1 pair Silver sleve buttons, 1 1/2 doz. Gold basket ditto; 4 doz: coat, 3 doz.
small buttons, 3 cork screws, 1 pair scissors, 1 nutmeg grater, 1 Seal, 3 Ivory two horn
combs, 1 tooth brush, 3 Ink stands, 2 brushes, 1 file and pair shearers, 2 flutes, 2 hats, 1
shaving box, 2 pocket books, 5 Books, 1 portmanteau, 3 pair shoes, 1 pair slippers, pair
boots; 1 teapot, 3 bowles 1 Walnut chest, 1 portmanteau trunk, 1 curry comb & brush, 1
Silver watch, 1 Sadle and bridle, 2 false queu's, 1 Masonic Apron   Total L. 54...0...0.
The above Appraisement of WILLIAM LUDEMANs Effects done the 18th of April 1786
                              JOHN STEWART
                              Dd. LAMBERT
                              JOHN GUNN
Returned into the Court of Hustings for the City of Richmond the 18th day of April
1786 and ordered to be recorded   Teste ADAM CRAIG, C.C.

PP   (On margin: BYRD's Trustee to HARRISON)
70-   THIS INDENTURE made this twenty fourth day of September in the year of our
71   Lord one thousand seven hundred and Eighty five Between CHARLES CARTER
         Esquire, Surviving Trustee of the late WILLIAM BYRD, Esquire, deceased, of one
part and BENJAMIN HARRISON Esquire of BERKLEY, of other part; Witnesseth that
CHARLES CARTER in consideration of the sum of One shilling current money to him in
hand paid by BENJAMIN HARRISON, as well as for the cause and consideration of a
Lottery Tickett, number Two thousand nine hundred and eleven, formerly drawn in a
Lottery of said WILLIAM BYRD and intitled to demand and have as a prize in the said
Lottery a lot of land in the City of Richmond, distinguished in the Original Plan by the
number Five hundred & Twelve, and containing one half acre, said CHARLES CARTER in
pursuance of an Act of the General Assembly held the fifth day of November one thousand seven hundred and eighty one intitled, "An Act to secure to Persons who derive
titles to lotts, lands or Tenements under the Lottery, or under the Deed of Trust of the
late WILLIAM BRYD Esquire, a fee simple Estate therein,", by these presents doth bargain and sell unto BENJAMIN HARRISON his heirs the lot of land in the City of Richmond known in the plan thereof by the number Five hundred and Twelve and containing half acre with all priviledges and appurtenances, To have and to hold the one
half acre lot of land with all its appurtenances unto BENJAMIN HARRISON his heirs, In

Witness whereof the said CHARLES CARTER hath to these presents set his hand and affixed his seal the day and year first above written
Signed Sealed and delivered in presence of
            JNO: W. PRICE, JAMES BUCHANAN,   CHARLES CARTER
            JNO: McKEAND, NATHANIEL SELDEN
   At a Court of Hustings for the City of Richmond held at the Public Buildings in the said City on Monday the 15th of May 1786   This Indenture was proved by the Oaths of JOHN W. PRICE, JAMES BUCHANAN and NATHANIEL SELDEN, witnesses thereto, and ordered to be recorded   Teste ADAM CRAIG, C.C.

p.   (On margin: JNO: BRYAN's Appmt.)
72   AN INVENTORY of the slaves and personal Estate of JNO: BRYAN, deced.
      One Negro woman Sarah (L. 60..0..0); One ditto girl Patt (L. 27..0..0); One horse (L. 7..0..0); One Cow & Calf (L. 3...10...0); one Cart & gear (L. 2..0..0); one Bed, bedstead & furniture (L. 4..10..0); one corner cupboard, seven chairs, two old Pine tables, six plates of Q. Ware, 2 old dishes, 2 old flax wheels and one cotton ditto; 6 candle moulds, 1 kettle, pot and pan, 1 Dutch oven, 1 box and two flat irons, 2 tubs and one pale; iron pot racks, looking glass, old Silver spoon, side saddle, sundry Old Books, clothes press; Total. L. 113...19...0.
   City of Richmond. Pursuant to an Order of the Court of Hustings of the 18th April 1786; We have apppraised the Estate of JOHN BRYAN deced. to L. 113...19...0; Witness our hands this 6th May 1786.   DABNEY MINOR
                                SAMUEL DOBIE
                                WILLIAM COCKE SENR.
   Returned into the Court of Hustings of the City of Richmond on Monday the 15th day of May 1786 and ordered to be recorded
            Teste ADAM CRAIG, C.C.

pp.   (On margin: BUCHANAN &c.. to ISAACS)
73-   THIS INDENTURE made this twenty seventh day of September in the year of our
74   Lord one thousand seven hundred and eighty five between JAMES BUCHANAN, DAVID PATTESON and ELIZABETH ANNE his Wife of one part and ISAIAH ISAACS of the other part; Witnesseth that in consideration of Thirty pounds current money of Virginia by ISAIAH ISAACS unto JAMES BUCHANAN, DAVID PATTESON and ELIZA: ANNE his Wife in hand paid, by these presents do bargain sell and confirm unto ISAIAH ISAACS his heirs a certain half acre lot of land lying in City of Richmond known by the plan of said City by the number 359 (three hundred and fifty nine), To have and to hold the half acre lot with all its appurtenances thereunto belonging to ISAIAH ISAACS his heirs and JAMES BUCHANAN, DAVID PATTESON and ELIZABETH ANN his Wife the half acre lot with all appurtenances against any person to ISAIAH ISAACS his heirs shall warrant and forever defend by these presents. In Witness whereof they the said JAMES BUCHANAN, DAVID PATTESON and ELIZABETH ANNE his Wife have hereunto set their hands and affixed their seals the day and year above written
Signed Sealed & Delivered in the presence of us
            JOHN LYNE, JNO: W. PRICE,   JAMES BUCHANAN
            JNO: GRAHAM, NAT: SELDEN   DAVID PATTESON
                                ELIZA: A. PATTESON
   At a Court of Hustings for the City of Richmond held at the Courthouse of the said City on Monday the 17th July 1786   This Indenture was acknowledged by JAMES BUCHANAN, one of the parties thereto, and proved as to DAVID PATTESON, another of the

parties thereto by the Oaths of JOHN W. PRICE, JOHN GRAHAM and NATHANIEL SELDEN, three of the witnesses thereto, & ordered to be recorded
                              Teste ADAM CRAIG, C. C.

p.   (On margin: HOPKINS to KEMP & STILL)
74   KNOW ALL MEN by these presents that whereas a suit is depending in the Court
          of HENRICO between GEORGE HOPE and myself and SETH FOSTER and as my lawful
and necessary business occasions my immediate absence out of this State which may
prevent my attending on the day it may probably come to issue, I do hereby impower
JAMES KEMP or BASSETT STILL to act for me in any matter of Appeal respecting the said
suit, warranting and authorising either of them the said JAMES KEMP or BASSETT STILL
to sign my name to any Bond or any other Instrument of Writing in Law that may be
necessary to establish an Appeal in the same, hereby ratifying and confirming either
of them doing so, to be equally binding on me my heirs &c. as if the same was personally done by myself. In Witness whereof I have hereunto set my hand and seal this 29th
day of July 1786
Signed Sealed and Delivered in presence of
    ROBERT POINDEXTER   JNO: HOPKINS
  At a Court of Hustings for the City of Richmond held at the Courthouse on Monday the
21st day of August 1786   This Power of Attorney was proved by the Oath of ROBERT
POINDEXTER, the witness thereto, & ordered to be recorded
                              Teste ADAM CRAIG, C. C.

p.   (On margin: GILBERT to CHARLTON) (Two pages numbered 74)
74   THIS INDENTURE made this Sixth day of June in the year of our Lord one thou-
          sand seven hundred and Eighty six Between ROBERT GILBERT of City of Rich-
mond of one part and JANE CHARLTON of the same City of the other part; Witnesseth
that ROBERT GILBERT in consideration of a Debt due from the said ROBERT to the said
JANE, amounting to Three hundred pounds specie, said ROBERT GILBERT by these presents doth bargain sell and deliver unto JANE CHARLTON six Negroe slaves as follows;
Anthony, Jack, George, Sampson, Hannah and her Child Annaka; To have and to hold
the slaves unto JANE CHARLTON her heirs and ROBERT GILBERT the Negroes with their
future increase to the use of JANE CHARLTON her heirs against every person shall
warrant and forever defend by these presents; PROVIDED Always, that if ROBERT GIL-
BER shall pay or cause to be paid unto JANE CHARLTON or assigns the aforesaid sum of
Three hundred pounds specie on or before the first day of October next, that then these
presents shall cease determine and be utterly void but if default be made in payment of
the same or any part thereof, then these presents shall remain in full force and virtue
Signed sealed and delivered in presence of
    ADAM CRAIG,   ROBT. GILBERT
    CLAIBORNE WATKINS, WILLIAM WHITLOCK
  At a Court of Hustings for the City of Richmond held at the Courthouse on Monday the
21st of August 1786.   This Mortgage was proved by the Oaths of ADAM CRAIG, CLAI-
BORNE WATKINS and WILLIAM WHITLOCK, witnesses thereto, and ordered to be recorded
                              Teste ADAM CRAIG, C. C.

p.   (On margin: MORRIS to PATTERSON)
75   THIS INDENTURE made this fourth day of May one thousand seven hundred and
          eighty six Between JOSHUA MORRIS of City of Richmond of one part and JAMES
PATTERSON of said City of other part; Witnesseth that JOSHUA MORRIS in consideration

of the sum of One hundred and ten pounds to him in hand paid, by these presents do
bargain and confirm unto JAMES PATTERSON his heirs a certain parcel of ground in
City of Richmond containing Twenty four feet in front, on the Main Street (leading
over the Bridge) and One hundred and six in the rear, on lot Six hundred & sixty one, on
which lot said MORRIS now lives, the said twenty four feet in front beginning on the
upper part of said lot on which a House sixteen feet square to him the said PATTERSON
his heirs, And JOSHUA MORRIS against the lawful claim of any person claiming under
him the said twenty four feet in front and one hundred in the rear with all appurtenances to JAMES PATTERSON his heirs by these presents shall warrant and forever
defend; In Witness whereof the said JOSHUA MORRIS hath hereunto set his hand and
affixed his seal the day and year above written
Signed Sealed and delivered in presence of
      JOHN COURTNEY,   JOSHUA MORRIS
      RICHARD NEALE, BERNARD NEALE
1786. May 9th. Received of Mr. JAMES PATTERSON one hundred and ten pounds
Teste RICHD. NEALE,   JOSHUA MORRIS
      JOHN COURTNEY, BERNARD NEALE
  At a Court of Hustings for the City of Richmond held at the Courthouse on Monday the
21st of August 1786   This Indenture with the Receipt hereon indorsed were acknowledged by JOSHUA MORRIS, party thereto, and ordered to be recorded
                    Teste ADAM CRAIG, C.C.

pp   (On margin: CARTER to CARTER)
76-   THIS INDENTURE made this thirtieth day of January one thousand seven hun-
75   dred and eighty six Between THOMAS CARTER of the City of Richmond of one part
        and WILLIAM CARTER of City of WILLIAMSBURG of other part. Whereas by cer-
tain Articles of Agreement heretofore made and subsisting between the said parties
entered into the twenty sixth day of June in the year of our Lord one thousand seven
hundred and eighty four, a Partnership was concluded between them in the Practice of
Physick and Surgery, and the Establishment of an Apothecary's & Druggist Shop in the
City of Richmond, which said Partnership commenced on the first day of July in the
same year and by the terms thereof was to continue in force for the term of five eyars
at the joint and equal expence of said parties; And Whereas by a subsequent Agreement
bearing date the Sixth day of December last and one other supplemental thereto
bearing date the fourteenth day of this present month of January made between the
said parties, it has been considered and determined that the said Partnership shall be
dissolved from and after the first day of February next ensuing the day of the date of
these presents, that all property of whatever nature and all the Drugs Medicines and
Material belonging to the Partnership shall be equally divided, and each party to take
his equal proportion of the same, that the Debts contracted on Account of the Shop (ex-
clusive of a Sterling Debt due to Messrs. SLATER and COMPANY of LONDON) shall be first
paid and that THOMAS CARTER should assure and convey unto WILLIAM CARTER all his
Estate and property both real and personal of whatsoever nature in Trust for the payment of his, the said THOMAS CARTER's full moiety of the said Sterling Debt due to
Messrs. SLATER & COMPANY of LONDON, and to indemnify WILLIAM CARTER for his
responsibility for the said Debt in case of the default of said THOMAS CARTER in the
payment of his full moiety thereof as aforesaid; NOW THIS INDENTURE WITNESSETH that
in consideration of the sum of Five shillings in hand paid by WILLIAM CARTER to THO-
MAS CARTER as also in consideration of the Agreement recited, said THOMAS CARTER by
these present doth bargain sell and enfeoff unto WILLIAM CARTER his heirs all said

THOMAS CARTER's full moiety and proportion of the Drugs, Medicines and Materials of the Partnership according to an Inventory thereof to be taken and subscribed by each of the said parties at the time of the dissolution of the Partnership and also the Estate and prperty following, to wit, a Negro wench named Fanny, three tables, one bedstead, one looking glass, one chest of drawers, one dozen Silver Tea Spoons, ten spoons, one do. of Windser Chairs, two fenders tongs and poker, two saucepans, three iron pots. And moreover THOMAS CARTER by these presents doth bargain sell and set over unto WILLIAM CARTER his heirs all said THOMAS CARTER's right title or demand which he now has or may have in right of his Wife, ANNE, one of the Daughters of WILLIAM BROADNAX, late of the County of SUSSEX deceased, who died intestate to a distributive share of the slaves and personal estate of said WILLIAM BROADNAX deced., To have and to hold the Estate and effects hereby sold and all other the interest and Estate of THOMAS CARTER hereby set over unto WILLIAM CARTER his heirs, IN TRUST, NEVERTHELESS and upon this condition that if THOMAS CARTER shall bonafide pay his full moiety and proportion of the Debt due in Sterling money from the Partnership of THOMAS & WILLIAM CARTER unto Messrs. SLATER & COMPANY of LONDON, that then WILLIAM CARTER his heirs shall execute and pass unto THOMAS CARTER his heirs good and sufficient Deed or Deeds in the Law for the relinquishment and surrender of all the Estate and interest hereby granted; In Witness whereof the said THOMAS CARTER hath hereunto set his hand & affixed his seal the day and year first above written
Signed Sealed & Delivered in presence of
ANTHONY GEOGHAGAN, JOHN REILLY,   THOMAS CARTER
THOMAS OUSBY, WILLIAM CARTER JR.
At a Court of Hustings for the City of Richmond held at the Courthouse on Monday the 21st day of August 1786   This Indenture of Mortgage and Agreement was proved by the Oaths of ANTHONY GEOGHAGAN and JOHN REILLY, two of the witnesses thereto and ordered to be recorded   Teste ADAM CRAIG, C.C.

p.   (On margin: ANDERSON to BECKLEY)
78   KNOW ALL MEN by these presents that I GEORGE ANDERSON of the City of Richmond in consideration of the sum of Ninety eight pounds five shillings to me in hand paid by JOHN BECKLEY of said City, have bargained and sold unto JOHN BECKLEY his heirs a Negro woman named Lucy and her Child, Charles, and do hereby for the consideration aforesaid warrant and defend the right title property and possession of the said Negro woman, Lucy, and her Child, Charles, together with the future increase of the said Lucy unto JOHN BECKLEY his heirs against the title claim or demand of all persons claiming under me the said GEORGE ANDERSON; In Witness whereof I have hereunto set my hand and affixed my seal this 18th day of April 1786
G. ANDERSON
At a Court of Hustings for the City of Richmond held at the Courthouse on Monday the 18th of September 1786. This Bill of Sale was acknowledged by GEORGE ANDERSON, party thereto & ordered to be recorded   Teste ADAM CRAIG, C.C.

pp.   (On margin: COLES to YOUNGHUSBAND)
78-   THIS INDENTURE made this twelfth day of April in the year of our Lord one
80   thousand seven hundred and eighty six Between JOHN COLES of the County of ALBEMARLE of one part and ISAAC YOUNGHUSBAND of the City of Richmond of other part; Witnesseth Whereas JOHN COLES of the County of HENRICO deced., was in his life time and at the time of his death, together with other real and personal estate, seized and possessed in fee of the lots of land after mentioned lying in City of Richmond, who by his Last Will and Testament did among other bequests and legacies devise

the same in manner following, that is to say, "Also its my desire all the land lots & houses belonging to me below the Hill where I live on in the Town of Richmond shall be equally divided between my three Sons, WALTER, JOHN & ISAAC COLES, to them and their heirs forever," and by said Last Will and Testament duly proved and recorded in the County Court of HENRICO; And whereas WALTER COLES, with privity and consent of the said JOHN & ISAAC COLES in the said devise mentioned did sell and dispose of to said ISAAC YOUNGHUSBAND for the consideration of Forty pounds, two of the lots of land devised to them as aforesaid, known and distinguished by the numbers of Twenty seven /27/ and Twenty eight /28/, together with all the appurtenances thereunto belonging; but WALTER COLES having departed this life without any conveyance or assurance of said lotts and appurtenances being made to ISAAC YOUNGHUSBAND and JOHN COLES being willing and desirous to convey to ISAAC YOUNGHUSBAND all his right and title thereunto, being one third part thereof, NOW THIS INDENTURE WITNESSETH that JOHN COLES in consideration of one third of the premsies and also for the sum of five shillings to him in hand paid by ISAAC YOUNGHUSBAND by these presents doth bargain and sell unto ISAAC YOUNGHUSBAND and his heirs one third part of the aforesaid two lots of land with the appurtenances; To have and to hold the one third part of said two lots of land unto ISAAC YOUNGHUSBAND his heirs and JOHN COLES doth for himself his heirs agree with ISAAC YOUNGHUSBAND his heirs that JOHN COLES will warrant & forever defend the title of said one third part of said two lots hereby conveyed against the claim or demand of himself his heirs; In Witness whereof the said JOHN COLES hath hereunto set his hand and affixed his seal the day and year above written
Signed Sealed and delivered in presence of
    SARAFINO FORMIEOLA,   JOHN COLES
    JOSHUA HUMPHREYS, WILLIAM DUNCAN
At a Court of Hustings for the City of Richmond held at the Courthouse on Monday the 18th of September 1786   This Indenture was proved by the Oaths of SARAFINO FORMIEOLA, JOSHUA HUMPHREYS and WILLIAM DUNCAN, the witnesses thereto and ordered to be recorded   Teste ADAM CRAIG, C.C.

pp.   (On margin: COLES to YOUNGHUSBAND)
80-   THIS INDENTURE made this thirtieth day of January in the year of our Lord one
81   thousand seven hundred and eighty six Between ISAAC COLES of County of HALI-
      FAX of one part and ISAAC YOUNGHUSBAND of City of Richmond of other part;
Whereas JOHN COLES of County of HENRICO deced., was in his life time and at the time of his death together with other real and personal estate seized and possessed in fee of the Lots of Land after mentioned lying in City of Richmond, who by his Last Will and Testament did among other bequests and Legacies devise the same in manner following, that is to say, "Also its my desire all the land lots and houses belonging to me below the Hill where I live on in the Town of Richmond shall equally be divided betweeen my three Sons, WALTER, JOHN & ISAAC COLES, to them and their heirs forever," as by said Last Will and Testament duly proved and recorded in the County Court of HENRICO, & whereas said WALTER COLES with the privity and consent of the said JOHN and ISAAC COLES in the said devise mentioned did sell and dispose of to ISAAC YOUNGHUSBAND for the consideration of Forty pounds two of the lots of land devised to them as aforesaid known and distinguished by the numbers Twenty seven /27/ and Twenty eight /28/, together with all appurtenances thereunto belonging; But the said WALTER COLES having departed this life without any conveyance or assurance of said lots and appurtenances being made to ISAAC YOUNGHUSBAND and the aforesaid ISAAC COLES being willing and desirous to convey to ISAAC YOUNGHUSBAND all his right and title thereto, being one

third part thereof; NOW THIS INDENTURE WITNESSETH that ISAAC COLES in consideration of one third of the premises and also in consideration of the sum of Five shillings
to him in hand paid by ISAAC YOUNGHUSBAND, by these presents doth bargain and sell
unto ISAAC YOUNGHUSBAND and his heirs one third part of the aforesaid two lotts of
land with the appurtenances; To have and to hold the said one third part of said two lots
of land unto ISAAC YOUNGHUSBAND his heirs, And ISAAC COLES doth for himself his
heirs agree with ISAAC YOUNGHUSBAND his heirs that he will warrant and forever defend the title of said one third part of the two lots hereby conveyed against the claim or
demand of himself his heirs; In Witness whereof said ISAAC COLES hath hereunto set
his hand and affixed his seal the day and year above written
Signed Sealed & Delivered in presence of
    SAML: TROWER,   ISAAC COLES
    WILLIAM DUNCAN, SARAFINO FORMIEOLA
  At a Court of Hustings for the City of Richmond held at the Courthouse on the 18th of
September 1786   This Indenture was proved by the Oaths of SAMUEL TROWER, WIL-
LIAM DUNCAN and SERAFINA FORMIEOLA, the witnesses thereto, and ordered to be
recorded   Teste ADAM CRAIG, C. C.

pp.   (On margin: YOUNGHUSBAND to PLEASANTS. Commission for taking Mrs.
81-   MARY YOUNGHUSBANDs acknowledgment recorded in County Court
82   Book No. 4.)
    THIS INDENTURE made this 18th day of September in the year of our Lord one
thousand seven hundred and eighty six Between ISAAC YOUNGHUSBAND SENR. and
MARY his Wife of City of Richmond of one part and ISAAC WEBSTER PLEASANTS of
County of GOOCHLAND of other part; Witnesseth that ISAAC YOUNGHUSBAND in consideration of the sum of Twenty pounds current money of Virginia in hand paid; by these
presents do bargain sell and confirm unto ISAAC WEBSTER PLEASANTS one certain half
acre of land number Twenty seven /27/ lying on Main Street in the City of Richmond
with all houses gardens profits commodities and hereditaments; To have and to hold the
lott of land with all the appurtenances to ISAAC WEBSTER PLEASANTS his heirs; and
ISAAC YOUNGHUSBAND and MARY his Wife will warrant and forever defend the title of
the said half acre lot of land hereby conveyed against the claim of himself his heirs.
In Witness whereof the said ISAAC YOUNGHUSBAND and MARY his Wife hath hereunto
set their hands and seals the day and year above written
Sealed and Delivered in presence of
    (no witnesses recorded)   ISAAC YOUNGHUSBAND
  At a Court of Hustings for the City of Richmond held at the Courthouse on Monday the
18th day of September 1786   This Indenture was acknowledged by ISAAC YOUNGHUS-
BAND, party thereto, and ordered to be recorded
              Teste ADAM CRAIG, C. C.

pp.   (On margin: HAY & Ux to HAY's Exors)
82-   THIS INDENTURE made this eighteenth day of September in the year of our
84   Lord one thousand seven hundred and eighty six Between WILLIAM HAY of the
        City of Richmond and ELIZABETH his Wife of one part and WILLIAM HAY and
GEORGE NICOLSON, Executors of the Last Will and Testament of JOHN HAY deced., all of
the said City of other part; Whereas WILLIAM HAY in his own right and the said WIL-
LIAM HAY and GEORGE NICOLSON as Executors of said JOHN HAY deced., are possessed of a
Lot with Improvements being part of the Tenement belonging to DAVID ROSS & CO., and
by them conveyed to said WILLIAM HAY one half in his own right & the other half to

said WILLIAM HAY and GEORGE NICOLSON, Executors as aforesaid, by Deed bearing date
the Ninth day of July in the year of our Lord one thousand seven hundred and eighty
five and of Record in the General Court, which lot and improvements has been valued
by consent of parties by JAMES BUCHANAN, Col. TURNER SOUTHALL & DABNEY MINOR to
the sum of Fourteen hundred pounds current money in order to enable the said WIL-
LIAM HAY to convey his moiety to said WILLIAM HAY & GEORGE NICOLSON for the benefit of the Estate of JOHN HAY deceased; NOW THIS INDENTURE WITNESSETH that WILLIAM
HAY and ELIZABETH his Wife in consideration of Seven hundred pounds current money
by WILLIAM HAY and GEORGE NICOLSON, Executors as aforesaid, to WILLIAM HAY in
hand paid, by these presents bargain and sell unto WILLIAM HAY and GEORGE NICOLSON
Executors as aforesaid, the moiety of the aforesaid lot of land improvements belonging
to WILLIAM HAY in his own right, to them and their heirs and all buildings profits and
appurtenances to said moiety belonging; and the rents and issues thereof; Nevertheless
the use of the Cellar and the floor above it in the Lumber House to said WILLIAM HAY
for one year commencing the first day of June last past; To have and to hold the moiety
of the lott and improvements to WILLIAM HAY and GEORGE NICOLSON, Executors as
aforesaid, and their heirs; And WILLIAM HAY and Elizabeth his Wife do covenant for
themselves and their heirs the moiety of the lot and improvements to WILLIAM HAY
and GEORGE NICOLSON, Executors as aforesaid, and their heirs against them and all persons claiming under them lawfully to warrant and forever defend by these presents;
In Witness whereof they have hereunto set their hands and affixed their seals the day
and year first above written
Sealed and Delivered in the presence of
(no witnesses recorded)   WM. HAY
                                                BETSY HAY
    At a Court of Hustings for the City of Richmond held at the Courthouse on Monday the
18th of September 1786   This Indenture was acknowledged by WILLIAM HAY, party
thereto, and ordered to be recorded Teste ADAM CRAIG, C.C.

pp.   (On margin: MILLER to STOCKDELL. Deld. WM. MARSHALL JR.)
84-   THIS INDENTURE made this fifth day of September in the year of our Lord one
86   thousand seven hundred and Eighty six Between DABNEY MILLER of the City of
         Richmond of one part and JOHN STOCKDELL of the same City of other part; Wit-
nesseth that DABNEY MILLER in consideration of the sum of Two hundred and fifty
pounds to him in hand paid by JOHN STOCKDELL, as also in consideration of the yearly
rent and covenants hereafter in and by these presents reserved and contained, on the
part of JOHN STOCKDELL and assigns to be paid and performed by these presents doth
demise lease and to farm let unto JOHN STOCKDELL his heirs three half acre lots or Tenements of land lying on SHOCKOE HILL in City aforesaid with the houses and improvements thereon, being the same now occupied by said DABNEY MILLER, with full power
and Licence to said JOHN STOCKDELL or those claiming under him to build such other
houses or improvements as he they or either of them may think proper at his or their
own costs and charges and the rents issues and profits thereof; to have and receive the
rent hereafter reserved always excepted, To have and to hold the demised premises unto
JOHN STOCKDELL his heirs during the time of Twenty years from the day of the date of
these presents paying unto DABNEY MILLER his heirs on the fifth day of December in
the year of our Lord one thousand seven hundred and eighty eight and on the same day
in every suceeding year, the sum of Two hundred pounds current money, and for the
last year from the fifth day of December until the fifth day of September then next
ensuing when this lease will expire after the same rate; to be paid at his or their option

either in money of actual gold and silver or in bonds or notes for money then actually
due and by him or them to be assigned to DABNEY MILLER his heirs, And the said DAB-
NEY and his heirs the demised premises during the time aforesaid unto said JOHN his
heirs against all persons shall warrant and defend; In Witness whereof the said parties
to these presents have hereunto set their hands and affixed their seals the day and year
first herein written
Signed Sealed and delivered in the presence of
                    (no witnesses recorded)   DABNEY MILLER
                                                               JNO: STOCKDELL
    At a Court of Hustings for the City of Richmond held at the Courthouse on Monday the
18th of September 1786   This Indenture of Lease was acknowledged by DABNEY
MILLER and JOHN STOCKDELL, parties thereto, and ordered to be recorded
                              Teste ADAM CRAIG, C. C.

pp.   (On margin: COLEMAN & Ux. to PENNOCK)
87-   THIS INDENTURE made this tenth day of August in the year of our Lord one
88   thousand seven hundred and eighty six Between SAMUEL COLEMAN of County of
         HENRICO and SUSANNA his Wife of one part and WILLIAM PENNOCK of City of
Richmond in the same County, Merchant, of other part; Witnesseth that in consideration of the sum of Five hundred and thirty pounds current money of Virginia by WIL-
LIAM PENNOCK before the delivery of these presents to said SAMUEL and SUSANNA in
hand paid, said SAMUEL COLEMAN and SUSANNA do by these presents bargain & sell
unto WILLIAM PENNOCK his heirs a certain part of a lot of land in City of Richmond in
the occupation of WILLIAM RUSSELL & COMPANY, lying on a sixteen feet Alley or Lane
running from the Cross Street by JAMES SOUTHALL's Line towards SHOCKOE CREEK, and
containing Sixteen feet in front on the West side of said Alley and one hundred feet
deep thereon. Also one other part of a lot of land adjoining to the former and running
twenty feet on the aforesaid Cross Street in front now in occupation of THOMAS PEDLEY,
likewise one other part of land containing twenty feet in front on the same Street now
in the occupation of FREDERICK THOMAS with all houses warehouses and appurtenances
to the several pieces of land belonging; To have and to hold the several pieces of land
with all appurtenances to WILLIAM PENNOCK his heirs, that said SUSANNA is now seised
in her own right of a clear and unincumbered Estate in fee simple in the respective
lands and other premises and that WILLIAM PENNOCK his heirs shall occupy the same
and take the rents issues and profits thereof to his or their own use without the disturbance of any person; In Witness whereof the said SAMUEL COLEMAN and SUSANNA
his Wife have hereunto set their hands and affixed their seals the day and year first
herein written
Signed Sealed and delivered in presence of
         ROBERT MEANS, SMITH BLAKEY,   SAMUEL COLEMAN
         FRA: RATLIFF   SUSANNA COLEMAN
    Received 10th August 1786, from the within named WILLIAM PENNOCK the sum of five
hundred and thirty pounds, being the full consideration money for the within granted
premises
Teste SMITH BLAKEY   SAML: COLEMAN
                                                   SUSANNA COLEMAN
    At a Court of Hustings for the City of Richmond held at the Courthouse on Monday the
18th of September 1786   This Indenture together with the Receipt endorsed were
acknowledged by SAMUEL COLEMAN and SUSANNA his Wife, parties thereto (she
having been first privily examined as the Law directs) and ordered to be recorded
                              Teste ADAM CRAIG, C. C.

pp.   (On margin: COLEMAN & Ux. to RUSSELL & CO.)
89-   THIS INDENTURE made the fifteenth day of September in the year of our Lord
90   one thousand seven hundred and eighty six Between SAMUEL COLEMAN of Coun-
        ty of HENRICO and SUSANNA his Wife of one part and WILLIAM RUSSELL & COM-
PANY of City of Richmond, Merchants, of other part; Witnesseth that in consideration
of the sum of Three hundred pounds current money of Virginia by WILLIAM RUSSELL
& COMPANY to said SAMUEL and SUSANNA in hand paid; by these presents have bargained and sold unto WILLIAM RUSSELL & COMPANY their heirs a certain lot of land in
the City of Richmond twenty eight feet in front on the Cross Street, down to SAMUEL
COUCH's line, and on the East corner of a sixteen feet Alley, and joining a lot leased to
ROBERT MINS with all houses warehouses and appurtenances to the lot of land; To have
and to hold the piece of land with all other the premises and appurtenances to WIL-
LIAM RUSSELL & COMPANY their heirs and doth covenant that WILLIAM RUSSELL and
COMPANY their heirs shall occupy the same and take the rents issues and profits there-
of to their own proper benefit without the disturbance of any person; In Witness
whereof the said SAMUEL COLEMAN and SUSANNA his Wife have thereunto set their
hands and affixed their seals the same day and year first herein written
Signed Sealed and delivered in presence of
            (no witnesses recorded)   SAMUEL COLEMAN
                                                             SUSANNA COLEMAN
    At a Court of Hustings for City of Richmond held at the Courthouse on Monday the 18th
of September 1786   This Indenture was acknowledged by SAMUEL COLEMAN &
SUSANNA his Wife, parties thereto, (she having been first privily examined as the Law
directs), and ordered to be recorded   Teste ADAM CRAIG, C.C.

pp.   (On margin: COLEMAN to COUCH)
90-   THIS INDENTURE made this fifteenth day of September in the year of our Lord
92   one thousand seven hundred and eighty six Between SAMUEL COLEMAN of the
        County of HENRICO and SUSANNA his Wife of one part and SAMUEL COUCH of the
City of Richmond in the same County, Merchant, of the other part; Witnesseth that in
consideration of the sum of Two hundred and Eighty two pounds current money of Virginia by SAMUEL COUCH to said SAMUEL and SUSANNA in hand paid, said SAMUEL COLE-
MAN and SUSANNA his Wife do by these presents bargain and sell unto SAMUEL COUCH
his heirs a certain part of a lot of land in City of Richmond five feet of ground in the
front on Main Street and Ninety four feet deep, joining that end of the lot next to the
Bridge that the said COUCH bought of JOHN RUSSELL, and joining that lot leased to JOHN
STOCKDELL to a sixteen feet Alley, Also one other lot laying on the Main Street joining
the upper end of the lot bought by said COUCH of JOHN RUSSELL and joining the lot that
is now leased to GEORGE PICKETT, containing in front on the Main Street eighteen feet
and ninety four feet deep from the line of the Main Street to a sixteen feet Ally, with all
houses warehouses and appurtenances to said several pieces of land and the rents
issues and profits thereof; To have and to hold the several pieces of land with all other
the premises and appurtenances to SAMUEL COUCH his heirs and SAMUEL COLEMAN and
SUSANNA his Wife for themselves their heirs do hereby covenant with SAMUEL COUCH
his heirs that SAMUEL COUCH his heirs shall hold the same without the disturbance of
any person; In Witness whereof the said SAMUEL COLEMAN and SUSANNA his Wife
have hereunto set their hands and affixed their seals the same day and year first
herein written
Signed Sealed and delivered in the presence of
            (no witnesses recorded)   SAMUEL COLEMAN
                                                             SUSANNA COLEMAN

Received the 15th of September 1786 from the within named SAMUEL COUCH two hundred and eighty two pounds being the full consideration money of the within granted premises
Teste JNO: GRAHAM   SAMUEL COLEMAN
    At a Court of Hustings for the City of Richmond held at the Courthouse on Monday the 18th of September 1786   This Indenture together with the Receipt endorsed, were acknowledged by SAMUEL COLEMAN and SUSANNA his Wife, parties thereto, (she having been first privily examined as the Law directs) and ordered to be recorded
                        Teste ADAM CRAIG, C.C.

pp.   (On margin: SCHERER to SCOTT)
92-   THIS INDENTURE made this 2d. day of June in the year of our Lord one thousand
93   seven hundred and Seventy seven Between NICHOLAS SCHERER of one part and
           ANN SCOTT of the other part; Witnesseth that NICHOLAS SCHERER in considera-
tion of the sum of Sixteen pounds, one shillings and six pence, hath bargained and sold
by these presents a part of a tract of land lying in HENRICO County containing Ten
acres and three quarters; beginning at a corner black Oak saplin on WILLIAM NEW's
line, thence North forty degrees East fifty one poles to a Branch, thence up the Branch
forty poles to a corner Pine, thence South forty one and a quarter West forty poles to a
corner two small Oak saplins, thence South sixty and an half East thirty five poles to the
beginning; To have and to hold the tract of land to ANN SCOTT and her heirs. And
NICHOLAS SCHERER has hereunto set his hand and seal the day and year above written
Signed Sealed and delivered in presence of
       WILLIAM RICHARDSON,   NICH: SCHERER
       FREDERICK THOMAS
 HENRICO County August Court 1777.
   This Deed from NICHOLAS SCHERER to ANN SCOTT was acknowledged in Court and
admitted to Record   Teste WILLIAM WHITE D.C.C.
   At a Court of Hustings for the City of Richmond held at the Courthouse on Monday the
18th of September 1786   This Indenture (the Record of which having been destroyed
by the enemy) was presented in Court and with the Certificate of the acknowledgment
thereof, ordered to be again recorded   Teste ADAM CRAIG, C.C.

pp   (On margin: SCOTT to BETTIS)
93-   THIS INDENTURE made this eighteenth day of September in the year of our Lord
94   one thousand seven hundred and eighty six Between ANNE SCOTT of County of
           HENRICO of one part and BEN a free Mulatto, sometimes called BEN BETTIS, of the
same County of other part; Witnesseth that said ANNE SCOTT in consideration of the sum
of Twenty pounds to her in hand paid by these presents doth bargain sell and confirm
unto said BEN BETTIS his heirs all that parcel of land lying in County of HENRICO and
within the limits of the Jurisdiction of the City of Richmond, beginning at a corner
black Oak saplin on WILLIAM NEW's line, thence running North forty degrees East fifty
one poles to a Branch, thence up the Branch forty poles to a corner Pine, thence South
forty one degrees and a quarter West forty poles to a corner two small Oak saplins,
thence South sixty one and a half degrees East thirty five poles to the beginning; being
the same parcel of land heretofore conveyed by NICHOLAS SHERER to ANNE SCOTT by
Deed bearing date the second day of June 1777; To have and to hold the parcel of land
and appurtenances unto BEN BETTIS his heirs freely and clearly exonerated from all
incumbrances whatsoever; And ANNE SCOTT for herself her heirs doth covenant with
BEN BETTIS his heirs that she will warrant and forever defend against the title claim or

demand of all persons; In Witness whereof the said ANNE SCOTT hath hereunto set her
hand and affixed her seal the day and year first above written
Signed Sealed and delivered in presence of
     JOHN BECKLEY,   ANNE her mark   /   SCOTT
     GEO: ANDERSON, ARCHIBALD ROSE
    At a Court of Hustings for the City of Richmond held at the Courthouse on Monday the
18th of September 1786   This Indenture was proved by the Oaths of JOHN BECKLEY,
GEORGE ANDERSON and ARCHIBALD ROSE, witnesses thereto, and ordered to be recorded
                          Teste ADAM CRAIG, C.C.

pp.   (On margin: COLEMAN & Ux. to PICKETT)
94-   THIS INDENTURE made the first day of September Anno Domini one thousand
96   seven hundred and eighty six Between SAMUEL COLEMAN of County of HENRICO
        and SUSANNA his Wife of one part and GEORGE PICKETT of the City of Richmond
of other part; Witnesseth that in consideration of the sum of Five shillings current
money of Virginia by GEORGE PICKETT in hand paid to said SAMUEL COLEMAN and
SUSANNA his Wife, said SAMUEL COLEMAN and SUSANNA his Wife for themselves jointly
and severally and for each of their joint and several heirs, particularly the heirs of the
said SUSANNA, by these presents do bargain sell and confirm unto GEORGE PICKETT and
his heirs a certain lot of ground in City of Richmond on the North West side of SHOCKOE
CREEK, Beginning on the Main Street at JOHN WALKER's Corner, thence with WALKER's
Line ninety four feet to a fifteen feet Alley, thence up the line of said Alley twenty one
feet to SAMUEL COUCH's Corner, thence with COUCH's line ninety four feet to the Main
Street aforesaid, thence down the said Main Street twenty one feet to the beginning; To
have and to hold by him said GEORGE PICKETT and his heirs of SAMUEL COLEMAN and
SUSANNA his Wife, together with the appurtenances thereunto belonging; SUBJECT
NEVERTHELESS to an annual Ground Rent and for the further consideration of the sum
of Twenty one pounds of Gold and Silver Coin as received in the Treasury of Virginia to
be paid yearly on the first day of January (the first payment to be made the first day of
January next ensuing) by GEORGE PICKETT his heirs; In Witness whereof the said
SAMUEL COLEMAN and SUSANNA his Wife have hereunto severally set their hands and
seals the day & year first above written
Signed Sealed and Delivered in presence of
    (no witnesses recorded)   SAMUEL COLEMAN
                                SUSANNA COLEMAN
    At a Court of Hustings for the City of Richmond held at the Courthouse on Monday the
16th of October 1786   This Indenture of Lease was acknowledged by SAMUEL COLEMAN
and SUSANNA his Wife, parties thereto (she having been first privily examined as the
Law directs), and ordered to be recorded
                        Teste ADAM CRAIG, C.C.

pp.   (On margin: COLEMAN & Ux. to MEANS)
97-   THIS INDENTURE made this first day of September Anno Domini one thousand
98   seven hundred and eighty six Between SAMUEL COLEMAN of County of HENRICO
        and SUSANNA his Wife of one part and ROBERT MEANS of City of Richmond of
other part; Witnesseth that in consideration of the sum of Five shillings current money
of Virginia by ROBERT MEANS in hand paid to SAMUEL COLEMAN and SUSANNA his Wife
said SAMUEL COLEMAN and SUSANNA his Wife for themselves jointly and severally and
for each of their joint and several heirs particularly the heirs of the said SUSANNA, by
these presents do bargain sell and confirm unto ROBERT MEANS and his heirs a lot of

Ground in the City of Richmond on the North West side of SHOCKOE CREEK, Beginning on
the Cross Street at the Corner of the Tenement now in possession of GEORGE PICKETT,
thence the line of said Tenement forty two feet to SAMUEL COUCHes line, thence the said
COUCHes line twenty four feet to WILLIAM RUSSELL and COMPANY's corner, thence the
said WILLIAM RUSSELL & COMPANY's line forty two feet to the Cross Street aforesaid as
now fixed, thence the line of said Cross Street twenty four feet to the beginning; To
have and to hold by said ROBERT MEANS and his heirs of SAMUEL COLEMAN and SUSAN-
NA his Wife their heirs jointly and the heirs of the said SUSANNA with the houses together with the appurtenances belonging. Subject Nevertheless to an annual Ground
Rent and the further consideration of the sum of Twenty pounds Gold or Silver Coin
received in the Treasury of Virginia to be paid yearly on the first day of January, the
first payment to be made the first day of January next ensuing; In Witness whereof the
said SAMUEL COLEMAN and SUSANNA his Wife have hereunto severally set their hands
& seals the day and year first before written
Signed Sealed and Delivered in the presence of
(no witnesses recorded)   SAMUEL COLEMAN
                                                 SUSANNA COLEMAN
   At a Court of Hustings for the City of Richmond held at the Courthouse on Monday the
16th of October 1786   This Indenture of Lease was acknowledged by SAMUEL COLE-
MAN and SUSANNA his Wife parties thereto (she having been first privily examined as
the Law directs) and ordered to be recorded
                         Teste ADAM CRAIG, C. C.

pp.   (On margin: COLEMAN & Ux. to COLIN. See CARRINGTON vs. OTIS 4 Gratt 235)
99-   THIS INDENTURE made this first day of September Anno Domini one thousand
101   seven hundred and Eighty six Between SAMUEL COLEMAN of HENRICO County
        and SUSANNA his Wife of one part and DIDIER COLLIN of City of Richmond of
other part; Witnesseth that in consideration of the sum of Five shillings current
money of Virginia by DIDIER COLLIN in hand paid to SAMUEL COLEMAN and SUSANNA
his Wife said SAMUEL COLEMAN and SUSANNA his Wife for themselves jointly and
severally & for each of their joint and several heirs, particularly the heirs of the said
SUSANNA, by these presents do bargain sell and confirm unto DIDIER COLLIN and his
heirs a certain Lot of Ground in the City of Richmond on the North West side of SHOCKOE
CREEK near the Bridge. Beginning on the bank of said Creek in the line of the Main
Street, thence up the said Main Street to (blank) Corner, thence Southwardly at right
angles with said Main Street & with the line of said (blank) corner, thence Southwardly
at right angles with the said Main Street & with the line of said (blank) ninety four feet
to a fifteen feet Alley, thence down the Alley to the aforesaid SHOCKOE CREEK, thence up
the Creek to the beginning; To have and to hold to said DIDIER COLLIN and his heirs of
said SAMUEL COLEMAN and SUSANNA his Wife and their heirs jointly and the heirs of
said SUSANNA with the houses together with the appurtenances thereunto belonging
and the rents issues and profits thereof. Subject Nevertheless to an Annual Ground
Rent and for the further consideration of Twenty five pounds of Gold and Silver Coins
by weight as received in the Treasury of Virginia to be paid yearly on the first day of
January (the first payment to be made on the first day of January next ensuing) by
DIDIER COLLIN and his heirs; In Witness whereof the said SAMUEL COLEMAN and
SUSANNA his Wife have hereunto severally set their hands and seals the day and year
first before written
Signed Sealed and Delivered in the presence of us
(no witnesses recorded)   SAMUEL COLEMAN
                                                 SUSANNA COLEMAN

At a Court of Hustings for the City of Richmond at the Courthouse on Monday the 16th of October 1786   This Indenture of Lease was acknowledged by SAMUEL COLEMAN & SUSANNA his Wife, parties thereto (she having been first privily examined as the Law directs and ordered to be recorded   Teste ADAM CRAIG, C C

pp.   (On margin: COLEMAN & Ux. to DUNN)
101-   THIS INDENTURE made the first day of September Anno Domini one thousand
103   seven hundred and Eighty six Between SAMUEL COLEMAN of County of HENRICO
       and SUSANNA his Wife of one part and JOEL DUNN of the County aforesaid of
other part; Witnesseth that in consideration of the sum of Two hundred pounds specie money of Virginia by JOEL DUNN in hand paid to SAMUEL COLEMAN and SUSANNA his Wife said SAMUEL COLEMAN and SUSANNA his Wife for themselves jointly and severally and for each of their joint and several heirs, particularly the heirs of said SUSANNA, by these presents do bargain sell and confirm unto JOEL DUNN and his heirs a certain Lot of Ground lying in County aforesaid near ROCKETS LANDING, being part of a Lot of Ground conveyed by CHARLES LEWIS to said SAMUEL COLEMAN on Ground Rent and bounded, Beginning on the Main Road leading from Richmond to FOUR MILE CREEK at that point which is just three feet from the end of a House built by said SAMUEL COLE-MAN, thirty six feet long and twenty four feet wide, thence a line parallel to said end up the Hill to said CHARLES LEWIS's line, thence with LEWIS's line seventy nine feet Northwesternly, thence a line parallel to the first mentioned line, down the hill to the Main Road aforesaid, thence down the Main Road seventy nine feet to the beginning; To have and to hold by JOEL DUNN and his heirs of SAMUEL COLEMAN and SUSANNA his Wife and their heirs jointly and the heirs of said SUSANNA with the houses thereon together with the appurtenances thereunto belonging and the rents issues and profits thereof, Subject Nevertheless to an annual Ground Rent and for the further consideration of Twenty pounds specie current money of Virginia to be paid yearly on the first day of January (the first payment to be made the first day of January next insuing) by JOEL DUNN his heirs; In Witness whereof the said SAMUEL COLEMAN and SUSANNA his Wife have hereunto severally set their hands & seals the day and year above written Signed Sealed & Delivered in the presence of us
              (no witnesses recorded)   SAMUEL COLEMAN
                                                   SUSANNA COLEMAN

At a Court of Hustings for the City of Richmond held at the Courthouse on Monday the 16th of October 1786   This Indenture of Lease was acknowledged by SAMUEL COLEMAN and SUSANNA his Wife parties thereto, she having been first privily examined as the Law directed and ordered to be recorded
              Teste ADAM CRAIG, C.C.

pp.   (On margin: PLEASANTS & Ux. to MONTGOMERY &c.)
104-   THIS INDENTURE made this thirteenth day of October in the year of our Lord
105   one thousand seven hundred and Eighty six Between ISAAC WEBSTER PLEASANTS
       & his Wife, JANE, of County of GOOCHLAND, of one part and ALEXANDER MONT-
GOMERY & COMPANY of City of Richmond of other part; Witnesseth that ISAAC WEBSTER PLEASANTS and his Wife, JANE, in consideration of the sum of Two hundred and fifty pounds current money of Virginia in hand paid, by these presents do bargain sell and confirm unto ALEXANDER MONTGOMERY and COMPANY, one certain parcel of Ground being part of the Lot number Twenty seven (27) in the City of Richmond, beginning at the intersection of the Main & Cross Streets and containing in front down the said Main Street thirty four feet and running thence back towards the River on a parallel with

-42-

RICHMOND CITY HUSTINGS COURT DEEDS 1782-1792

the Cross Street one hundred and sixty five feet, thence running parallel with the Main
Street thirty four feet to the aforesaid Cross Street, thence along the Cross Street to the
beginning, with all houses gardens profits & hereditaments whatsoever; To have and to
hold the parcel of Ground with all appurtenances to ALEXANDER MONTGOMERY and
COMPANY their heirs; And ISAAC WEBSTER PLEASANTS will warrant and forever defend
the title of said parcel of Ground hereby conveyed against the claim of every person; In
Witness whereof the said ISAAC WEBSTER PLEASANTS and his Wife, JANE, hath hereunto set their hands & seals the day and year above written
Sealed & Delivered in presence of
     JAMES PLEASANTS JUNR.,   JOS: W. PLEASANTS
     THOMAS W. PLEASANTS,   JANE PLEASANTS
     JOS: W. PLEASANTS, JOS: MILNER
  At a Court of Hustings for the City of Richmond held at the Courthouse on Monday the
16th of October 1786   This Indenture was proved by the Oaths of JOSEPH W. PLEA-
SANTS, JAMES PLEASANTS and JOSEPH MILNER, witnesses thereto, and ordered to be
recorded   Teste ADAM CRAIG C. C.

pp.   (On margin: BYRD's Trustees to COCKE)
105-   THIS INDENTURE made this twenty eighth day of March in the year of our Lord
106   one thousand seven hundred and eighty six Between CHARLES CARTER Esqr., of
      County of CHARLES CITY, only acting surviving Trustee of the Honourable
WILLIAM BYRD Esquire, deceased, of one part and WILLIAM COCKE of City of Richmond
of other part; Witnesseth that CHARLES CARTER pursuant to the directions of an Act of
Assembly intituled, "An Act to secure persons who derive titles to Lots Lands and Tenements under the Lottery or under a Deed of Trust of the late WILLIAM BYRD Esquire a
fee simple Estate therein," And for the consideration of the sum of Ten pounds current
money to him in hand paid by WILLIAM COCKE by these presents doth bargain and sell
unto WILLIAM COCKE and to his heirs one half acre lot of Ground lying in City of Richmond and County of HENRICO and denoted in the plan of the Lottery of said WILLIAM
BYRD by the numbers or figures (682) Six hundred and eighty two, and all profits advantages and appurtenances to the premsies belonging and the rents and issues thereof; To have and to hold the lot and premises with the appurtenances unto WILLIAM
COCKE his heirs and CHARLES CARTER for himself and his heirs the lot and premises
unto WILLIAM COCKE his heirs against all persons lawfully claiming under him to war-
rant and forever defend by these presents; In Witness whereof the said CHARLES CAR-
TER hath hereunto set his hand and affixed his seal the day and year first above written
Sealed and Delivered in the presence of
     ALEXR: BUCHANAN, GEORGE WEIR,   CHARLES CARTER
     JOHN W. PRICE, NATHL: SELDEN
  At a Court of Hustings for the City of Richmond held at the House of Mr. STEPHEN
TANKARD in the said City on Monday the 1st of November 1786
This Indenture was proved by the Oaths of ALEXANDER BUCHANAN, JOHN W. PRICE and
NATHANIEL SELDEN, witnesses thereto, and ordered to be recorded
             Teste ADAM CRAIG, C. C.

pp.   (On margin: GRAVES to STOCKDELL)
106-   THIS INDENTURE made and entered into this Fifteenth day of May in the year of
109   our Lord one thousand seven hundred and Eighty six Between FRANCIS GRAVES
      of City of Richmond of one part and JOHN STOCKDELL of the same City of other
part; Witnesseth that FRANCIS GRAVES in consideration of the yearly rent herein after

mentioned to be paid by JOHN STOCKDELL his heirs by these presents doth demise lease
and to farm let unto JOHN STOCKDELL and to his heirs a part of a lot of land lying in said
City and on the corner of the Street leading from SHOCKOE WAREHOUSES to MESSRS.
PENNOCK and strikes the BRICK STORE on the other Corner of said Stret, which part of
lot measures sixty feet front on said Street, eighty feet on the Street known by the name
of CARY STREET, which will appear by the plan of the Town, with all houses and all
other appurtenances priviledges and immunities to the said moiety, And also a part of a
lot of land lying in the Main Street in the City aforesaid and beginning at the East corner of MESSRS. PENNOCK and SKIPWITHs BRICK STORE and running down said Main
Street twenty feet to the corner of NELSON HERON & CO. STORE HOUSE, now occupied by
Mr. SAMUEL PAYNE and CO., thence back forty feet and is the parcel of ground purchased of FULWAR SKIPWITH, together with the house erected thereon & lately occupied by Messrs. LOTT, HIGBEE & CO., with free ingress & egress to and from the said Store;
To have and to hold the premises with the appurtenances unto JOHN STOCKDELL his
heirs during the term of Five years from the above date on his paying therefor the
yearly rent of nine hundred and thirty three Spanish Milled Dollars and one third of a
Spanish Milled Dollar to FRANCIS GRAVES his heirs by equal quarterly payments, viz.
the sum of Two hundred and thirty three Spanish Milled Dollars and one third of a
Spanish Milled Dollar on the fifteenth day of August next ensuing and a like sum on the
fifteenth day of November, and a like sum on the fifteenth day of February and a like
sum on the fifteenth day of May each year and JOHN STOCKDELL his heirs will pay and
satisfy all Public dues taxes assessments and impositions which shall be assessed on said
demised premises and at the expiration of said term leave and render up the demised
premises in good order and repair as they are at this present time to FRANCIS GRAVES
his heirs, natural decay, injury or destruction by fire, tempest or other such like
unavoidable accidents always excepted; In Witness whereof the said parties to these
presents have hereunto set their hands and seals the day and year first above written
Signd. Seald. and deliverd. in presence of

    E. CARROLL,   FRANCIS GRAVES
    E: DAVIS, JOHN PUGGETT   JNO: STOCKDELL

  At a Court of Hustings for the City of Richmond continued and held at the House of Mr.
STEPHEN TANKARD in the said City on Tuesday the 21st of November 1786
This Indenture of Lease was proved by the Oaths of EDWARD CARROLL, EDWARD DAVIS
and JOHN PUGGETT witnesses thereto and ordered to be recorded
             Teste ADAM CRAIG, C.C.

pp.   (On margin: BYRD's Trustee to HAY)
109-   THIS INDENTURE made this fifteenth day of July in the year of our Lord one
110   thousand seven hundred and eighty six Between COLO. CHARLES CARTER of
        SHIRLEY in County of CHARLES CITY Esqr., only acting surviving Trustee of the
Honble: WILLIAM BYRD of WESTOVER, deceased, of one part and WILLIAM HAY of the
City of Richmond of other part; Whereas by an Act of Assembly passed in the November
session held in the year one thousand seven hundred and Eighty one the said CHARLES
CARTER Esqr. as being the only acting surviving Trustee of the said WILLIAM BYRD
Esqr. is impowered and requested to execute Deeds of Conveyance for Lotts, Lands and
Tenements to purchasers who derive their titles under the Lottery or Deed of Trust of
said WILLIAM BYRD Esqr. as by reference being had to said Act may appear; NOW THIS
INDENTURE WITNESSETH that CHARLES CARTER Esqr. in consideration of the sum of Five
pounds current money of Virignia by WILLIAM HAY to CHARLES CARTER Esqr. in hand
paid by these presents doth bargan and sell unto WILLIAM HAY his heirs one Lot or

half acre of Ground lying in City of Richmond and County of HENRICO and distinguished
in the plan of the Prizes of the Lottery, called BYRDs LOTTERY, by the numbers or
figures 601/Six hundred and one/ as by said Plan remaining filed among the Records of
the Court of County of HENRICO; with all buildings profits advantages & appurtenances
to said lot appertaining; To have and to hold the lot and premises with appurtenances
unto WILLIAM HAY his heirs; In Witness whereof the said CHARLES CARTER Esqr. hath
hereunto set his hand and affixed his seal the day and year above written
Sealed and Delivered in presence of
     JAMES WARINGTON, LEWIS PRICE,   CHARS: CARTER
     BENJA: RAWLINGS, GEO: PICKETT,
     BENJ: HARRISON JR. ROBERT ALLEN
   At a Court of Hustings for the City of Richmond held at the Courthouse in the said City
on Monday the 18th of September 1786   This Indenture was proved by the Oaths of
LEWIS PRICE and BENJAMIN RAWLINGS, two of the witnesses thereto, And at another
Court held for the said City the 17th day of January 1787, the same was further proved
by the Oath of ROBERT ALLEN, another witness thereto, and ordered to be recorded
                   Teste ADAM CRAIG C. C.

pp.   (On margin: MATTHEW MOODY Bond as Serjt.)
110-   KNOW ALL MEN by these presents that we MATTHEW MOODY and EDWARD VOSS
111   of the City of Richmond and JAMES PRICE, BARRET PRICE and ELISHA PRICE of
      County of HENRICO are held and firmly bound unto the Mayor, Recorder, Alder-
men and Common Council of said City in the sum of One thousand pounds current
money to which payment well and truly to be made we bind ourselves our heirs firmly
by these presents: Witness our hands & seals this seventeenth day of January one thousand seven hundred and eighty seven & in the 11th year of the Commonwealth
  THE CONDITION of the above obligation is such that Whereas the above bound
MATTHEW MOODY hath been appointed SERJEANT of the City of Richmond, Now if the
said MATTHEW MOODY shall duly and faithfully execute the Duties of his said Office according to Law and shall well and truly demean himself therein, Then this obligation to
be void, otherwise to remain in full force and virtue
Sealed and Delivered in the presence of
     The Court   MATTHEW MOODY
                              EDWARD VOSS
                              JAMES PRICE
                              BARRET PRICE
                              ELISHA PRICE
   At a Court of Hustings continued for the City of Richmond & held at the Courthouse on
Wednesday the 17th of January 1787   This Bond was acknowledged by the Obligors
and ordered to be recorded Teste ADAM CRAIG, C. C.

pp.   (On margin: MAYO to BECKLEY)
111-   KNOW ALL MEN by these presents that I JOHN MAYO of County of HENRICO by
112   these presents do make and appoint JOHN BECKLEY, Esquire, of City of Richmond,
      my true and lawful Attorney for me and in my name to pray for an appeal from
any Judgment or Decree which shall be rendered in any suit now depending against me
in the Court of the County of HENRICO and in the Court of Hustings of the City of Richmond and for me and in my name to sign seal and deliver all such Bonds and other
Securites as shall be necessary to procure such Appeals and carry them into effect
when obtained; And I do hereby authorize said JOHN BECKLEY Esquire or his Attorney

appointed under him to act and do in the premises as fully and amply to all intents and
purposes as I could were I personally present hereby ratifying and confirming all that
said JOHN BECKLEY shall legally do in the same; In Witness whereof I have hereunto set
my hand & seal this twenty first day of October 1786
Sealed and Ackd. in the presence of
    CHARLES HAY   JOHN MAYO
At a Court of Hustings for the City of Richmond held at the Courthouse the 19th of
February 1787.   This Power of Attorney from JOHN MAYO to JOHN BECKLEY was proved
by the Oath of CHARLES HAY, a witness thereto, & ordered to be recorded
                Teste ADAM CRAIG, C.C.

pp.   (On margin: BUCHANAN & SADLER to STEWART & HILL)
112-   TO ALL WHOM THESE PRESENTS may come, Whereas WILLIAM JOHNSTON of
113   DOWN County in Kingdom of IRELAND, by his Deed duly executed bearing date
        the Eighth of August in the year one thousand seven hundred and eighty three
duly recorded in the Court of the City of Richmond in the County of HENRICO and Commonwealth of Virginia, and hereunto prefixed, did appoint us whose names are hereunto subscribed to be his true and lawful Attorney for him and in his name to ask sue
for and receive all such sums of money dues or demands then owing to him in America
by any person and to take all lawful ways and means for the recovery thereof; KNOW YE
therefore that we the said JAMES BUCHANAN and HENRY SADLER by this present writing do appoint in our place ARTHUR STEWART and WILLIAM HILL of City of Richmond,.
Merchants, and HENRY SADLER of NEW YORK in America, Merchant, jointly, or any one
of them to be our lawful substitutes on behalf of WILLIAM JOHNSTON; In Witness whereof we have hereunto set our hands and affixed our seals this tenth day of June in the
year of our Lord one thousand seven hundred and eighty six
Signed Sealed and Delivered in presence of
    JOHN McKEAND,   JAMES BUCHANAN
    ALEXANDER BUCHANAN   HENRY SADLER
At a Court of Hustings for the City of Richmond held at the Courthouse on Monday the
19th of February 1787   This Power of Attorney was proved by the Oath of ALEXANDER
BUCHANAN, a witness thereto, and ordered to be recorded
                Teste ADAM CRAIG, C.C.

pp.   (On margin: COLEMAN to SCOTT)
113-   THIS INDENTURE made this first day of September Anno Domini one thousand
115   seven hundred and eighty six Between SAMUEL COLEMAN of County of HENRICO
        and SUSANNA his Wife of one part and THOMAS SCOTT of City of Richmond of
other part; Witnesseth that in consideration of the sum of Five shillings current
money of Virginia by THOMAS SCOTT in hand paid to SAMUEL COLEMAN and SUSANNA
his Wife said SAMUEL COLEMAN and SUSANNA his Wife for themselves jointly and
severally and for each of their joint and several heirs, particularly the heirs of said
SUSANNA, by these presents do bargain sell and confirm unto THOMAS SCOTT his heirs a
certain Lot of Ground in City of Richmond on the North West side of SHOCKOE CREEK, Beginning on the Main Street at DIDIER COLIN's Corner, thence his line Ninety four feet
to a fifteen feet Alley, thence up the line of said Alley twenty four feet to JOHN WAL-
KER's Corner, thence WALKER's line ninety four feet to the Main Street, thence down
the Main Street twenty four feet to the beginning; To have and to hold by him said THO-
MAS SCOTT and his heirs of SAMUEL COLEMAN and SUSANNA his Wife and their heirs
jointly and the heirs of said SUSANNA, with the house thereon together with the appur-

tenances theretunto belonging; Subject Nevertheless to an annual Ground Rent and for the further consideration of Eighteen pounds of Gold and Silver Coins by weight as received in the Treasury of Virginia to be paid every year on the first day of January, the first payment to be made the first day of January next ensuing by THOMAS SCOTT his heirs to SAMUEL COLEMAN and SUSANNA his Wife and their heirs; In Witness whereof the said SAMUEL COLEMAN and SUSANNA his Wife have hereunto set their hands and seals severally the day and year first before written
Signed Sealed and delivered in the presence of us
    (no witnesses recorded)   SAMUEL COLEMAN
                                      SUSANNA COLEMAN

  At a Court of Hustings for the City of Richmond held at the Courthouse on Monday the 26th of March 1787   This Indenture of Lease was acknowledged by SAMUEL COLEMAN and SUSANNA his Wife, parties thereto, (the said SUSANNA having been first privily examined as the Law directs) and ordered to be recorded
                          Teste ADAM CRAIG, C. C.

pp.   (On margin: COLEMAN to COLEMANs)
115-   TO ALL TO WHOM these presents shall come, I SAMUEL COLEMAN of HENRICO
116   County send Greeting. Know ye that I SAMUEL COLEMAN in consideration of the
       natural affecton which I bear my two Daughters, to wit, ELIZABETH WYATT
COLEMAN and SARAH STORRS COLEMAN, and for divers other good causes and considerations me hereunto moving, by these presents do give and grant unto my two Daughters jointly all my Negroes, to wit, Catchina a woman about twenty six years of age, Judy a girl about four year of age, and Elizabeth an Infant girl about nine months old, To have hold and enjoy jointly until my Daughter ELIZABETH WYATT shall arrive at the age of Twenty one years or until either of them shall marry, in either case the said Negroes and their increase shall as near as possible be equally divided having respect to their value between my said two Daughters their heirs, And I said SAMUEL COLEMAN the aforesaid Negroes and their issue to my Daughters their heirs against all persons shall warrant and forever defend by these presents; In Witness whereof I have hereunto set my hand and seal this 12th day of January 1787
Teste JNO: RUSSELL,   SAMUEL COLEMAN
     GERVAS STORRS
  At a Court of Hustings held for the City of Richmond on Monday the 26th of March 1787 This Deed of Gift was acknowledged by SAMUEL COLEMAN as his act and deed and ordered to be recorded   Teste DAM CRAIG, C C.

pp.   (On margin: MINOR & Ux. to PICKET. Deld. to CHAS: HOPKINS)
116-   THIS INDENTURE made this twenty fourth day of March in the year of our Lord
118   one thousand seven hundred and Eighty seven Between DABNEY MINOR and
       ANNE his Wife of City of Richmond of one part and GEORGE PICKETT and CHARLES
HOPKINS, Merchants, in the City aforesaid of other part; Witnesseth that DABNEY MINOR and ANN his Wife in consideration of Five hundred pounds current money of Virginia to them in hand paid by said GEROGE PICKETT and CHARLES HOPKINS said DABNEY MINOR and ANNE his Wife by these presents do bargain sell and confirm unto GEORGE PICKET and CHARLES HOPKINS their heirs a certain half acre lot of land lying in City of Richmond known by the number Six hundred and five (#605), as laid down in the plan of said City, it being the same which DABNEY MINOR purchased of CHARLES CARTER the only surviving Trustee of the Honble. WILLIAM BYRD deceased, by Deed bearing date the fifteenth day of March one thousand seven hundred and eighty six

Together with all houses and hereditaments to half acre lot number six hundred and
five belonging; To have and to hold the half acre lot to GEORGE PICKET and CHARLES
HOPKINS their heirs (as Tenants in Common and not as Joint Tenants), And DABNEY
MINOR and ANNE his wife for themselves their heirs the sold premises to GEORGE
PICKETT and CHARLES HOPKINS their heirs against all persons claiming under them
shall warrant and forever defend by these presents; in Witness whereof the the said
DABNEY MINOR and ANNE his Wife have hereunto set their hands and fixed their seals
the day and year first written.
Signed Sealed and delivered in the presence of
    FRANCIS JAMES,   DABNEY MINOR
    AW. DUNSCOMBE, CHARLES MARSHALL   ANN MINOR
  The Commonwealth of Virginia to RICHARD ADAMS, JOHN MARSHALL and JOHN HAR-
VIE, Gentlemen, Justices of the Court of Hustings for the City of Richmond, Greeting:
Whereas (the Commission for the privy examination of ANN, the Wife of DABNEY MINOR); Witness
ADAM CRAIG, Clerk of our said Court at the Courthouse the 26th day of March 1787 in
the 11th year of the Commonwealth   ADAM CRAIG
  City of Richmond, to wit. In Obedience to the within Dedimus to us directed, we have
this day waited on the within named ANN MINOR and have shewn and explained to her
privily and apart from her Husband, the annexed Deed, and have also examined her
privily concerning it; the said ANN then declared to us that she willingly signed and
sealed the said writing and that she gives her full assent to its being recorded. Given
under our hands and seals this twenty sixth day of March in the year one thousand
seven hundred and Eighty seven   JOHN MARSHALL
                             JOHN HARVIE
  At a Court of Hustings for the City of Richmond at the Courthouse on Monday the 26th
of March 1787   This Indenture was proved by the Oaths of FRANCIS JAMES, ANDREW
DUNSCOMB and CHARLES MARSHALL, the witnesses thereto, and together with the Commission annexed and the Certificate of the execution thereof, ordered to be recorded
            Teste ADAM CRAIG, C.C.

pp.   (On margin: TURPIN to HARVIE & Trustee. Deld. Col: HARRISONs Order)
119-   THIS INDENTURE made this 20th day of May one thousand seven hundred and
120   eighty six Between DOCTOR PHILIP TURPIN of County of POWHATAN of one part
        and JOHN HARVIE In Trust to and for the Subscribers to Mr. QUESNAYS ACADE-
MY in the City of Richmond of the other part; Witnesseth that PHILIP TURPIN in consideration of the sum of Three hundred pounds to him in hand paid by JOHN HARVIE by
these presents doth bargain and sell unto JOHN HARVIE in Trust to and for the use of
the Subscribers to Mr. QUESNAY's ACADEMY a certain tract of land containing about
three acres and three quarters of an acre more or less being part of what was WATSONs,
now TURPINs Tenement and bounded; Beginning at a corner Stone on the Gully at the
East side of the Cross Street below GREENHOW's Lotts, thence South thirty five degrees
West two hundred and five feet and a half to a corner Pig Iron, thence South fifty five
degrees East one hundred and eighty feet to a corner Pig Iron, thence South thirty five
degrees West ninety one feet to a corner Stone on TURPIN, thence South fifty five
degrees East three hundred and five feet to a corner Stone, thence North thirty five
degrees East four hundred and seventy four feet to a small corner Pine on a Gully
leading into SHOCKOE CREEK, thence up the Gully as it meanders to the Beginning, And
said TURPIN doth covenant that the Main Street on SHOCKOE HILL shall be extended and
ever after kept open for the whole interest of the said three acres and three quarters of
an acre that borders thereon; he also agrees that a Dam or Dams may be established

across the Gully now the dividing boundary for the purpose of raising a head of water for the benefit of the ACADEMY Garden; To have and to hold the three acres and three quarters of an acre be the same more or less with the priviledges herein before granted to JOHN HARVIE in Trust for the ACADEMY and PHILIP TURPIN doth agree with JOHN HARVIE that he will warrant and defend the title of the same to JOHN HARVIE in Trust to and for the Subscribers to Mr. QUESNAY's ACADEMY and to his heirs against the claim of every person; In Witness whereof the said PHILIP TURPIN hath hereunto set his hand and seal the day and year above written
Test   CHARLES LEWIS, JNO: P. THOMAS,   PHILIP TURPIN
           SAML. M. CRAW. JOHN TUCKER
    At a Court of Hustings held for the City of Richmond at the Courthouse on Monday the 26th of March 1787   This Indenture was proved by the Oaths of CHARLES LEWIS, SAMUEL M. CRAW and JOHN TUCKER, three of the witnesses thereto and ordered to be recorded   Teste ADAM CRAIG, C. C.

pp.   (On margin: RUSSELL & Ux. to ALISON)
120-   THIS INDENTURE made this twenty seventh day of March in the year of our
122   Lord one thousand seven hundred and eighty seven Between JOHN RUSSELL of
          the County of HENRICO and HANNAH his Wife of one part and FRANCIS ALISON of
the other part; Witnesseth that JOHN RUSSELL and HANNAH his Wife in consideration of the sum of Three hundred pounds current money of Virginia to said JOHN RUSSELL by FRANCIS ALISON before the sealing and delivery of these presents in hand paid, said JOHN RUSSELL and HANNAH his Wife by these presents do bargain and sell unto FRAN-CIS ALISON his heirs all that parcel of land in City of Richmond containing Thirty two thousand eight hundred and fifty five square feet being part of YOUNGHUSBANDs Tene-ment, known by the number Three hundred and Thirty seven in the plan of the said City, And Beginning at a corner Stone on the Street next to the River, running thence North thirty six degrees and a half East one hundred and sixty five feet to a Corner Stone on SAMUEL COLEMANs line, thence South fifty three degrees and a half East one hundred and ninety seven feet to SHOCKOE CREEK,thence down the Creek as it meanders one hundred and sixty seven feet to the River Street, thence up said Street North fifty three degrees and a half West two hundred and two feet to the beginning, with all houses improvements thereunto belonging with the rents issues and profits thereof; To have and to hold the granted land premises and appurtenances unto FRANCIS ALISON his heirs and the said JOHN and HANNAH their heirs the granted premises against all persons claiming an estate therein shall warrant and forever defend to said FRANCIS his heirs; In Witness whereof the said JOHN RUSSELL and HANNAH his Wife have hereunto set their hands and seals the day and year first herein written
Signed Sealed and delivered in presence of
          (no witnesses recorded)   JOHN RUSSELL
                                                             HANNAH RUSSELL
    Received March 26th 1787 of FRANCIS ALISON, the sum of Three hundred pounds being the full consideration money within mentioned   JNO: RUSSELL

KNOW ALL MEN by these presents that Whereas I SUSANNA STORRS, Widow of JOSHUA STORRS deced. am intitled to and seised of Dower in the Land by the within Deed granted and conveyed, I do hereby in consideration of Five shilling current money to me in hand paid by FRANCIS ALISON within named bargain sell and release to said FRANCIS his heirs all my right title and estate dower or claim of Dower or other demand in all or any part of the land and appurtenances in the within Deed mentioned; To have and to

hold the bargained premises to said FRANCIS his heirs to his and their use; In Witness
whereof I have hereunto set my hand and seal this 26th day of March in the year of our
Lord one thousand seven hundred and eighty seven
Signed Sealed and Delivered in presence of
      SAM: COLEMAN,   SUSANNA STORRS
      JOHN BROOKE, BARTLETT STILL
   At a Court of Hustings held for the City of Richmond at the Courthouse on Monday the
26th of March 1787   This Indenture and the receipt endorsed were acknowledged by
JOHN RUSSELL and HANNAH his Wife, parties thereto (she having been first privily
examined as the Law directs) and together with the acknowledgment of SUSANNA
STORRS thereon also indorsed, which was proved by the Oaths of SAMUEL COLEMAN,
JOHN BROOKE and BARTLETT STILL, the witnesses thereto, ordered to be recorded
               Teste ADAM CRAIG, C. C.

pp.   (On margin: PENNOCK to RUSSELL & CO.)
122-   THIS INDENTURE made this first day of January Anno Domini one thousand
125   seven hundred and Eighty seven Between WILLIAM PENNOCK, Merchant of the
       City of Richmond of one part and WILLIAM RUSSELL & CO., Merchants of the
same City of other part; Witnesseth that in consideration of the sum of Five shillings
current money of Virginia in hand paid by WILLIAM RUSSELL & CO., to WILLIAM PEN-
NOCK, said WILLIAM PENNOCK by these presents doth bargin sell and confirm unto
WILLIAM RUSSELL & COMPANY and their heirs a certain lot of Ground lying in City of
Richmond and bounded; Beginning at a Corner made by the Cross Street (leading from
the Main Street between the Tenements now occupied by SAMUEL TROWER and GEORGE
PICKET to the River Street) and a fifteen feet Alley (leading from the said Cross Stree to
SHOCKOE CREEK), thence the line of said Alley one hundred feet to SAMUEL COLEMAN's
Corner, thence said COLEMAN's line sixteen feet to THOMAS PEDLEYs Corner, thence said
PEDLEY's line one hundred feet to the aforesaid Cross Street, thence up the said Cross
Street sixteen feet to the beginning, with all the appurtenances thereunto belonging;
To have and to hold of WILLIAM PENNOCK and his heirs by WILLIAM RUSSELL and COM-
PANY and their heirs; On the further consideration of the sum of Ten pounds of cur-
rent gold and silver Coin of Virginia as received in the Treasury thereof annually to be
paid by WILLIAM RUSSELL and COMPANY their heirs to WILLIAM PENNOCK his heirs,
the first payment to be made the first day of January one thousand seven hundred and
eighty eight as a Ground Rent by WILLIAM RUSSELL & COMPANY their heirs, said
WILLIAM PENNOCK for himself his heirs warranting and defending to WILLIAM RUS-
SELL & COMPANY their heirs the parcel of ground with appurtenances against any
other right title or demand of any person; In Witness whereof the said WILLIAM PEN-
NOCK hath hereunto set his hand & affixed his seal the day and year first above written
Signed Sealed & delivered in presence of
      JAMES QUIGG,   WM. PENNOCK
      LITTLEBERRY STOVALL, JOHN BECKLEY
  At a Court of Hustings held for the City of Richmond on Monday the 26th of March 1787
This Indenture of Lease was proved by the Oaths of JAMES QUIGG, LITTLEBERRY
STOVALL and JOHN BECKLEY, witnesses thereto, and ordered to be recorded
               Teste ADAM CRAIG, C. C.

pp.   (On margin: PENNOCK to THOMAS)
125-   THIS INDENTURE made this nineteenth day of March in year of our Lord one
128   thousand seven hundred and eighty seven Between WILLIAM PENNOCK, Mer-
       chant and ANN his Wife of City of Richmond of one part and FREDERICK THOMAS

of the same City of other part; Witnesseth that in consideration of the sum of Five shillings current money of Virginia in hand paid by FREDERICK THOMAS to WILLIAM PENNOCK and ANN his Wife said WILLIAM PENNOCK and ANN his Wife by these presents doth bargain sell and confirm unto FREDERICK THOMAS his heirs a certain lot of land lying in City of Richmond, bounded. Beginning at THOMAS PEDLEY's Corner on the Cross Street (leading from the Main Street between the Tenements now occupierd by SAML: TROWER and GEORGE PICKETT to the River Street), thence along said PEDLY's line one hundred feet to SAMUEL COLEMAN's line, thence with COLEMAN's line twenty feet to FRANCIS ALLISON's line, thence said ALLISON's line one hundred feet to the Cross Street, thence up said Street twenty feet to the beginning, with all the appurtenances thereunto belonging; To have and to hold of said WILLIAM PENNOCK and ANN his Wife their heirs by FREDERICK THOMAS his heirs; On the further consideration of the sum of fifteen pounds of current gold or silver Coin in Virginia as received in the Treasury thereof annually to be paid by FREDERICK THOMAS his heirs to WILLIAM PENNOCK and ANN his Wife their heirs, the first payment to be made on the first day of January one thousand seven hundred and Eighty eight said WILLIAM PENNOCK and ANN his Wife for themselves their heirs warranting and defending to said FREDERICK his heirs the lot of ground with all appurtenances against any other right title or demand of any person; In Witness whereof the said WILLIAM PENNOCK and ANN his Wife have hereunto set their hands and affixed their seals the day and year before written
Signed Sealed & Delivered in presence of
        (no witnesses recorded)   WILLIAM PENNOCK
                                                         ANN PENNOCK
    At a Court of Hustings held for the City of Richmond on Monday the 26th of March 1787 This Indenture of Lease was acknowledged by WILLIAM PENNOCK and ANN his Wife parties thereto (she having been first privily examined as the Law directs), and ordered to be recorded   Teste ADAM CRAIG, C. C.

pp.   (On margin: PENNOCK to PEDLEY)
128-   THIS INDENTURE made this nineteenth day of March in the year of our Lord
131   one thousand seven hundred and eighty seven Between WILLIAM PENNOCK,
        Merchant, and ANN his Wife of City of Richmond of one part and THOMAS PEDLY
of said City of other part, Witnesseth that in consideration of the sum of Five shillings current money of Virginia in hand paid by THOMAS PEDLY to WILLIAM PENNOCK and ANN his Wife said WILLIAM PENNOCK and ANN his Wife by these presents doth bargain sell and confirm unto THOMAS PEDLY his heirs a certain lott of ground lying in City of Richmond and bounded; Beginning at WILLIAM RUSSELL and COMPANY's Corner on the Cross Street (leading from the Main Street between the Tenements now occupied by SAMUEL TROWER and GEORGE PICKETT to the River Street), thence said RUSSELL and COMPANY's line one hundred feet to SAMUEL COLEMAN's line, thence the said COLE-MAN's line twenty feet to FREDERICKS THOMAS's Corner, thence said THOMAS's line one hundred feet to the Cross Street, thence up said Street twenty feet to the beginning; with all the appurtenances thereunto belonging; To have and to hold of WILLIAM PENNOCK and ANN his Wife and their heirs by THOMAS PEDLY his heirs; On the further consideration of the sum of Fifteen pounds current gold and silver Coin in Virginia as received in the Treasury thereof annually to be paid by THOMAS PEDLY his heirs to WILLIAM PENNOCK his heirs, the first payment to be made the first day of January one thousand seven hundred and eighty eight as a Ground Rent by THOMAS PEDLY his heirs to WILLIAM PENNOCK his heirs said WILLIAM PENNOCK and ANN his Wife for themselves their heirs warranting and defending to THOMAS PEDLY his heirs the lot of

ground with the appurtenances against any other person. In Witness whereof said
WILLIAM PENNOCK and ANN his Wife have hereunto set their hands and affixed their
seals the day and year above written
Signed Sealed & delivered in presence of
         (no witnesses recorded)   WILLIAM PENNOCK
                                                       ANN PENNOCK

   At a Court of Hustings held for the City of Richmond on Monday the 26th of March 1787
This Indenture of Lease was acknowledged by WILLIAM PENNOCK and ANN his Wife
parties thereto (she having been first privily examined as the Law directs) and ordered
to be recorded   Teste ADAM CRAIG, C. C.

pp.   (On margin: ORR to DUGARD. Delivered CH: COPLAND Esqr. 29 Oct. 98)
131-   THIS INDENTURE made this twenty sixth day of March in the year of our Lord
132   one thousand seven hundred and eighty seven Between JOHN ORR of City of
         Richmond of one part and ABRAHAM DUGARD of the same City of other part:
Witnesseth that JOHN ORR in consideration of the sum of One hundred and forty pounds
current money of Virginia to him in hand paid by ABRAHAM DUGARD, said JOHN ORR
by these presents doth bargain sell and confirm unto ABRAHAM DUGARD his heirs one
certain parcel of land lying in City of Richmond and part of a lott distinguished and
known in the plan of said Town by number (49) Forty Nine, lying in the Corner of said
lott bounded by the Cross and Back Streets and containing Eighty four feet on Cross
Street and Forty feet on the Back Street, with all buildings profits and appurtenances to
said parcel of land belonging; To have and to hold the parcel of land with the appurtenances unto ABRAHAM DUGARD his heirs; And JOHN ORR his heirs the parcel of land
against all persons to ABRAHAM DUGARD his heirs shall warrant and forever defend by
these presents; In Witness whereof the said JOHN ORR hath hereunto set his hand and
affixed his seal the day and year above written
Signed Sealed and Delivered in the presence of
         G. WEBB JUNR.,   JOHN ORR
         BD: WEBB, ROGER GREGORY JUNR.
At a Court of Hustings held for the City of Richmond on Monday the 26th of March 1787
This Indenture was acknowledged by JNO: ORR as his act and deed and ordered to be
recorded   Teste ADAM CRAIG, C. C.

pp.   (On margin: WORKMAN to SHERMER. Deld. SHERMER)
133-   KNOW ALL MEN by these presents that we THOMAS WORKMAN and WILLIAM
134   BRUMELL of BASINGHALL STREET LONDON, Warehousemen, for divers good
         causes us hereunto moving by these presents do make and appoint WILLIAM
SHERMER of GRAFTON STREET in County of MIDDLESEX, Gentleman, now is about to sail
for Virginia in North America, our true and lawful Attorney for us and in our names to
ask demand recover and receive of and from Messrs. FULWAR SKIPWITH and COMPANY,
late of LONDON, Merchants, or Messrs. PENNOCK, NICHOLSON and SKIPWITH of Richmond
in Virginia or any of them engaged in the copartnership or trade with Messrs. FULWAR
SKIPWITH and COMPANY or who may be liable to pay the same the sum of One hundred
and twenty six pounds, sixteen shillings and eleven pence being the balance of a Debt
due to us for goods sold and delivered to Messrs. FULWAR SKIPWITH and COMPANY and
upon receipt to execute sufficient Receipts; giving our Attorney full power in the
premises to act and do all such matters and things that may be necessary in and about
the premises as fully and effectually as we might or could do were we personally present; In Witness whereof we the said THOMAS WORKMAN and WILLIAM BRUMELL have

hereunto set our hands and seals this twenty third day of February in the year of our
our Lord one thousand seven hundred and eighty seven
Sealed and Delivered (being first duly stampt) in the presence of
      SAML: MILFORD,   THOMAS WORKMAN
      ANTHONY DREWIDZ   for self & WM. BRUMELL
  At a Court of Hustings continued and held for the City of Richmond at the Courthouse
on Wednesday the 30th of May 1787, agreeable to Adjournment   This Power of Attorney was proved by the Oath of SAMUEL MILFORD, a witness thereto, and ordered to be
recorded   Teste ADAM CRAIG, C. C.

pp.   (On margin: COURT to SHERMER)
134-   TO ALL TO WHOM these present shall come, DAVID COURT of the TRINITY HOUSE
135   LONDON, Esquire, sendeth Greeting. Whereas SAMUEL BEALL of the City of
        WILLIAMSBURG in Virginia, one of the Thirteen United States of North America,
Merchant, made his first, second and third Bills of Exchange all of them dated at WIL-
LIAMSBURG on the twentieth day of December one thousand seven hundred and eighty
three by each of which he directed Messrs. CLIFTON and TYSON, Merchants in LONDON,
at sixty days after sight of said Bills of Exchange (the others of the same tenour and date
not being paid) to pay to Mr. WILLIAM SHERMER or Order the sum of Six hundred
pounds Sterling for Eight hundred pounds current money there received, and directed
that at the time they should make payment and place the same to the account of said
SAMUEL BEALL, And Whereas the said SAMUEL BEALL made his first second and third of
a certain other Bill of Exhange all of them also dated at WILLIAMSBURG on the twenty
first day of December one thousand seven hudnred and eighty three by each of which
he directed the said Messrs. CLIFTON and TYSON at sixty days after sight of said Bills of
Exchange (the others of the same tenor and date not being paid) to pay to WILLIAM
SHERMER or Order the sum of Six hundred pounds Sterling for eight hundred pounds
current money there received and directed that at the time they should make payment
and place the same to the account of said SAMUEL BEALL, And whereas said WILLIAM
SHERMER to whom or to whose order the said two sets of Bills of Exhange were payable
afterwards paid and indorsed the same to said DAVID COURT and said Messrs. CLIFTON
and TYSON having refused or declined to accept and pay each of the Bills of Exchange,
said DAVID COURT sometime since transmitted the first of each of them to WILLIAM
MURRAY of PETERSBURG in Virginia, Merchant, to receive and recover the same, And
Whereas WILLIAM SHERMER being about to embark for Virginia, said DAVID COURT is
desirous that he should receive for said DAVID COURT the monies payable upon said Bills
of Exchange; NOW KNOW ALL MEN that for the considerations aforesaid and divers other
cause said DAVID COURT thereunto moving by these presents doth appoint WILLIAM
SHERMER (now of GRAFTON STREET in County of MIDDLESEX, Gentleman) his true and
lawful Attorney to ask demand recover and receive of WILLIAM MURRAY or any other
persons hold said Bills of Exchange and recover and receive of SAMUEL BEALL his
Executors or any other persons liable to pay the same the money's comprized in said
Bills of Exchange; In Witness whereof DAVID COURT hath hereunto set his hand and
seal this Twenty sixth day of February in the year of our Lord one thousand seven
hundred and eighty seven
Signed Sealed and Delivered (being first duly stampt) in the presence of
      SAML: MILFORD,   DAVID COURT
      ANTHONY DREWIDZ

At a Court of Hustings continued and held for the City of Richmond at the Courthouse
on Wednesday the 30th of May 1787, agreeable to Adjournment
This Power of Attorney was proved by the Oath of SAMUEL MILFORD a witness thereto
and ordered to be recorded   Teste ADAM CRAIG, C.C.

pp.   (On margin: WRIGGLESWORTH to SHERMER. Deld. SHERMER)
138-   TO ALL TO WHOM these presents shall come, BENJAMIN WRIGGLESWORTH of
142   BUCKLERSBURY in City of LONDON, Warehouseman, sendeth Greeting; Whereas
           by a certain Bill of Lading dated at Virginia in North America the nineteenth
day of December one thousand seven hundred and eighty three and signed by GEORGE
GOOSLEY, then Master and Commander of the Ship, "NEPTUNE," it is affirmed that fifty
hogsheads of Tobacco marked and numbred as in the margin thereof and as follows vizt.
(S. B. No. 1 to 50), were shipped in good order and well conditioned by SAMUEL BEALL of
WILLIAMSBURG in Virginia, Merchant, in and upon the sd. Ship, "NEPTUNE," then
riding at anchor in JAMES RIVER and bound for LONDON, and which were to be delivered in the like good order and well conditioned at the Port of LONDON (the dangers of
the Sea only excepted) unto WILLIAM SHERMER (now of GRAFTON STREET in County of
MIDDLESEX, Gentleman) or to his assigns he or they paying freight for said goods after
the rate of Thirty five Shillings Sterling per hogshead with primage and average
accustomed; And Whereas by a certain other Bill of Lading dated also at Virginia the
nineteenth day of December one thousand seven hundred and eighty three and signed
by the said GEORGE GOOSLEY, it is affirmed that fifty other Hogsheads of Tobacco markt.
and numbred as in the margin thereof and as follows, vizt., S. B. No. 51 to 100, were
shipped in good order and well conditioned by said SAMUEL BEALL in and upon the Ship
"NEPTUNE," then riding at anchor in JAMES RIVER and bound for LONDON and which
were to be delivered in like good order and well conditioned at the Port of LONDON (the
dangers of the Sea only excepted) unto WILLIAM SHERMER or his assigns he or they
paying freight for the said goods after the Rate of Thirty five Shillings p. Hogshead and
primage and average accustomed as in and by said Bills of Lading relation being thereunto had will appear; And Whereas in each of said Bills of Lading it was affirmed that
two other of the same tenor and date being also signed by GEORGE GOOSLEY, the one of
them being accomplished, the other two were to stand void; And Whereas the recited
Bills of Lading have become the property of BENJAMIN WRIGGLESWORTH by virtue of
certain assignments or Indorsements thereon from WILLIAM SHERMER to BENJAMIN
WRIGGLESWORTH: And whereas the Ship, "Neptune," after she sailed from JAMES RIVER
put into the Port of NEW YORK at which place said one hundred hogsheads of tobacco
comprized in the two recited Bills of Lading were sold by the Order of SAMUEL BEALL,
GEORGE GOOSLEY and NICHOLAS LOW of NEW YORK, Merchant, or some or one of them for
the neat sum of Three thousand and sixty six pounds two shillings and eleven pence,
NEW YORK Currency, instead of being brought to and delivered at the Port of LONDON
according to the tenor and effect of said Bills of Lading, whereby the said BENJAMIN
WRIGGLESWORTH hath been deprived of all benefits and advantage arising therefrom;
And whereas BENJAMIN WRIGGLESWORTH some time since by a certain Letter of Attor-
ney or Instrument under his hand and seal appointed WILLIAM MURRAY of PETERS-
BURG in Virginia, Merchant, his Attorney to proceed against the proper parties in Vir-
ginia for the recovery of the amount of said Bills of Lading. And whereas WILLIAM
SHERMER being about to embark for Virginia, said BENJAMIN WRIGGLESWORTH is de-
sirous of appointing him his Attorney in the place and stead of said WILLIAM MURRAY
for the purposes hereinafter mentioned. NOW KNOW ALL MEN that BENJAMIN WRIG-
GLESWORTH hath appointed WILLIAM SHERMER his true and lawful Attorney to apply to

WILLIAM MURRAY and receive the said Bills of Lading in case the same shall not have
been satisfied. but in case the same or either of them hath been paid then for BENJA-
MIN WRIGGLESWORTH and in his name to ask demand recover and receive of WILLIAM
MURRAY such sums of money or such tobacco or other commodities or produce as WIL-
LIAM MURRAY may have received on account of said Bills of Lading (This Letter of
Attorney continues for three more pages, and also contains a Memorandum for WILLIAM SHERMER to
prosecute and appoint additional attornies.)
Sealed and Delivered in the presence of us
    SAML: MILFORD,   BENJA: WRIGGLESWORTH
    ANTHONY DREWIDZ
   At a Court of Hustings continued and held for the City of Richmond at the Courthouse
on Wednesday the 30th of May 1787 agreeable to Adjournment
This Power of Attorney together with the Memorandum endorsed were proved by the
Oath of SAML. MILFORD. al witness thereto, and ordered to be recorded
            Teste ADAM CRAIG, C. C.

pp.   (On margin: SCHERER & Ux. to PEDLEY)
143-   The Commonwealth of Virginia to RICHARD ADAMS, ROBT. BOYD and F. WEBB,
144   Gent., Justices of the City of Richmond, Greeting, Whereas SAMUEL SCHERER
     and HANNAH his Wife by their certain Indenture of Bargain and Sale bearing
date the eighteenth day of October in the year one thousand seven hundred and eighty
three have sold and conveyed unto THOMAS PEDLEY a certain tract of land with the
appurtenances lying in City of Richmond, And whereas the said HANNAH cannot conveniently travel to our said Court of Hustings to make acknowledgment of the said conveyance; Therefore we do give unto you are any two or more of you power to receive
the acknowledgment which the said HANNAH shall be willing to make before you of the
conveyance aforesaid (the Commission for the privy examination of HANNAH, the Wife of
SAMUEL SCHERER); Witness ADAM CRAIG, Clerk of our said Court at the Courthouse in
Richmond the 27th day of February 1787 in the 11th year of the Commonwealth
              ADAM CRAIG
   Pursuant to the within Commission, we have this day examined HANNAH SCHERER
privily and apart from her Husband, SAMUEL, and find she acknowledges her right to a
Lot on the Main Street as expressed in the annexed Deed and is willing the same should
be admitted to Record without the threats or persuasions of her said Husband; Given
under our hands and seals this 30th of April 1787   ROBT: BOYD
                                F. WEBB JR.
   At a Court of Hustings for the City of Richmond held at the Courthouse on Monday the
28th of May 1787   This Commission together with the Certificate of the execution
thereof indorsed was this day returned & ordered to be recorded
            Teste ADAM CRAIG. C. C.

pp.   (On margin: PEDLEY to STRUBEA. Dld. STRUBEA)
144-   THIS INDENTURE made this (blank) day of (blank) in the year of our Lord one
147   thousand seven hundred and Eighty seven Between THOMAS PEDLY of City of
     Richmond and MARY his Wife of one part and JOHN STRUBEA of the same City of
other part; Witnesseth that in consideration of the sum of Two hundred and fifty
pounds current money of Virginia by JOHN STRUBEA before the sealing and delivery of
these presents to said THOMAS and MARY in hand paid; by these presents do bargain
sell and confirm unto JOHN STRUBEA his heirs a certain peice of ground or part of a lot
of land in City of Richmond situate on and running along the South side of the Main

street thirty six feet in front, thence back from each corner in equal angles eighty five feet in depth so as to form in the rear a line parrallel with the Main Street twenty five feet in length, being the same peice of ground (two feet in front running back to a point excepted) which THOMAS PEDLEY formerly purchased from SAMUEL SCHERER and JACOB THOMAS in several parcels as by their respective Deeds bearing date the eighteenth day of October in the year one thousand seven hundred and eighty three of Record in the Court of Hustings of said City may more fully appear; with all houses improvements and appurtenances on said granted parcel of land belonging; and all the rents issues and profits thereof; To have and to hold the land and all other the premises with the appurtenances unto JOHN STRUBEA his heirs free and clear from all incumbrance whatsoever and the said THOMAS and his heirs the land and premises with the appurtenances unto JOHN STRUBEA his heirs shall warrant and forever defend; In Witness whereof the said THOMAS PEDLEY and MARY his Wife have hereunto set their hands and affixed their seals the same day and year first herein writtn
Signed Sealed & Delivered in the presence of

> FITZWHYLSONN   THOMAS PEDLY
> WM: BOOKER   MARY PEDLEY

At a Court of Hustings for the City of Richmond held at the Courthouse on Monday the 28th of March 1787   This Indenture was acknowledged by THOMAS PEDLY & MARY his Wife, parties thereto, (she having been first privily examined as the Law directs), & ordered to be recorded   Teste ADAM CRAIG, C.C.

pp.   (On margin: Commission for Sale of Public Lands to VOSS)
147-   THIS INDENTURE made this Twenty third day of April in the year of our Lord
148   one thousand seven hundred and eighty seven Between NATHANIEL WILKINSON,
         MILES SELDEN JR., JOHN HARVIE, THOMAS PROSSER and WILLIAM FOUSHEE,
Commissioners appointed by an Act of Assembly entituled, "An Act directing the sale of the Public Lands and other property in or near the City of Richmond," Witnesseth that said Commissioners in confirmity with the terms of said Act and in consideration of the sum of Two hundred and twenty nine pounds specie, the payment whereof has been secured as by the Act is prescribed, by these presents do bargain and sell unto EDWARD VOSS of City of Richmond one intire lot of ground distinguished in the Plan of said City by the number Three hundred and Thirty Four and called COUTTS, a peice of ground near the ROCK LANDING annexed to a Tenement, also numbred in said Plan Three hundred and Thirty Four and called COUTTS's, and which under the Operation of an Act of Assembly intituled, "An Act conerning Escheats and Forfeitures of British Subjects," was escheated to the Commonwealth of Virginia as being the proper Estate of COCKRANE CUNNINGHAME & COMPANY, as British Subjects, as by inquest of Office remaining of Record in the General Court will appear; Together with all houses and improvements thereon, and the rents issues and profits thereof; To have and to hold the said peice of ground with all houses and improvements thereon to EDWARD VOSS his heirs; In Witness whereof we have hereunto set our hands and affixed our seals the day and year above written
Signed Sealed & Acknowledged in presence of

> GEO: PICKETT   NATHL: WILKINSON
> JOHN GROVES,   MILES SELDEN
> R. B. VOSS, WILLIAM DUNCAN   W. FOUSHEE

At a Court of Hustings for the City of Richmond held at the Courthouse on Monday the 28th of May 1787   This Indenture was proved by the Oaths of JOHN GROVES, ROBERT B. VOSS and WILLIAM DUNCAN, witnesses thereto, and ordered to be recorded
                    Teste ADAM CRAIG, C.C.

pp.   (On margin: VOSS & Ux. to COLSTON. Deld. Mr. WM. MARSHALL 14th April 1792)
149-   THIS INDENTURE made this Twenty fourth day of April in the year of our Lord
152   one thousand seven hundred and eighty seven Between EDWARD VOSS and JANE
         his Wife of City of Richmond of one part and RAWLEIGH COLSTON of County of
FREDERICK and Commonwealth of Virginia of other part; Witnesseth that EDWARD VOSS
and JANE his Wife in consideration of the sum of Two hundred pounds current money
of Virginia to them in hand paid by RAWLEIGH COLSTON, by these presents do bargain
sell and confirm unto RAWLEIGH COLSTON his heirs one intire lott or peice of ground
lying in City of Richmond distinguished in the plan of said City by the number Three
hundred and Thirty Four (334), and called COUTTS, being a peice of ground near the
ROCK LANDING annexed to a Tenement, also numbered in the Plan Three hundred and
Thirty Four (334), and called COUTTS, as by reference to said plan will more fully appear
being all that lott or peice of ground purchased by EDWARD VOSS of the Commissioners
for the sale of Public Land and other property in and near the City of Richmond &
conveyed to EDWARD VOSS by a Deed of Bargain and Sale bearing date the 23rd day of
April 1787; To have and to hold the lott or parcel of ground to RAWLEIGH COLSTON his
heirs and EDWARD VOSS and JANE his Wife their heirs shall warrant and for ever defend by these presents; In Witness whereof they the said EDWARD VOSS and JANE his
Wife have hereunto set their hands and affixed their seals the day and year first above
written
Signed Sealed and delivered in presence of
         FRANCIS JAMES,   EDWARD VOSS
         JS: MARSHALL,   JANE VOSS
         CHARLES LEWIS, CHARLES MARSHALL
   The Commonwealth of Virginia to JOHN HARVIE and JOHN MARSHALL Gent., Justices of
the Court of Hustings for the City of Richmond, Greeting. Whereas (the Commission for the
privy examination of JANE, the Wife of EDWARD VOSS); Witness ADAM CRAIG, Clerk of our
said Court at the Courthouse in Richmond 16th day of June 1787 in the 11th year of the
Commonwealth   ADAM CRAIG
   City of Richmond. Sct. Agreeable to the within Commission to us directed from the
Worshipfull, the Court of Hustings for the said City, we have examined the within
mentioned JANE privately and apart from said EDWARD VOSS her Husband (the return of
the execution of the privy examination of JANE VOSS); Given under our hands and seals the
16th day of June 1787   J. MARSHALL
                                              JOHN HARVIE

   At a Court of Hustings for the City of Richmond held at the Courthouse on Monday the
28th of May 1787   This Indenture was proved by the Oaths of JAMES MARSHALL,
CHARLES LEWIS and CHARLES MARSHALL, witnesses thereto, and together with a Commission annexed and the Certificate of the execution thereof are ordered to be recorded
                      Teste ADAM CRAIG, C. C.

pp.   (On margin: EGGLESTON to BLAIR. Deld. LEIGH CLAIBORNE)
152-   KNOW ALL MEN by these presents that I JOHN EGGLESTON of County of CHESTER-
153   FIELD in consideration of the sum of Five shillings by ARCHIBALD BLAIR of the
         City of Richmond to me in hand paid have bargained and sold set over and deli-
vered to said ARCHIBALD the four slaves following, viz. Primus, Bob, Fanny and Luke;
To have and to occupy as the proper slaves of said ARCHIBALD in Trust and Special Confidence, nevertheless, that said ARCHIBALD shall apply all the clear profits arising
from the labour of the said slaves in the suport and maintenance of my Wife, MARION,
Sister to said ARCHIBALD, and of our Children, including the expence of their education

and at my death shall distribute the slaves and their increase, if any, among them in the same proportion as the Law disposes of them in cases of intestacy, the whole to be subject, however, to such debts as I may owe at this time; In Testimony whereof I have subscribed my hand & affixed my seal this twenty first day of January in the year of our Lord one thousand seven hundred and eighty six
Sealed and Delivered in the presence of

    ROBERT THOMSON,   JOHN STONE,   JOHN EGGLESTON
    ANNE BLAIR

  Richmond January 31, 1786. Received of ARCHIBALD BLAIR the sum of five shillings current money for the Deed of Trust this day executed by me

                               JOHN EGGLESTON

  At a Court of Hustings for the City of Richmond held at the Courthouse on Monday 28th of May 1787   This Deed of Trust together with the Receipt thereon endorsed was acknowledged by JOHN EGGLETON and ordered to be recorded

                    Teste ADAM CRAIG, C.C.

pp.   (On margin: COLEMAN to COUCH)
154-   TO ALL TO WHOM these presents shall come, I SAMUEL COLEMAN of HENRICO
155   County and Commonwealth of Virginia send Greeting; Know ye that I SAMUEL
       COLEMAN in consideration of the conjugal affection which I bear my Wife,
SUSANNA COLEMAN, and the especial trust and confidence which I place in SAMUEL COUCH, Merchant of Richmond, and divers other good causes and considerations me hereunto moving, by these presents do give and grant unto SAMUEL COUCH for the use of my Wife, SUSANNA COLEMAN, a certain double riding Chair and harness, the body of which is painted of a London Brown Colour and the Carriage and Wheels of a pale yellow, together with one black gelding about six years of age, his hind feet white, near five feet high, a star in his forehead and branded on the near buttock S.C., To have hold and enjoy the said double riding chair, harness and gelding unto SAMUEL COUCH or assigns for the use of SUSANNA COLEMAN her heirs; and I the said SAMUEL COLEMAN for the use of and in trust for SUSANNA COLEMAN her heirs against all persons shall warrant and forver defend by these presents; In Witness whereof I have hereunto affixed my seal and subscribed my name this twenty first day of April one thousand seven hundred and eighty seven

                    SAMUEL COLEMAN

  At a Court of Hustings for the City of Richmond held at the Courthouse on Monday the 28th of May 1787   This Deed of Trust was acknowledged by SAMUEL COLEMAN as his act and deed, and ordered to be recorded

                    Teste ADAM CRAIG, C.C.

pp.   (On margin: RANDOLPH to FORMICOLA. Deld. FORMICOLA)
155-   I HARRISON RANDOLPH do hereby bargain and sell unto SERAFINA FORMICOLA
156   in consideration of Three hundred and Ninty pounds 13/4, in Military Certifi-
       cates and in consideration of Five shillings current money to me in hand paid
by SERAFINA FORMICOLA, one Negroe man named Matt, also one Negroe man named Casar; To have and to hold the said Matt and said Casar to him the said SERAFINA FORMICOLA his heirs upon this nevertheless, that if HARRISON RANDOLPH shall pay unto SERAFINA FORMICOLA on or before the first day of July next the sum of Three hundred and ninty pounds 13/4 in Military Certificates that then said SERAFINA FORMICOLA will reconvey the said slaves unto HARRISON RANDOLPH, If I said HARRISON RANDOLPH should fail to pay him the said sum in Military Certificates issued to the Officers &

Soldiers by the Authority of an Act of Assembly made for that purpose, that SERAFINA
FORMICOLA will expose to sale the said slaves giving publick notice at least ten days
before the day of the sale which is to be for Military Certificates issued as before mentioned and will pay to me HARRISON RANDOLPH so much as the said slaves shall sell for
over and above the said sum of Three hundred and ninty pounds 13/4 in Military Certificates; in Witness whereof I the said HARRISON RANDOLPH have hereunto set my hand
and seal this thirty first day of March 1787
Test SAML: TROWER,   HARRISON RANDOLPH
        WILLIAM DUNCAN
    At a Court of Hustings for the City of Richmond continued and held at the Couthouse on
Tuesday the 24th of July 1787   This Mortgage was proved by the Oaths of SAMUEL
TROWER & WILLIAM DUNCAN, witnesses thereto, and ordered to be recorded
                           Teste ADAM CRAIG, C.C.

pp.   (On margin: DAVID EAST's Will)
156-   GODS WILL BE DONE. I DAVID EAST of City of Richmond in the Parish and Coun-
158   ty of HENRICO being weak of body but of sound mind and memory do make and
           ordain this my Last Will and Testament in manner and form following, that is to
say, Imprimis. It is my Will and Desire to have all my just debts paid by my Executors
(hereafter named), and to enable my said Executors duly and fully to perform the same,
it is my Will that the Lease of the House which I now hold of Mr. RICHARD ADAMS at a
consideration of Twelve pounds pr. Ann: ground Rent forever, be sold as likewise the
body and carriage of a double chair which is now in the work shop, which I rent of Mr.
GABRIEL GALT as likewise all my tools and whatever else belongs to me in ye said Shop;
   Item. The overplus arising from the above sale after my Debts are paid is to be equally
divided between my beloved Wife, ANN EAST, and my Son, WILLIAM EAST, for the
benefit of them and their heirs forever;
   Item. I give and bequeath unto my said Son and his heirs my pair of Gold sleeve
buttons.
   Item. It is my Will that my Executors as soon after my decease as they shall judge
necessary do take an Inventory of all my wearing apparrel, household furniture and
whatever else I may die psosses of except the things I have allotted to be sold and have
the same valued by two Appraisers and equally divided between my said Wife and Son,
that portion belonging to my Son still to continue in my Wife's possession until he becomes of age unless she my said Wife shall marry again, in which case they are to be
immediately deliver'd up to his Guardians hereafter named;
   Item. If my said Son die before he becomes of age, I ordain and appoint my said Wife to
be his sole heir and Executrix.
   Item. I appoint my said Wife and worthy Friend, WILLIAM LIPSCOMB, Guardians to my
said Son;
   Item. I lastly appoint my said Wife and my said beloved Friend, WILLIAM LIPSCOMB,
and my valuable Friend, JOHN CLARK, as Executors of this my Last Will and Testament,
declaring all other Wills to be void and unlawful. In Witness whereof I have hereunto
set my hand and affixed my Seal this sixteenth day of March in the year of our Lord one
thousand seven hundred and eighty seven and the Eleventh year of the Independence
of America
Signed and Sealed in presence of
        THOS: SOWELL, JOHN BURTON,   DAVID his mark X EAST
        M: his mark X ADAMS

At a Court of Hustings for the City of Richmond continued & held at the Courthouse on Tuesday the 29th of May 1787   This Will was presented in Court and proved by the Oaths of THOMAS SOWELL and MALLORY ADAMS, two of the witnesses thereto, and ordered to be recorded; And on the motion of WILLIAM LIPSCOMB, one of the Executors therein named, who made Oath according to Law, & together with JOHN CLARK & THOMAS WARREN, his Securities, entered into and acknowledged their Bond in the penalty of Three hundred pounds conditioned as the Law directs, Certificate was granted him for obtaining a Probat thereof in due form, Liberty being reserved to the other Executors named in the said Will to join in the Probat when they shall think fit
                              Teste ADAM CRAIG. C.C.

pp.   (On margin: JOSEPH BROWN's Inventory.)
158-   INVENTORY of Sundrys belonging to JOSEPH BROWN, deceased, taken the 27th
159   of February 1787.   1 Silver Watch No. 63; 11 Brocade silk patterns for Shoes
         and Trimmings, 2 pr. Boots, 1 compleat set Shoemakers Tools, 1 green Coat, 1 drab
ditto, 1 nankeen ditto, 1 brown great Coat, 1 black velvet Jacket, 1 Corderoy ditTo, 1
white ditto, 1 coating ditto, 1 pr. nankeen breeches, 1 pr. overalls, 3 shirts, 5 stocks, 1
pr. gloves; 3 pr. stockings, 3 black silk handkerchiefs, 2 remnants blk. Catimanco, 7 yds;
1 ditto green ditto 4 yds., 1 bolt blk. Binding, 1 rasor case, shaving box & strap, 1 yd.
Rusia sheeting, 1 Chest, 1 blk. & white hat   Total 15..5..3.
                              ROBT. MACARTNEY
                              JOHN V. KAUTZMAN
                              GEORGE NICHOL
Returned into Court of Hustings for the City of Richmond on Monday the 26th of
March 1787. And ordered to be recorded
                              Teste ADAM CRAIG. C.C.

pp.   (On margin: COLEMAN & Ux. to WALKER)
159-   THIS INDENTURE made this first day of September Anno Domini one thousand
162   seven hundred and eighty six Between SAMUEL COLEMAN of County of HENRICO
         and SUSANNA his Wife of one part and JOHN WALKER of City of Richmond of
other part; Witnesseth that in consideration of the sum of Five shillings current
money of Virginia by JOHN WALKER in hand paid to SAMUEL COLEMAN and SUSANNA
his Wife at and before the sealing and delivery of these presents; said SAMUEL COLEMAN and SUSANNA his Wife for themselves jointly and severally and particularly the
heirs of the said SUSANNA, by these presents do bargain sell and confirm unto JOHN
WALKER and his heirs a certain parcel or lot of ground in City of Richmond on the
North West side of SHOCKOE CREEK, Beginning on the Main Street at THOMAS SCOTTs corner, thence his line ninety four feet to a fifteen feet Alley, thence up said Alley forty
one feet to JOHN WALKERs corner, thence said WALKERs line ninety four feet to the
Main Street, thence down the Main street forty one feet to the beginning; To have and
to hold by JOHN WALKER and his heirs of SAMUEL COLEMAN and SUSANNA his Wife and
their heirs and the heirs of said SUSANNA with the houses thereon together with the
appurtenances thereunto belonging and the resnts issues and profits thereof, Subject
nevertheless to an Annual Ground Rent and for the further consideration of the sum of
Thirty pounds fifteen shillings of Gold and Silver Coin as received in the Treasury of
Virginia to be paid yearly on the first day of January (the first payment to be made the
first day of January next ensuing), In Witness whereof the said SAMUEL COLEMAN and
SUSANNA his Wife have hereunto set their hands and seals the day and year first
before written

Signed Sealed & Delivered in the presence of us
        (no witnesses recorded)
                                        SAMUEL COLEMAN
                                        SUSANNA COLEMAN

At a Court of Hustings for the City of Richmond held at the Courthouse on Monday the
25th of June 1787   This Indenture was acknowledged by SAMUEL COLEMAN and
SUSANNA his Wife, parties thereto (she having been first privily examined as the Law
directs), and ordered to be recorded Teste ADAM CRAIG, C.C.

pp.   (On margin: MITTART to GILES &c. Delivered WM. GILES)
162-   THIS INDENTURE made this fifth day of April in the year of our Lord one thou-
164   sand seven hundred and eighty seven Between JACOB MITTART of City of Rich-
         mond of one part and WILLIAM GILES, JOHN NEW and WILLIAM GEDDY of County
of HENRICO of other part. Whereas JACOB MITTART hath obtained an Appeal to the
General Court from a Judgment obtained against him in the Court of HENRICO County
for the sum of Three hundred and fifty pounds and costs of suit by Sir PEYTON SKIP-
WITH, and the above named WILLIAM GILES, JOHN NEW and WILLIAM GEDDY having
become Securities in the Appeal Bond given by JACOB MITTART and thereby made
themselves liable for the amount of said Judgment and costs with lawful Interest thereon in case the said Judgment should be affirmed, and JACOB MITTART being desirous of
securing to his said Securities property sufficient to reimburse them in case they
should be hereafter compelled to pay the above mentioned sum of money and costs with
the Interest thereon; NOW THIS INDENTURE WITNESSETH that JACOB MITTART in consideration of the premises and also in consideration of the sum of five shillings to him
paid by WILLIAM GILES, JOHN NEW and WILLIAM GEDDY, by these presents doth bargain sell and confirm to WILLIAM GILES, JOHN NEW and WILLIAM GEDDY and their
heirs a certain lot of land containing one quarter of an acre lying in County of HEN-
RICO in the bottom between SHOCKOE and RICHMOND HILLS and near the Mill upon
SHOCKOE CREEK belonging to Colo. RICHARD ADAMS and the LIVERY STABLE belonging
to THOMAS ADAMS, being the lot of land on which JACOB MITTART now at the time of the
sealing and delivering of this Indenture resides with all houses and other appurtenances thereunto belonging; To have and to hold the lot of land to WILLIAM GILES,
JOHN NEW and WILLIAM GEDDY their heirs upon the express condition that if JACOB
MITTART shall well and truly pay the said Sir PEYTON SKIPWITH the amount of the
Judgment abovementioned with all costs and the legal Interest thereon in case the
Judgment shall be affirmed or the Appeal obtained by JACOB MITTART shall not be
prosecuted with effect, that then this Indenture shall be utterly void; In Witness
whereof the said JACOB MITTART hath hereunto put his hand & affixed his seal the day
and year above written
Sealed and Delivered in presence of us
        CHARLES HAY,   JACOB MITTERT
        ZENAS TAIT, JOHN RALEY
Richmond April 5th 1787. Receive of WILLIAM GILES, JOHN NEW and WILLIAM GEDDY
Five shillings current money of Virginia being the consideration within mentioned
Witness CHARLES HAY   JACOB MITTERT
At a Court of Hustings for the City of Richmond held at the Courthouse on Monday the
25th of June 1787   This Indenture of Mortgage together with the Receipt & Memoran-
dum thereon endorsed were proved, the said Mortgage by the Oaths of CHARLES HAY,
ZENAS TAIT and JOHN RALEY, and the Receipt & Memorandum by the Oaths of said
CHARLES HAY, witness thereto, and ordered to be recorded
                        Teste ADAM CRAIG, C.C.

pp.   (On margin: COLEMAN & Ux. to WALKER)
164-   THIS INDENTURE made this sixteenth day of October in the year of our Lord one
167   thousand seven hundred and Eighty six Between SAMUEL COLEMAN of HENRICO
         and SUSANNA his Wife of one part and JOHN WALKER of City of Richmond of
other part; Witnesseth tht in consideration of the sum of Five shillings current money
of Virginia by JOHN WALKER in hand paid to SAMUEL COLEMAN and SUSANNA his Wife,
at and before the sealing and delivery of these presents, said SAMUEL COLEMAN and
SUSANNA his Wife for themselves jointly and severally of their joint and several heirs,
particularly the heirs of the said SUSANNA, by these presents do bargain sell and confirm unto JOHN WALKER his heirs a certain lot of ground in City of Richmond on the
North West side of SHOCKOE CREEK, Beginning on the Main Street at the Corner of
GEORGE PICKETTs Tenement, formerly JOHN STOCKDELLs,, thence down the Main Street
toward SHOCKOE CREEK forty one feet to the upper line of the other Lot which said JOHN
WALKER purchased of SAMUEL COLEMAN and SUSANNAH his Wife, thence on the line
back ninety four feet to a fifteen foot Alley, thence up the Alley forty one feet to
GEORGE PICKETTs corner on said Alley, thence th said PICKETTs line ninety four feet to
the Main Street to the beginning. To have and to hold by said WALKER his heirs of
SAMUEL COLEMAN and SUSANNA his Wife and their heirs jointly and the heirs of the
said SUSANNA with all the appurtenances thereunto belonging and the rents issues and
profits thereof, Subject nevertheless to an Annual Ground Rent and for the further
consideration of Thirty pounds fifteen shillings of Gold or Silver Coin as received in the
Treasury of Virginia to be paid yearly on the first day of January, the first payment to
be made the first day of January next ensuing by JOHN WALKER his heirs to SAMUEL
COLEMAN and SUSANNA his Wife and their heirs, said SAMUEL COLEMAN and SUSANNA
his Wife warranting and defending the ground to JOHN WALKER his heirs against any
person: In Witness whereof said SAMUEL COLEMAN and SUSANNA his Wife have hereunto severally set their hands & affixed their seals the day and year first above written
Signed Sealed and Delivered in the presence of us
         (no witnesses recorded)   SAMUEL COLEMAN
                                                          SUSANNA COLEMAN
   At a Court of Hustings for the City of Richmond held at the Courthouse on Monday the
25th of June 1787   This Indenture was acknowledged by SAMUEL COLEMAN & SUSAN-
NA his Wife parties thereto, (she having been first privily examined as the Law directs)
and ordered to be recorded   Teste ADAM CRAIG, C.C.

pp.   (On margin: BENNET to McROBERTS)
167-   KNOW ALL MEN whom it may concern, that I JAMES BENNET commonly called
168   JAMES BENNET of WESTHAM, being indebted to ALEXANDER McROBERTS of City of
         Richmond, Merchant, in the sum of Fifty pounds current money of Virginia,
bearing an interest of Five per centum per Annum from the (blank) for securing the
payment thereof and in consideration of the sum of One Shilling like money to me in
hand paid by ALEXANDER McROBERTS, I the said JAMES BENNET by these presents do
bargain and sell unto ALEXANDER McROBERTS Two Negroe slaves, to wit, Clit and Jane,
women: To have and to hold the said Negroes and each of them unto ALEXANDER
McROBERTS his heirs; PROVIDED always that if I said JAMES BENNET or any person in
my behalf, shall pay ALEXANDER McROBERTS or assigns the sum of Fifty pounds with all
interest due in Gold or Silver current Coin on or before the first day of January next
ensuing the date hereof that then the right and estate of said ALEXANDER McROBERTS
his heirs in the Negroes shall cease and be done away; In Witness whereof, I have
hereunto set my hand & seal this seventh day of July one thousand seven hundred and
eighty seven

The within writing signed sealed and delivered
by JAMES BENNET therein named in our presence
                    JOHN McCOLL,   JAMES BENNET
                    G. H. BASKERVILL,
    Received 7th July 1787 from ALEXANDER McROBERTS, the sum of One shilling in full of
the consideration money for the within mentioned Negroes
Teste   JOHN McCOLL,   JAMES BENNET
        G. H. BASKERVILL
    At a Court of Hustings for the City of Richmond held at the Courthouse the 24th of July
1787   This Mortgage together with the Receipt thereon endorsed was proved by the
Oath of GEORGE H. BASKERVILL, a witness thereto and ordered to be recorded
                    Teste ADAM CRAIG, C. C.

pp.   (On margin: COUTTS's Exors. to DePRIEST)
168-   THIS INDENTURE made July 15th one thousand seven hundred and Eighty seven
169   Between BENJAMIN LEWIS, JOHN McKEAND & ALEXANDER McROBERTS, Executors
       of WILLIAM COUTTS deceased, of one part and JOHN DePRIEST of other part; Wit-
nesseth that BENJAMIN LEWIS, JOHN McKEAND and ALEXANDER McROBERTS, Executors
as aforesaid, and by virtue of an authority vested in them by the Last Will and Testament of their Testator, WILLIAM COUTTS, do by these presents sell and confirm unto
JOHN DePRIEST his heirs one half acre Lot No. 451 lying on SHOCKOE HILL in the City of
Richmond in County of HENRICO, together with the appurtenances thereunto belonging. To have and to hold the half acre with all appurtenances to JOHN DePRIEST his
heirs; In Witness whereof we do hereunto affix our hands & seals this 16th day of July
Anno Dom: one thousand seven hundred & eighty seven
                                    JOHN McKEAND
                                    BENJA: LEWIS
                                    A. McROBERTS
    At a Court of Hustings held for the City of Richmond at the Courthouse the 25th of July
1787   This Indenture was acknowledged by JOHN McKEAND, BENJAMIN LEWIS and
ALEXANDER McROBERTS, Executors of WILLIAM COUTTS, deceased, parties thereto, and
ordered to be recorded   Teste ADAM CRAIG C. C.

pp.   (On margin: WM. McCLOUD's Appraismt.)
170-   INVENTORY and APPRAISMENT of the Estate of WM. McCLOUD deced.
171   3 Coats, 10 & 1 fronts of Waistcoats, 4 shirts, overalls, stocks & 2 handkerchiefs,
        a remnant of Linnen, 1 Nankeen Coat, 2 pr. Breeches, 2 hats, 4 pr. Stockings, 1
pr. shoes, 1 box of Silk & Thread & sundry articles, 1 shaving box & 2 Razors & 1 snuff
box, sundry taylors tools, chest, 2 case bottles, set of Buckles, pr. Buckles, Pocket Book,
Blanket, Match Coat; Cash L. 9...2...0.   Total: L. 22...0...1.
                                    WILLIAM COCKE SENR.
                                    JOHN SIMS
                                    JOHN BRYAN
    The above mentioned articles were sold on the 14th Instant to the highest bidders for
the sum of L. 12...2...9 1/4.   THOS: ELLIOTT, Admor. July 23d. 1787.
    Returned into the Court of Hustings for the City of Richmond the 25th. day of July 1787
and ordered to be recorded   Teste ADAM CRAIG, C. C.

pp.   (On margin: DIDDEP vs. MANN)
171-   THIS INDENTURE WITNESSETH that JAMES DIDDEP of City of Richmond, Orphan of
172   ARCHIBALD DIDDEP deceased, hath put himself and by these presents doth
         voluntarily and of his own free will and accord put himself Apprentice to
HENRY MANN of the said City, Cabinet Maker, to learn the Art, Trade and Mystery and
after the manner of an Apprentice to serve said HENRY MAN from the day of the date
hereof until he shall attain the full age of Twenty one years during all which term the
said Apprentice his said Master shall faithfully serve; And the said Master shall use the
utmost of his Endeavours to teach or cause to be taught or instructed the said Apprentice in the Trade or Mistery of a Cabinet Maker, also learn the said Apprentice to read
write and common Arithmetick and procure and provide for him sufficient meat drink
cloaths washing and lodging fitting for an Apprentice during said term and at the end
thereof pay him the Customary Freedom Dues and for the true performance of all the
covenants aforesaid the parties bind themselves each unto the other firmly by these
presents; In Witness whereof the said parties have interchangeably set their hands
and seals hereunto dated the 24th day of July in the year of our Lord one thousand
seven hundred and Eighty seven and in the 12th year of the Commonwealth
Sealed and Delivered in the presence of
         CLAI. WATKINS   JAMES DIDDEP
                                                    HENRY MANN
   At a Court of Hustings for the City of Richmond held at the Courthouse the 25th day of
July 1787   This Indenture of Apprenticeship was with the consent of the Court executed and acknowledged by the parties thereto and ordered to be recorded
                   Teste ADAM CRAIG, C.C.

pp.   (On margin: GRAVES to NEALE)
172-   THIS INDENTURE made and entered into this Thirteenth day of December one
175   thousand seven hundred and Eighty six Between FRANCIS GRAVES of the City of
         Richmond of one part and JANE NEALE of K. WM. County of other part; Witnes-
seth that in consideration of the Rent herein after mentioned to be paid by JANE NEALE
to FRANCIS GRAVES, said FRANCIS GRAVES by these presents doth grant demise and to
farm let unto JANE NEALE all that lot of land belonging to FRANCIS GRAVES in City of
Richmond adjoining the lots where JOHN STOCKDELL and WILLIAM NICOLSON now lives,
being the lot he purchased of FOSTER WEBB JUNR. of said City and where Mrs. ELIZA-
BETH DONALDSON now resides, with all houses gardnes rights priviledges & appurtenances thereon appertaining; To have and to hold the demised premises unto JANE
NEALE from the first day of March one thousand seven hundred and Eighty seven
during the term of four years thence next ensuing; Provided said JANE NEALE shall so
long live and in case of the death of said JANE NEALE within said term, then to her
Executors during the residue of said term unexpired at the time of her decease, if they
shall think proper to retain the same, and shall at any time within twenty days after
the death of said JANE NEALE signify such assent in Writing to FRANCIS GRAVES his
heirs, otherwise this present writing and any clause therein to be immediately after
the death of the said JANE NEAL null and void, paying unto FRANCIS GRAVES his heirs
yearly the sum of One hundred pounds current money of Virginia, Spanish Milled
Dollars at the rate of Six shillings each or in other Silver or Gold Coin at like value and
proportion without deductions for Taxes or other causes on the last day of February in
each year In Witness whereof the said parties to these presents have set their hands &
seals the day and year first written

Signed Sealed and delivered in presence of
    RICHARD NEALE,   FRANCIS GRAVES
    EDWARD CARROLL,   EDWARD DAVIS   JANE NEALE
At a Court of Hustings for the City of Richmond held at the Courthouse on Tuesday the
24th of July 1786   This Indenture of Lease was proved by the Oaths of EDWARD CARROL
and EDWARD DAVIS, two of the witnesses thereto, and ordered to be recorded
               Teste ADAM CRAIG, C. C.

pp.   (On margin: GRAVES & Ux. to WARRINGTON). (No page numbered 177)
175-   THIS INDENTURE made this sixteenth day of October in the year of our Lord one
179   thousand seven hundred and Eighty six Between FRANCIS GRAVES of the City of
       Richmond and MARTHA his Wife of one part and JAMES WARRINGTON of the
same City of other part; Witnesseth that FRANCIS GRAVES and MARTHA his Wife in
consideration of the sum of Six hundred & thirty four pounds current money of Virginia to them in hand paid by JAMES WARRINGTON, by these presents do bargain sell
and confirm unto JAMES WARRINGTON his heirs a certain parcel of ground lying in
City of Richmond containing Six thousand seven hundred and Eighty three square feet
and bounded; Beginning at a corner Pig Iron in the Main Street, thence South thirty
seven degrees West one hundred and nineteen feet to a Stone under (blotted) House,
thence South eight two degrees West four feet to the corner of the Kitchen, thence
South thirty seven and one half degrees West forty feet four inches to corner of the
Stable on a 21 foot Alley, thence along said Alley South fifty seven degrees East sixty
five feet six inches to a Stake on the said Street, thence North thirty five and one half
degrees East sixty feet to a Stake at the corner of a small Stable, thence North forty five
and one quarter degrees West thirteen feet, thence North thirty six degrees East fifteen
feet seven inches to a corner Stone on GRAVES's Lot, thence North thirty seven degrees
East one hundred one and an half feet to the corner of GRAVES's upper Store House on
the Main Street, thence up the Main Street twenty seven feet to the place begun at, together with all appurtenances and the rents issues and profits thereof; To have and to
hold the land and premises with the appurtenances unto JAMES WARRINGTON his heirs;
And FRANCIS GRAVES for himself and heirs doth agree with JAMES WARRINGTON his
heirs that the land and premises unto JAMES WARRINGTON his heirs against all persons
claiming right title or property in the same shall warrant and by these presents defend; In Witness whereof the said parties to these presents have hereunto set their
hands and affixed their seals the day and year first above written
Signed Sealed and Delivered in the presence of
    LAIN J. JOHNSON,   FRANCIS GRAVES
    EDWARD DAVIS, EDWARD CARROLL   MARTHA GRAVES
 The Commonwealth of Virginia to ROBERT BOYD, FOSTER WEBB JUNR., & ALEXANDER
McROBERTS Gent., Justices of the Hustings Court for the City of Richmond, Greeting,
Whereas (the Commission for the privy examination of MARTHA, the Wife of FRANCIS GRAVES);
Witness ADAM CRAIG, Clerk of our said Court at the Courthouse in Richmond, the 9th
day of May 1787 in the 11th year of the Commonwealth   ADAM CRAIG
By Virtue of the within Commission to us directed, we did personally go to the within
mentioned MARTHA, the Wife of the within named FRANCIS GRAVES, and examined her
privily and apart from her said Husband touching her acknowledgment of the conveyance contained in the Indenture hereunto annexed (the return of the execution of the
privy examination of MARTHA GRAVES); Given under our hands and seals this sixteenth day
of May one thousand seven hundred and eighty seven
                     FOSTER WEBB JR.
                     ALEXANDER McROBERTS

At a Court of Hustings for Richmond County held at the Courthouse the 24th of July
1787   This Indenture was proved by the Oaths of LAIN J. JOHNSON, EDWARD DAVIS
and EDWARD CARROLL, the witnesses thereto, and together with the Commission annexed and Certificate of the execution thereof returned are ordered to be recorded
Teste ADAM CRAIG, C. C.

pp,   (On margin: COUTTS's Exors. to JACKSON)
179-   THIS INDENTURE made this Eleventh day of June in the year of our Lord one
180   thousand seven hundred and eighty seven Between JOHN McKEAND & ALEXAN-
        DER McROBERTS, of City of Richmond, BENJAMIN LEWIS of County of HENRICO,
Executors of WILLIAM COUTTS deceased, of one part and TOBY JACKSON of City aforesaid
of other part; Witnesseth that in consideration of the sum of Fifty pounds Virginia
currency to them the said JOHN McKEAND, ALEXANDER McROBERTS and BENJAMIN
LEWIS, Executors of said WM. COUTTS deceased, in hand paid, by these presents do bargain sell and confirm unto TOBY JACKSON his heirs a certain half acre lot lying in City
aforesaid and known in the plan of said City by the number Six hundred & Four, To
have and to hold the half acre lot with all houses improvements and appurtenances
thereunto belonging to TOBY JACKSON his heirs; And JOHN McKEAND, ALEXANDER
McROBERTS and BENJAMIN LEWIS, the Executors to WM. COUTTS deceased, doth hereby
warrant and will forever defend the title against all persons claiming under them; In
Witness whereof the said JOHN McKEAND, ALEXANDER McROBERTS and BENJAMIN
LEWIS, Executors of said WM. COUTTS deced., have hereunto set their hands and affixed
their seals this day and year first above written
Signed Sealed & delivered in the presence of us
        (no witnesses recorded)   JNO: McKEAND
                                                        A: McROBERTS
                                                        BEN: LEWIS
    At a Court of Hustings for the City of Richmond held at the Courthouse on Monday the
24th of September 1787   This Indenture was acknowledged in Court by JOHN McKEAND
BENJAMIN LEWIS & ALEXANDER McROBERTS, Executors of WILLIAM COUTTS deced., as
their act and deed, & ordered to be recorded
                    Teste ADAM CRAIG, C. C.

pp,   (On margin: McCOUTTS's Exors. to PENNOCK. Deld. GEO: NICOLSON)
180-   THIS INDENTURE made this (blank) day of May in the year of our Lord one
181   thousand seven hundred and Eighty seven Between BENJAMIN LEWIS, ALEXAN-
        DER McROBERTS and JOHN McKEAND, Executors of the Last Will and Testament of
the REVEREND WILLIAM COUTTS deceased, of one part and WILLIAM PENNOCK of City of
Richmond, Merchant, of other part; Witnesseth that in consideration of the sum of
Twenty five pounds current money of Virginia to BENJAMIN LEWIS, ALEXANDER
McROBERTS and JOHN McKEAND, Executors of said WILLIAM COUTTS deceased, in hand
paid by WILLIAM PENNOCK, by these presents do bargain sell and confirm unto WIL-
LIAM PENNOCK his heirs a certain plot of ground lying in City of Richmond in the
Parish and County of HENRICO, known in the plan of said City by the number Five
hundred and Ninety Eight, in figures by the number 598, containing one half acre of
land be the same more or less with all appurtenances thereunto belonging; To have and
to hold the half acre lot with appurtenances unto WILLIAM PENNOCK his heirs; And
BENJAMIN LEWIS, ALEXANDER McROBERTS & JOHN McKEAND, Executors as aforesaid, by
a power in them vested by the Last Will and Testament of WILLIAM COUTTS recorded in
the County Court of HENRICO, against all persons claiming under them as Executors as

aforesaid shall warrant and forever defend by these presents; In Witness whereof the
said BENJAMIN LEWIS, ALEXANDER McROBERTS and JOHN McKEAND, have hereunto
respectively affixed their hands and seals the day and year above written
Signed Sealed and delivered in the presence of us
    (no witnesses recorded)   BEN: LEWIS
                                              JNO: McKEAND
                                            A: McROBERTS

    At a Court of Hustings for the City of Richmond held at the Courthouse on Monday the
24th day of September 1787   This Indenture was acknowledged by BENJAMIN LEWIS,
JOHN McKEAND & ALEXANDER McROBERTS, Executors of WILLIAM COUTTS, deceased, as
their act & deed and ordered to be recorded
                   Teste ADAM CRAIG, C. C.

pp.   (On margin: BLANKENSHIP & Ux. to THOMAS)
181-   THIS INDENTURE made this second day of February in the year of our Lord one
182   thousand seven hundred and eighty seven Between STEPHEN BLANKENSHIP and
        JANE his Wife of one part and JACOB THOMAS of the other part. Witnesseth that
in consideration of the sum of Fifty pounds current money to them in hand paid, hath
bargained and sold unto JACOB THOMAS his heirs one certain lot of Ground in City of
Richmond containing twenty two and a half feet in front and one hundred & twenty six
back, being part of a lot known in the plan of said City by the number (blank) and
bounded by NICOLSON's, STROBIA's and sd. THOMAS's lots, To have and to hold the lot of
ground with all appurtenances unto JACOB THOMAS his heirs and STEPHEN BLANKEN-
SHIP and JANE his Wife for themselves their heirs will warrant and defend the lot of
ground unto JACOB THOMAS his heirs against the claim of all persons; In Witness
whereof they have hereunto set their hands and affixed their seals the day and year
above written
Signed Sealed and delivered in presence of
    THOS. NICOLSON,   STEPHEN X BLANKENSHIP
    GEO: RICHARDSON,   JANEY BLANKENSHIP
    B. DAWSON
    At a Court of Hustings for the City of Richmond held at the Courthouse on Monday the
24th of September 1787   This Indenture was acknowledged by STEPHEN BLANKEN-
SHIP and JANE his Wife,. parties thereto (she having been first privily examined as the
Law directs), and ordered to be recorded
                   Teste ADAM CRAIG, C. C.

pp.   (On margin: STOCKDELL & Ux. to ALEXANDER)
182-   THIS INDENTURE made on the Nineteenth day of March in the year of our Lord
185   one thousand seven hundred & Eighty seven Betwixt JOHN STOCKDALE and
        ELIZABETH STOCKDALE his Wife of City of Richmond of one part and WILLIAM
ALEXANDER of County of HENRICO of other part; Witnesseth that in consideration of the
sum of One thousand three hundred and Eighty seven pounds, Ten shillings in specie
which JOHN STOCKDELL has heretofore borrowed of said WILLIAM ALEXANDER &
honestly desires to secure and pay to him the sum & in farther consideration of the sum
of Five shillings like money to JOHN STOCKDELL & his Wife in hand paid by WILLIAM
ALEXANDER, said JOHN STOCKDELL and ELIZABETH his Wife by these presents doth bargain sell & confirm to WILLIAM ALEXANDER his heirs that part of a lot or tenement of
land lying in City of Richmond with the houses and improvements thereon & being the
same now occupied by JOHN STOCKDELL with all appurtenances belonging and the

benefits and profits of said lot; To have and to hold the lot and premises unto WILLIAM
ALEXANDER his heirs and JOHN STOCKDELL and his Wife, ELIZABETH, and their heirs
shall warrant and forever defend the lot and premises unto WILLIAM ALEXANDER his
heirs against every person. Upon Trust and as an additional security for said Loan said
JOHN STOCKDELL doth demise lease and to farm let three half acre lots or tenements of
land lying on SHOCKOE HILL in City aforesaid with the houses and improvements thereon being the same now occupied by DABNEY MILLER and by him leased to said JOHN
STOCKDELL for the term of Twenty years as appears by an Indenture of Lease executed
by DABNEY MILLER to JOHN STOCKDELL bearing date September 5th 1786 to said WIL-
LIAM ALEXANDER his heirs; To have and to hold the premises as the lots are demsied to
JOHN STOCKDELL by DABNEY MILLER which Lease shall be exonerated from those payments which have been or may be made by JOHN STOCKDELL before the 8th November
1787, In Witness whereof the said JOHN STOCKDELL and ELIZABETH STOCKDELL his Wife
and WILLIAM ALEXANDER have hereunto set their hands & seals on the day above
written
Signed & Sealed in presence of
      SIMON M. STOCKDELL,   JNO: STOCKDELL
      GEORGE GRAY,   ELIZABETH STOCKDELL
      RICHARD VERNON, J. B. DANDRIDGE   W. ALEXANDER
  At a Court of Hustings for the City of Richmond held at the Courthouse on Monday the
24th of September 1787   This Indenture was proved by the Oaths of SIMON M. STOCK-
DELL, GEORGE GRAY & JULIUS B. DANDRIDGE, witnesses thereto & ordered to be recorded
                  Teste ADAM CRAIG, C.C.

pp.   (On margin: DePRIEST & Ux. to HYLTON)
185-   THIS INDENTURE made this fourth day of October in the year of our Lord one
187   thousand seven hundred and eighty seven Between JOHN DePRIEST of County of
         HENRICO and City of Richmond and SARAH his Wife of one part and RALPH HYL-
TON of State of Virginia of other part; Witnesseth that in consideration of the sum of
Five shillings current money of Virginia by RALPH HYLTON to said JOHN and SARAH in
hand paid, said JOHN DePRIEST and SARAH his Wife do by these presents bargain and
sell unto RALPH HYLTON his heirs a certain parcel of land containing half an acre
lying in City of Richmond and described in the plan of said City by the number Four
hundred and Fifty One, with all the houses and appurtenances to said lott of land belonging and the rents issues and profits thereof; To have and to hold the lott of land
with all appurtenances to RALPH HYLTON his heirs and JOHN DePRIEST and SARAH his
Wife for themselves their heirs do promise RALPH HYLTON his heirs shall occupy the
same without let or disturbance at any time by an person; In Witness whereof the said
JOHN DePRIEST and SARAH his Wife have hereunto set their hands and affixed their
seals the day and year first herein written
Signed Sealed and delivered in presence of
    J. PRYOR,   JNO: DePRIEST
    JOHN CRINGAN, HUGH MUNRO   SARAH DePRIEST
  The Commonwealth of Virginia to JOHN HARVIE, WILLIAM FOUSHEE and WILLIAM
HAY, Gent., Justices of the Court of Hustings for the City of Richmond, Greeting; Where-
as (the Commission for the privy examination of SARAH, the Wife of JOHN DePRIEST); Witness
ADAM CRAIG, Clerk of our said Court at the Courthouse the 4th day of October 1787 in the
12th year of the Commonwealth   ADAM CRAIG
  Richmond Sct. Pursuant to the within Commission we have examined SARAH DePRIEST
Wife of JOHN DePRIEST, privily and apart from her Husband, and hereby certify that

she executed the Deed hereunto annexed freely and voluntarily and consents that the
same should be recorded as her act & deed; Given under our hands and seals the 5th
October 1787   W: FOUSHEE
                                      WM: HAY
   At a Court of Hustings for the City of Richmond held at the MASONS HALL in the said
City on Monday the 22d. of October 1787   This Indenture was proved by the Oath of
HUGH MONRO, a witness thereto; And at a Court of Hustings for the said City continued
and held at the MASONS HALL the day following, to wit, on Tuesday the 23d. of October
1787, the same was further proved by the Oath of JOHN PRYOR, another witness thereto;
And at another Court held for said City at the MASONS HALL on Monday the 25th of
November 1787, the same was further proved by the Oath of JOHN CRINGAN, another
witness thereto and (together with the Commission annexed and the Certificate of the
execution thereof), ordered to be recorded
                          Teste ADAM CRAIG, C. C.

pp.   (On margin: HYLTON to NICOLSON. Deld. GEORGE NICHOLSON 7th March 1788)
188-   THIS INDENTURE made July 25th 1787, Between RALPH HYLTON of one part and
189   GEORGE NICOLSON of other part; Witnesseth that RALPH HYLTON in considera-
         tion of Five shillings to him in hand paid, said RALPH HYLTON does by these pre-
sents bargain sell and confirm unto GEORGE NICOLSON his heirs one half acre lott No.
451, formerly the property of JOHN DePRIEST lying on SHOCKOE HILL in City of Richmond in County of HENRICO together with the house and tenement thereunto belonging
To have and to hold the half acre, house and tenement with all appurtenances thereunto belonging to GEO: NICOLSON his heirs and RALPH HYLTON for him and his heirs the
lott house and tenement against every person to GEORGE NICOLSON his heirs shall warrant and forever defend by these presents; In Witness whereof I do hereunto affixed
my hand and seal this 25th day of July Anno Domini one thousand seven hundred and
eighty seven
Teste J. PRYOR,   RALPH HYLTON
       FORTUNATUS GREEN, T. WARREN,
       HUGH MUNRO
   Received 25th July 1787 of Mr. GEORGE NICOLSON, six hundred pounds being the full
consideration money for the within lott and house
Teste HUGH MUNRO   RALPH HYLTON
   At a Court of Hustings for the City of Richmond held at the MASONS HALL in the said
City on Monday the Twenty second of October 1787, This Indenture together with the
Receipt endorsed were proved by the Oath of HUGH MUNRO, a witness thereto, And at
another Court held for the said City at the MASONS HALL on Monday, the 26th of Novem-
ber 1787, The Indenture was further proved by the Oaths of JOHN PRYOR and THOMAS
WARREN, two other witnesses thereto, and together with the Receipt (which was before
proved by the Oath of HUGH MUNRO) ordered to be recorded
                          Teste ADAM CRAIG, C. C.

pp.   (On margin: ALEXR. THOMPSON's Appraismt.)
189-   INVENTORY and APPRAISMENT of the goods of the late ALEXR: THOMPSON de-
192   ceased.   1 Chest, 1 great Coat, 2 close do; 1 pr. black breeches and vest; 2
         trousers, 2 hats, 1 plaid, 2 pr. nankeen breeches, 6 vests, 6 pr. worsted hoes and
bag, 1 silk do, 18 hoes and 3 silk handkerchiefs, 7 stocks, 3 ruffled shirts, 3 plain do., 4
Oznabrigs do., 3 do. Trowsers, 6 hats, 1 pr. boots, spurs and whip, 3 boots, 8 Qr. Paper, 4
pr. mens shoes, 1 womens, 10 black balls, 2 lbs. shot, 1 double barrl Gun, 10 table

knives, 19 forks, 10 pr. buckles, 2 steel, 1/2 papers pins, 1/2 doz. Scissors, 8 Cutteau
knives, 5 Child's Buckles, 1do, mens Silver, 1 set buckle stock; 8 doz. coat buttons, 3
vests, 3 rols pomatum, 5 papers needles, 8 combs, 1 carpenters adz, 2 razors, 1 brass Ink-
stand, 3 do. Cocks, 2 shoe brushes, 11 check handkerchiefs, 2 3/4 lbs. nuns thread, 2 1/4
white do. 15 pr. thread hoes, 19 1/2 yds. Irish Linen, 2 3/4 yds. do. 2 1/2 yards do., 14
sheeting, 20 do., 26 Irish Linen, 5 printed do, 28 Pillow Fustian, 23 1/4 Durant, 8 Camblet,
1 empty hogshead, 13 1/2 yards brown Linen, 33 1/2 Oznabrigs, 3 lbs. bottle Mustd., 1
small do., 1 lump of Sugar 9 1/4 lb., 14 Loaves do. Wt. 127 10 oz., 13 lbs. Coffee, 3 1/2
bottles Snuff and Gin Case, 6 gall: Hollands do, 7 bottles cordial do, 31 gall. Brandy or
anniseed & cask; 39 lbs. Soap, 7 gall. Cherry Cordial and cask; 3/4 box Pipes, 1 Barrl.
Sugar 238 lb. wt., 19 gall. N. England Rum and cask; 2 barrels Fish, 9 galls. Clove Water
and cask, 64 Rum do. 2/4 barrel Fish, 55 gall. Molasses & cask, 111 do, do., 20 Brandy do.,
part of a barrel of Herrings, do with a little Pork, 67 lb. Rice, 47 Cheese, 15 gall. Molasses
and barrel. 4 1/2 Brancy & cask, 3/4 barrel Herrings, 208 lb. Sugar & barrel 118 Nt. Wt.,
2 chairs and 1 table, 9 blue & white tea pots; 10 Queens ware, 5 cold. milk pots, 32 Jugs, 3
mugs, 5 water bottles, 3 basons for do., 3 1/2 doz. cups and saucers, 2 button coats, 16
plates, 1 1/2 doz. Mustard and pepper boxes, 1 barrel bottles, 19 bottles porter, 5 do.
claret wine, 2 doz. and 8 womens heels, 1 small keg biscuit, 8 pricks Tobacco, 25 lb. Flour
and barrel, sundry small articles, 2 casks, 1 pr. Scales measures &c; Total L. 126...17...9
1/2.
  Cash. L. 35...10...0; Book Debts outstanding L. 40...9...11 1/2; a Silver Watch value
2...8...0: 2 Bills of Exchange 1 dated Glasgow 24th May 1767 on the Revrd: JAMES
THOMPSON, Virginia. in favor of JAMES THOMPSON, or order of above place for L. 8...2...8;
1 dated Annithill April 27th 1769 on the Revrd. JAMES THOMPSON, Virginia, in favor
JAMES THOMSPON or Order of above place for 23...2...9. Total: 31...5...5.
November 26th 1787.   WM: RUSSELL
          Richmond   JNO: LIVINGSTON
                                        THOS: SCOTT
                                        WM. McKECHNIE
  Returned into the Court of Hustings for the City of Richmond 26th of November 1787
and ordered to be recorded   Teste ADAM CRAIG, C.C.

pp.   (On margin: CARTER with TERNAN. Deld. WILLIAM WRAY)
192-   THIS AGREEMENT made Between WILLIAM CARTER SENR. of City of WILLIAMS-
194   BURG of one part and JAMES TERNAN of City of Richmond of other part; Witnes-
         seth that whereas said CARTER confiding in the honesty integrity and fidelity of
said TERNAN hath agreed to enter into a Copartnership and Joint Trade with him said
TERNAN for the establishment of an APOTHECARY's and DRUGGIST's SHOP in the City of
Richmond, And Whereas at the day of the date hereof a valuation hath been made by
said parties to these presents of the stock of Drugs and Medicines, and all matters and
things which are the stock and goods of said WILLIAM CARTER belonging to said Trade
and Occupation, they amount unto the sum of L. 86...2; Sterling; And whereas said JAMES
TERNAN hath for one moiety of said Stock and goods paid and secured to be paid to WIL-
LIAM CARTER SENR. the sum of L. 42...1; Sterling money of Great Britain, being the
moiety of said valuation; And given Bond for the faithful keeping and rendering a fair
account of the profits of said Shop. Now Therefore these presents witnesseth that after
the day next insuing the date hereof, WILLIAM CARTER SENR. and JAMES TERNAN shall
be Copartners and Joint Traders in the trade and business of APOTHECARIES or DRUG-
GISTS in City of Richmond and the partnership to continue for three years, from the
first day of October next ensuing if said parties shall so long live, On the Conditions and
limitations hereafter set down and expressed;

1st. WILLIAM CARTER stipulates and agrees to fix an APOTHECARY's or DRUGGIST's SHOP in City of Richmond by the first day of October, if possible, to amount of L. 86...2, Sterling;

2nd. The said CARTER further agrees to lend gratis for the use of said Shop all the necessary furnmiture, to wit, Druggiest's painted boxes, bottles, Ointment and Syrup, pots, mortars and what ever other utensils he may furnish during the continuance of the copartnership;

3lrd. In consideration of the above, JAMES TERNAN convenants and agrees to take upon himself the care and trouble of managing and conducting the said Shop without any charge or allowance for Wages or Salary, to the best of his power and abilities in every respect for the interest of the said Company; to open a set of Books under the firm of CARTER and TERNAN, which are to be kept under the direction and controul of said CARTER, subject to his inspection and superintendance to be laid before him whenever he shall require it. The Books of said copartnership to be settled quarterly by said TERNAN at which periods a fair and distinct estimate is to be made in said Books for the profit or loss of the copartnery, the said TERNAN further covenants and agrees to pay down L. 20 Currency of Virginia in hand to said CARTER in part of his moiety for the stock of medicines and other matters and things advanced by said CARTER and also to pay sixty per centum on one half of the full amount of the drugs, materials and medicines furnished as aforesaid as far as he is able from the end of one quarter to another, till the whole is paid off;

4th. It is mutually agreed between the parties that an Assistant or an Apprentice may be employed for the said Shop so soon as the increased business and profits of the copartnery requires and can afford such an aid; But no Apprentice is to be taken nor Assistant employed without the approbation of WILLIAM CARTER;

5th. The Shop Rent, dieting, washing, coal and candles and every other necessary expence incurred for the use of said Shop to be paid for out of the profits arising there-from;

6th. No purchases are to be made nor any debts to be contracted by or for the Company nor any part of the money belonging to the copartnery to be lent out or used without the express consent of both parties;

7th. The said WILLIAM CARTER SENR. reserves to himself the priviledge of either assigning his interest in said concern to his Son, WILLIAM CARTER JUNR., or to sell out at option, first giving the said TERNAN a refusal thereof. And the said CARTER stipulates that in case of his death, previous to the expiration of the term of the copartnery, the said Shop is to be continued to the end of three years for the benefit of his Family;

8th. At the end of every quarter or half year at the option of said CARTER, settlements are to be made and the profits divided between the parties;

9th. All the expences of transportation of medicines and every other expence incidental to this agreement to be jointly borne by the parties.

In Witness whereof both parties have hereunto set their hands and affixed their seals, this twelfth day of September in the year of our Lord 1787

Teste ANTHONY GEOGHEGAN,   WILLIAM CARTER SENR.
       JOHN GLYNN   JAMES TERNAN

At a Court of Hustings for the City of Richmond held at the MASONS HALL in said City on Monday the twenty sixth of November 1787   This Agreement was proved by the Oaths of ANTHONY GEOGHEGAN and JOHN GLYNN, witnesses thereto, and ordered to be recorded   Teste ADAM CRAIG, C. C.

pp.   (On margin: Commissioners to NELSON HERRON & CO.)
195-   THIS INDENTURE made this third day of May in the year of our Lord one thou-
196   sand seven hundred and eighty seven Between NATHANIEL WILKERSON, MILES
          SELDEN JUNR., JOHN HARVIE, THOMAS PROSSER and WILLIAM FOUSHEE, Commis-
sioners appointed by an Act of Assembly intituled, "An Act directing the Sale of the
Public Lands and other Property in or near the City of Richmond," Witnesseth that said
Commissioners in conformity with the terms of said Act and for the sum of Three hundred and Six pounds specie, the payment whereof has been secured as by the said Act is
prescribed; by these presents do bargain and sell unto NELSON HERON and COMPANY of
the City of Richmond two lotts of land lying on (blank) Alley, each lott being forty five
feet on said Alley and known by the numbers Seven and Eight (7 & 8), in the plan of the
Commissioners, the lott number seven being bounded to the East by the line of DOCTOR
WILLIAM FOUSHEE, and to the North by the lines of NELSON HERON & CO., purchased of
HUNTER, BANKS & CO., the lott or piece of ground number eight bounded to the East by
the line of lott number seven, to the North by the line of FRANCIS GRAVES's purchase
of HUNTER, BANKS & CO. to the Western side by the line of lott number nine purchased
by Mr. FRANCIS GRAVES to the said (blank) Alley, so as to run on said Alley ninety feet
on the two lotts, all which will more fully appear in the Commissioners plan in the
County Court of HENRICO and which under the operation of an Act of Assembly
intituled, "An Act concerning Escheats and Forfeitures from BRITISH SUBJECTS," was
escheated to the Commonwealth of Virginia as being the proper Estate of COCHRANE
CUNNINGHAM & COMPANY as British Subjects as by inquest of Office remaining of
Record in the General Court will appear, together with all houses and improvements
thereon and the rents issues and profits thereof; To have and to hold the piece of
ground with all houses and improvements thereon to said NELSON HERON & COMPANY
their heirs; In Witness whereof we have hereunto set our hands and affixed our seals
the day and year above written
Signed Sealed and Delivered in the presence of
          BENJA: BROWN,   NATHL: WILKINSON
          JAMES HERRON,   MILES SELDEN
          NATHL· MACGILL   JOHN HARVIE
                                                 THO: PROSSER
                                                 W: FOUSHEE

    At a Court of Hustings for the City of Richmond continued and held at the MASONS
HALL in the said City on Tuesday the 27th of November 1787   This Indenture was
proved by as to NATHANIEL WILKINSON, THOMAS PROSSER & WILLIAM FOUSHEE by
BENJAMIN BROWN, JAMES HERRON & NATHANIEL MACGILL, witnesses thereto & ordered
to be recorded   Teste ADAM CRAIG C. C.

pp.   (On margin: BYRD's Trustee to HERON)
196-   THIS INDENTURE made this seventeenth day of March in the year of our Lord
197   one thousand seven hundred and Eighty seven Between CHARLES CARTER, the
          only surviving Trustee of the Honourable WILLIAM BYRD, deced., of one part
and JAMES HERON, Merchant, of the other part; Witnesseth that CHARLES CARTER pursuant to the power vested in him by Act of Assembly as the only surviving Trustee of
the said WILLIAM BYRD deceased, and for the sum of Five shillings current money of
Virginia to him in hand paid, by these presents doth bargain sell and confirm unto
JAMES HERON his heirs a certain half acre lott lying in City of Richmond and known in
the plan of said City by number (565), Five hundred and Sixty Five, per Ticket number
6700. To have and to hold the half acre lott with all houses improvements and appurte-

nances thereunto belonging to the use of JAMES HERON his heirs and CHARLES CARTER
by virtue of the trust in him resposed against all persons claiming under him the half
acre lott and its appurtenances to JAMES HERON his heirs shall warrant and forever
defend; In Witness whereof said CHARLES CARTER the only surviving Trustee of WIL-
LIAM BYRD deceased, hath hereunto set his hand and affixed his seal, the day and year
above mentioned
Signed Sealed and delivered in presence of
       WILLIAM S PLUMMER,   CHAS: CARTER
       NATHL: MACGILL, WILLIAM DUNCAN
       SAML: PAINE, BENJA: BROWN, JAMES HERRON
   At a Court of Hustings for the City of Richmond continued and held at the MASONS
HALL in the said City on Tuesday the 27th of November 1787
This Indenture was proved by the Oaths of BENJAMIN BROWN, JAMES HERON &
NATHANIEL MACGILL, witnesses thereto, and ordered to be recorded

p.   (On margin: FELLOWSHIP FIRE COMPANY OPERATION)
198   WE the underwritten Subscribers taking into consideration the present de-
           fenceless situation of the City and our total inability to provide against accidents
by Fire unless Order and Discipline be introduced among the Citizens, do hereby asso-
ciate ourselves (under and Act of Assembly) into a Company to be known and called by
the name of THE FELLOWSHIP FIRE COMPANY of RICHMOND, and hereby agree to abide
by and perform all such Laws, Rules and Regulations as shall be enacted and agreed to
by a majority of the said Company; Witness our hands this Ninth day of January one
thousand seven hundred & Eighty eight

ANDREW RONALD	JAMES DALZEL	STEPHEN CROUCH
THO: P. JOHNSON	JOHN BOYD	WM: MITCHELL
W. FOUSHEE	JOHN KER	JOHN BEALL
GEORGE ESKRIGGE	JAMES MACOMB	JOHN HICKS
WILLIAM MUNRO	STEPHEN HOLLINGSWORTH	BENJA: HARRISON JR.
THOMAS RUTHERFORD	FRANCIS J. JAMES	ALEXR: QUARRIER
HARRY HETH	MOSES CUISTIN	WM. HAY
THOMAS WILLIAMS	EBEN: MACNAIR	J. HERON
CHARLES HOPKINS	JOHN WILSON	ROBT. RAWLINGS
GEO: PICKETT	WM. RICHARDSON	SAML: McCRAW
WILLM. GALT	WM: HASLETT	JOHN BECKLEY
ABRAM· LOTT	JOS: HIGBEE	J. MARSHALL
JAMES WARINGTON	FRANCIS GRAVES	ALEXR. McROBERTS
THOS: KEENE	SAMUEL COUCH	DAVID LAMBERT
	R. MITCHELL	

   At a Court of Hustings for the City of Richmond held at the Courthouse on Monday the
28th of January 1788   This Instrument of Writing composing the "FELLOWSHIP FIRE
COMPANY of RICHMOND" was exhibited into Court by THOMAS P. JOHNSON, one of the
Subscribers thereto, acknowledged by the said JOHNSON and proved by his Affirmation
as to the rest of the subscribers except JOHN KER & JOHN HICKS, which is ordered to be
recorded   Teste ADAM CRAIG, C. C.

p.   (On margin: HARRY HETH's Bond as Serjt. 1788)
199   KNOW ALL MEN by these presents that we HARRY HETH. DAVID VANDEWALL,
           JOHN GUNN, WILLIAM REYNOLDS, JOHN PRYOR, PLEASANT YOUNGHUSBAND
AND GILLEY LEWIS are held and firmly bound unto the Mayor, Aldermen and Com-

monalty of the City of Richmond in the sum of One thousand pounds current money to which payment well and truly to be made we bind ourselves our heirs jointly & severally firmly by these presents; Witness our hands & seals this 28th day of January one thousand seven hundred & Eighty eight & in the 12th year of the Commonwealth

THE CONDITION of the above Obligation is such that whereas the above bound HARRY HETH hath been appointed SERJEANT of the City of Richmond; Now if said HARRY HETH shall duly & faithfully execute the duties of his said Office according to Law, and shall well & truly demean himself therein, then the above Obligation to be void, otherwise to remain in full force and virtue

Sealed & Delivered in the presence of   HARRY HETH
   The Court   D. VANDEWALL
                JNO: GUNN
       W. REYNOLDS J: PRYOR
      P. YOUNGHUSBAND GILLEY LEWIS

At a Court of Hustings for the City of Richmond held at the Courthouse Monday the 28th of January 1788   This Bond was acknowledged in open Court by the Obligors and ordered to be recorded   Teste ADAM CRAIG, C. C.

pp. (On margin: SEPNOR to CLAIBORNE &c. Mortgage. Delivered Mr. Claiborne)
200- THIS INDENTURE made this first day of August in the year of our Lord one thou-
203 sand seven hundred and eighty seven Between HENRY SEPNOR of County of
  CHESTERFIELD of first part, and WILLIAM CLAIBORNE and JOHN STOCKDELL of County of HENRICO and MARGARET SMITH of County of CHESTERFIELD of second part, Whereas the above named HENRY SEPNOR stands justly indebted to said WILLIAM CLAIBORNE in a considerable sum of money for the Rent of part of the FALLS PLANTATION (now in possession of HENRY SEPNOR) for the present year 1787, And Whereas HENRY SEPNOR stands also justly indebted unto said MARGARET SMITH in the sum of Three hundred pounds being the balance due to said MARGARET upon an Account settled between said HENRY & MARGARET, And Whereas said WILLIAM CLAIBORNE and JOHN STOCKDELL have also become bound as securities for said HENRY SEPNOR in two Replevin Bonds, one granted to JAMES HAYES with a condition for the payment of Two hundred and fourteen pounds on the 19th day of May last past, and one other granted to PLEASANT THURMAN with a condition for the payment of fifty nine pounds on the (blank) And HENRY SEPNOR being desirous to secure said WILLIAM CLAIBORNE the payment of the money now due to him for the rent of said part of the FALLS PLANTATION and also the balance of the rent which will become due to the said WILLIAM CLAIBORNE at the expiration of the term of said HENRY SEPNOR, also to secure to the said MARGARET SMITH the payment of the said Three hundred pounds and to secure to WILLIAM CLAIBORNE and JOHN STOCKDELL so much of the property of him said HENRY SEPNOR as will reimburse and indemnify them in case they or either o them or the heirs of them should at any time be compelled to pay any sums of money or quantities of Tobacco in discharge of the Bonds above mentioned in which said WILLIAM CLAIBORNE and JOHN STOCKDELL have become bound as securities for HENRY SEPNOR or in discharge of any Judgments which may be obtained thereon. NOW THIS INDENTURE WITNESSETH that HENRY SEPNOR in consideration of the premises and also in consideration of the sum of Five shillings current money of Virginia to him in hand paid by these presents doth bargain and sell unto WILLIAM CLAIBORNE JOHN STOCKDELL and MARGARET SMITH and their heirs a certain lot containing (blank) lying in County of HENRICO near the MILL of COLONEL RICHARD ADAMS on SHOCKOE CREEK with all houses and appurtenances thereunto belonging; Also the following Negro slaves, to wit, Solomon, Esther, Patty, Ran-

dolph, Molly, Ned, Cint, Hugh, Isaac & Harry; ten beds & furniture, one Clock, twelve
chairs and all the rest of his household and kitchen furniture, twenty nine horses,
mares and colts, one hundred head of hogs, eighty head of cattle, three waggons and
geer, all his plows and gear, also all his Wheat, Oats and Hay in Barns or in Stacks on the
FALLS PLANTATION; To have and to hold the lot of land with the appurtenances, also
the slaves and other property herein mentioned to WILLIAM CLAIBORNE, MARGARET
SMITH and JOHN STOCKDELL and their heirs, Upon the express condition nevertheless,
that if HENRY SEPNOR his heirs shall pay WILLIAM CLAIBORNE on or before the first
day of January next the balance now due from the said SEPNOR for the Rent of part of
the FALLS PLANTATION, also such other parts of the rent which may become due for the
present year, and shall pay MARGARET SMITH on or before the twenty fifth day of
April next the sum of Three hudnrd pounds, And shall also pay WILLIAM CLAIBORNE
and JOHN STOCKDELL, or either of them or either of their heirs all sums of money and
quantities of Tobacco as they or either of them shall at any time be compelled to pay in
discharge of the above mentioned replevin Bonds or of Judgments which may be
obtained on them, Then this Indenture shall be void. In Testimony whereof said HENRY
SEPNORhath hereunto set his hand and seal this day and year first above written
Signed Sealed and delivered in presence of
          SAML. TROWER,   HENRY SEPNOR
          RICHD: BOWLER, JAMES SOUTHALL
   At a Court of Hustings for the City of Richmond held at the Courthouse on Monday the
25th day of February 1788   This Mortgage was acknowledged in Court by the said
HENRY SEPNOR as his act and deed and ordered to be recorded
          Teste ADAM CRAIG, C.C.

pp   (On margin: PLEASANTS &c. to JOHNSON)
203-   THIS INDENTURE made this twenty second day of November in the year of our
207   Lord one thousand seven hundred and eighty seven Between SAMUEL PLEA-
         SANTS of the City of PHILADELPHIA in the State of PENSYLVANIA, Merchant,
JOHN FIELD of the same City, Merchant, THOMAS EDDY of Town of FREDERICKSBURG in
State of Virginia, Merchant, GEORGE EDDY of the City of PHILADELPHIA, Merchant,
ABRAHAM LOT and JOSEPH HIGBEE of City of Richmond in Virginia, Merchants, con-
stituting the late Commercial House designated by the firm of LOT, HIGBEE and COMPANY
of City of Richmond, Merchants, and Partners of the one part and THOMAS POTTS JOHN-
SON of the same City, Merchant, of other part; Witnesseth that in consideration of the
sum of five shillings current money of Virginia by THOMAS POTTS JOHNSON to said
SAMUEL PLEASANT, JOHN FIELD, THOMAS EDDY, GEORGE EDDY, ABRAHAM LOTT and
JOSEPH HIGBEE in hand paid, the constituent members of the late House of LOTT, HIGBEE
and COMPANY do by these presents bargain sell and confirm unto THOMAS POTTS JOHN-
SON his heirs all that lot of land lying in City of Richmond which was formerly granted
and conveyed by CHARLES CARTER Esquire, only surviving Trustee of the late honourable WILLIAM BYRD Esquire deceassed, to the aforesaid LOT, HIGBEE and COMPANY in
fee simple by Deed of bargain and sale indented bearing date the twenty fourth day of
December in the year one thousand seven hundred and eighty four as by said Deed of
Record in HENRICO County Court will appear, which lot of land contains by estimation
fifteen hundred square feet and is the WAREHOUSE LOTT drawn in the Lottery of aforesaid WILLIAM BYRD Esqr., deceased, as an appendage to the tenement known in the
plan of the City by the name of YOUNGHUSBANDs TENEMENT, with all houses kitchens,
warehouses, storehouses lumber and appurtenances on said land belonging; To have
and to hold the lott of land with appurtenances to THOMAS POTTS JOHNSON his heirs and

(the members named above) will at all time herafter warrant and forever defend; In Witness whereof the said parties to these presents have hereunto set their hands and seals the same day and year first in this Indenture written
Signed Sealed and Delivered in the presence of us by the above named SAMUEL PLEASANTS, JOHN FIELD and GEORGE EDDY:

THOS: FRANKLIN,   ANDREW SPENCE,   SAML: PLEASANTS
HUGH COX,   JOHN FIELD
Signed Sealed & Delivered by the above mentd.   THOMAS EDDY
THOMAS EDDY in pressence of us WM. GEDDY,   GEORGE EDDY
CHARLES HUMANS, JAMES MACOMB, STEPHEN   ABRAM: LOTT
HOLLINGSWORTH, LAIN J. JOHNSON,   JOSEPH HIGBEE
Signed Sealed and Delivered by the above mentioned
ABRAM: LOTT & JOSEPH HIGBEE in presence of
RICHARD ADAMS, STEPHEN HOLLINGSWORTH, LAIN J. JOHNSON

The Eleventh day of December in the year of our Lord one thousand seven hundred and eighty seven before me THOMAS McKEAN, Chief Justice of the Supreme Court of the State of PENSYLVANIA, came SAMUEL PLEASANTS, JOHN FIELD and GEORGE EDDY in the within written Indenture named and acknowledged the same to be their several and respective acts and deeds and desired it may be recorded as such; Witness my hand and seal the day and year above said   THOS: McKEAN

PENSYLVANIA Sct.   The Supreme Executive Council of the Commonwealth of PENSYLVANIA. To all to whom these presents shall come Greeting.
(SEAL)   Know ye that the Honble. THOS. McKEAN Esqr. whose name is subscribed to the Instrument of Writing hereto annexed was at
P. MUHLENBERG   the time of subsribing the same, Chief Justice of the Supreme Court of the said Commonwealth, duly appointed and commissioned; And full faith is and ought to be given to him accordingly. Given in Council under the hand of the Honble. PETER MUHLENBERG, Vice President, and the Great Seal of the State at PHILADELPHIA this twelfth day of December in the year of our Lord one thousand seven hundred and eighty seven
Attest CHS: BODDLE, Secry.

Received 22d. November 1787 from THOMAS POTTS JOHNSON the sum of Five shillings current money of Virignia, being the full consideration for the land and other premises by the within Indenture convey'd: Witnesses present at the signing by SAML. PLEASANTS, JOHN FIELD & GEORGE EDDY:

THO: FRANKLIN,   SAML: PLEASANTS
ANDREW SPENCE   JOHN FIELD
                          GEORGE EDDY

At a Court of Hustings for the City of Richmond held at the Courthouse in the said City on Monday the 25th of February 1788   This Indenture together with the Receipt thereon endorsed were presented in Court and the same having been proved as to the within SAMUEL PLEASANTS, JOHN FIELD and GEORGE EDDY before the Honorable THOMAS McKEAN, Chief Justice of the Supreme Court of the State of PENSYLVANIA as appears by his Certificate endorsed and the annexed Certificate of the Honorable PETER MUHLENBERG, Vice President of the said State of PENSYLVANIA, under the Great Seal thereof; It is ordered that the same as to the said SAMUEL PLEASANTS, JOHN FIELD and GEORGE EDDY be recorded;

And at a Court of Hustings held for the said City at the PUBLIC BUILDINGS on Monday the 28th of April following, the said Indenture was further proved as to THOMAS EDDY, another of the parties by the Oaths of JAMES MACOMB, STEPHEN HOLLINGSWORTH and

LAIN J. JOHNSON, witnesses thereto and at the same time it was acknowledged by ABRAM LOTT and JOSEPH HIGBEE, the remaining parties thereto and ordered to stand fully recorded   Teste ADAM CRAIG, C.C.

pp.   (On margin: JOHN H. HOLTs Will)
207-   IN THE NAME OF GOD Amen. I JOEN HUNTER HOLT of the City of Richmond,
208   Printer, being sick in body but at the same time in my perfect senses, It is my
        desire that all my wearing apparel and two pair of pistols be given to my Cousin,
JOHN DIXON JUNR., a mourning Ring to my Aunt DIXON and my Sister, BARBOUR, which I
hope they will accept and keep for my sake, all the rest of my worldly property that I
may be possessed of at the time of my decease I desire may be given to my dear Sister,
ELIZABETH OSWALD. I should be glad if my Friends, JOHN and HENRY DIXON, would
qualify as Executors to this my Last Will and Testament and do desire the Court will allow
them to qualify as such without giving any security for their administration, knowing
the trouble attending that kind of business and being satisfied they will do justice to my
Estate Witness my hand this Twenty fourth day of December 1786
Sealed Signed and Acknowledged in presence of
        ALEXANDER McMILLAN   JOHN H. HOLT
        DANIEL BAXTER
  At a Court of Hustings for the City of Richmond held at the PUBLIC BUILDINGS on
Monday the 28th of April 1788   This Last Will and Testament of JOHN H. HOLT was
presented in Court and proved by the Oath of DANIEL BAXTER, a witness thereto, and
ordered to be recorded. And on the motion of JOHN DIXON, one of the Executors therein
named, who made Oath according to Law, and entered into and acknowledged his Bond
in the penalty of One thousand pounds conditioned as the Law directs, a Certificate was
granted him for obtaining a Probat thereof in due form, Liberty being reserved to the
other Executor named in the said Will to join in the Probat when he shall think fit.
                    Teste ADAM CRAIG C.C.
(On margin: Admon. de bonis non with the Will annexed granted JOHN W. MURDAUGH,
Febry. 28, 1833.)

pp.   (On margin: JOHNSON to PLEASANTS & FIELD)
208-   THIS INDENTURE made this twenty third day of November in the year of our
210   Lord one thousand seven hundred and eighty seven Between THOMAS POTTS
        JOHNSON of City of Richmond, Merchant, of one part and SAMUEL PLEASANTS
and JOHN FIELD of City of PHILADELPHIA in the State of PENSYLVANIA, Merchants, of
other part; Witnesseth that in consideration of the sum of five shillings current money
of Virginia by SAMUEL PLEASANTS and JOHN FIELD in hand paid to THOMAS POTTS JOHN-
SON, said THOMAS POTTS JOHNSON by these presents doth bargain sell and confirm unto
SAMUEL PLEASANTS and JOHN FIELD their heirs all that lott of land lying in City of
Richmond containing by estimation Fifteen hundred square feet which was heretofore
granted and conveyed by CHARLES CARTER Esquire, only surviving Trustee of the
Honourable WILLIAM BYRD Esquire, deceased, to LOTT, HIGBEE & COMPANY, Merchants
and Partners, and afterwards by the several constituent members of the said Company,
to wit, SAMUEL PLEASANTS, JOHN FIELD, THOMAS EDDY, GEORGE EDDY, ABRAHAM LOTT
& JOSEPH HIGBEE to THOMAS POTTS JOHNSON in fee simple with all houses kitchens warehouses, storehouses lumber and appurtenances on said lott of land and the rents issues
and profits thereof; To have and to hold the granted land premises with the appurtenances unto SAMUEL PLEASANTS and JOHN FIELD their heirs as Tenants in Common,
And THOMAS POTTS JOHNSON for himself and his heirs will warrant and forever defend

said SAMUEL & JOHN their joint or several heirs; In Witness whereof the said THOMAS
POTTS JOHNSON hath hereunto set his hand and seal the day and year first in this
Indenture written
Signed Sealed and Delivered in presence of
     (no witnesses recorded)   THOS: P. JOHNSON
  Received 23d. November 1787 from SAMUEL PLEASANTS and JOHN FIELD, the sum of
five shillings current money of Virginia being the full consideration money for the
land and other premises by the within Indenture conveyed   L. 0...5...0.
                 THO: P. JOHNSON
  At a Court of Hustings for the City of Richmond at the PUBLIC BUILDINGS on Monday
the 28th of April 1788   This Indenture together with the Receipt thereon endorsed
were acknowledged in Court by THOMAS P. JOHNSON as his act and deed and ordered to
be recorded   Teste ADAM CRAIG. C.C.

pp.   (On margin: DAVID EAST's Appraismt.)
210-   AN INVENTORY and Appraisment of the Estate of DAVID EAST deceased taken
211   this 26th July 1787. 1 Bed and Furniture and Bedstead; 1 Bed under Bed Blanket
       and old bed cover, the wooden work of the Carriage and body of a double Chair;
an Iron Screw clamp, 1 Walnut desk, 1 diaper table cloth, 2 Queens C. Dishes and 9 plates;
3 cloth coats at 4 8/, 6/ & 6/; 3 Waistcoats and 2 pr. Breeches; 2 pr. yarn stockings and 1
worsted Cap, 2 Hats, 1 great Coat, 1 looking glass, 1 large blk. Smiths vice, parcel of
tools, parcel old Iron, parcel old Juggs and bottles; a pot, pan, Dutch oven, tea kettle and
trivit, brass Skillet, 3 candle sticks and snuffers, 2 butter pots, 1 turean, tinn coffee pot
and some Q. China Ware, 3 knives and forks, 2 pewtr: plates & sugar dish, safe, p rcel
wheel fellows, old Musket, tub and 2 small pales &c., 2 tables, pr. flat irons, ginn case
and bottles, Walnut Cupboard, box, old trunk and four old Chairs Total: 43...8...6.
  Pursuant to an Order of the Court of Hustings for the City of Richmond, we the Subscribers being first sworn to value in current money the slaves and personal Estate of
DAVID EAST deced., do say that all the Estate which was shewn us is worth Forty three
pounds, eight shillings and Six pence and no more; Given under our hands the date
before mentioned   WM: WHITE
                   SMITH BLAKEY
                   FRANCIS PEARCE
  Returned into Court of Hustings for the City of Richmond the 26th of May 1788 and
ordered to be recorded   Teste ADAM CRAIG. C.C.

pp.   (On margin: WILSON to MITCHELL &c. Power of Atto.)
212-   KNOW ALL MEN by these presents that I JOSEPH WILSON, Surviving Partner of
213   WILLIAM JOHNSTON and late of Richmond in the State of Virginia, by these pre-
       sents do make and appoint my trusty and loving Friends, ROBERT MITCHELL
Esquire and Mr. JOHN GROVES, both of City of Richmond, my true and lawful Attorneys
for me and in my name to ask demand sue for levy recover and receive all sums of
money debts, rents goods wares dues accounts and other demands which are or shall be
owing to me or detained from me by WILLIAM ARMISTEAD, late Commercial Agent for
the State of Virginia or by the Executive Government of the State of Virginia by reason
of a contract entered into by WILLIAM ARMISTEAD for said State on or about the month
of September 1780 and which was ratified and signed by THOMAS JEFFERSON, Esqr., then
Governor of said State, to and with said WILLIAM JOHNSTON, since deceased, and me said
JOSEPH WILSON giving and granting unto my said Attorneys by these presents my full
and whole powers and authority in the premises and generally all and every other act

and acts in the Law necessary to be done for me in my name to execute and perform as I
might or could do if I were personally present allowing firm and effectual all my said
Attorneys shall lawfully do in the premises by virtue hereof; In Witness whereof I
have hereunto set my hand and seal this ninth dy of May in the Twelfth year of
American Independence Annoque Domini one thousand seven hundrd and eighty eight.
Sealed and delivered in the presence of us
   JAMS: CRAWFORD,   JOSEPH WILSON
   HUGH MOORE
 At a Court of Hustings for the City of Richmond held at the Courthouse on Monday the
26th of May 1788 This Power of Attorney was proved by the Oath of HUGH MOORE,
witness thereto, and ordered to be recorded
      Teste ADAM CRAIG, C. C.

pp. (On margin: BYRDs Trustee to McCRAW)
214- THIS INDENTURE made this fifth day of January in the year of our Lord one
215 thousand seven hundred and eighty eight Between CHARLES CARTER, the only
   surviving Trustee of the Honourable WILLIAM BYRD deceased, of one part and
SAMUEL McCRAW, of City of Richmond of other part; Witnesseth that CHARLES CARTER
pursuant to the power vested in him by Act of Assembly as the only surviving Trustee
of said WILLIAM BYRD deceased, and in consideration of a Lottery Ticket No. 7662, as
well as of Five shillings Sterling money to him in hand paid, by these presents do bargain sell and confirm unto SAMUEL McCRAW his heirs a certain half acre lot lying in
the City of Richmond number Six hundred and Seventy Nine, drawn a prize to the
Ticket Number Seven thousand six hundred and sixty two and known in the plan of said
City in figures by No. 679; To have and to hold the half acre lott with all houses improvements and appurtenances thereunto belonging to SAMUEL McCRAW his heirs;
And CHARLES CARTER by virtue of the trust in him reposed against all persons claiming
under him the half acre lot and its appurtenances to SAMUEL McCRAW his heirs by
these presents shall warrant and forever defend; in Witness whereof the said CHARLES
CARTER, the only surviving Trustee of WILLIAM BYRD deceased, hath hereunto set his
hand and affixed his seal the day and year above written
Signed Sealed and Delivered in presence of
   CHRISTO: FRY.   CHAS: CARTER
   JOSHUA PAINE, ORRIS PAINE
 At a Court of Hustings for the City of Richmond held at the Courthouse on Monday the
28th of January 1788 This Indenture was proved by the Oaths of CHRISTOPHER FRY
and JOSHUA PAINE, two of the witnesses thereto, And at another Court held for the said
City the 23d. of June following, the same was further proved by the Oath of ORRIS PAINE
another witness thereto and ordered to be recorded
      Teste ADAM CRAIG, C. C.

pp. (On margin: BYRDs Trustee to McCRAW)
215- THIS INDENTURE made this fifth day of January in the year of our Lord one
217 thousand seven hundred and eighty eight Between CHARLES CARTER, the only
   surviving Trustee of the Honourable WILLIAM BYRD deceased, of one part and
SAMUEL McCRAW, of City of Richmond of other part; Witnesseth that the said CHARLES
CARTER pursuant to the power vested in him by Act of Assembly as the only surviving
Trustee of said WILLIAM BYRD deceased and in consideration of the Lottery Ticket No.
7306, as well as of five shillings Sterling money to him in hand paid, by these presents
do bargain sell and confirm unto SAMUEL McCRAW his heirs a certain half acre lot

lying in City of Richmond number Six hundred and Fifty nine; To have and to hold the half acre lot with all houses improvements and appurtenances thereunto belonging to SAMUEL McCRAW his heirs; And CHARLES CARTER by virtue of the trust in him reposed against all persons claiming under him the half acre lot and its appurtenances to SAMUEL McCRAW his heirs by these prsents shall warrant and forever defend; In Witness whereof said CHARLES CARTER, the only surviving Trustee of WILLIAM BYRD deceased, hath hereunto set his hand and affixed his seal the day and year above written Signed Sealed and Delivered in presence of

CHRISTO. FRY,   CHARS: CARTER
JOSHUA PAINE, ORRIS PAINE

At a Court of Hustings for the City of Richmond held at the Courthouse on Monday the 28th of January 1788   This Indenture was proved by the Oaths of CHRISTOPHER FRY and JOSHUA PAINE, two of the witnesses thereto, And at another Court held for the said City the 23d. of June following, the same was further proved by the Oath of ORRIS PAINE another witness thereto, and ordered to be recorded

Teste ADAM CRAIG, C. C.

pp.   (On margin: BYRD's Trustee to McCRAW)
217-   THIS INDENTURE made this fifth day of January in the year of our Lord one
218   thousand seven hundred and eighty eight Between CHARLES CARTER, the only surviving Trustee of the Honble: WILLIAM BYRD deceased, of one part and SAMUEL McCRAW of City of Richmond of other part; Witnesseth that said CHARLES CARTER pursuant to the power vested in him by Act of Assembly as the only surviving Trustee of WILLIAM BYRD deceased, and in consideration of a Lottery Ticket No. 2061, as well as Five shillings Sterling money to him in hand paid, by these presents do bargain sell and confirm unto SAMUEL McCRAW his heirs a certain half acre lot lying in City of Richmond number Six hundred and sixty one and known in the plan of said City in figures by No. 661; To have and to hold the half acre lot with all houses improvements and appurtenances thereunto belonging to SAMUEL McCRAW his heirs, and CHARLES CARTER by virtue of the Trust in him reposed against all persons claiming under him the half acre lot and its appurtenances shall warrant and forever defend; In Witness whereof said CHARLES CARTER, only surviving Trustee of WILLIAM BYRD deceased, hath hereunto set his hand and affixed his seal the day & year above written Signed Sealed & Delivered in presence of

CHRISTO: FRY,   CHARS: CARTER
JOSHUA PAINE, ORRIS PAINE

At a Court of Hustings for the City of Richmond held at the Courthouse on Monday the 28th of January 1788   This Indenture was proved by the Oaths of CHRISTOPHER FRY and JOSHUA PAINE, two of the witnesses thereto, And at another Court held for the said City the 23rd. of June following, the same was further proved by the Oath of ORRIS PAINE another witness thereto and ordered to be recorded

Teste ADAM CRAIG, C. C.

pp.   (On margin: HARRY HETH's Bond as Collector of the City's Taxes for 1787)
219-   KNOW ALL MEN by these presents that we HARRY HETH, JOHN PRYOR, ROBERT
220   BOYD and WILLIAM REYNOLDS of City of Richmond are held and firmly bound unto the Mayor, Aldermen and Commonalty of the City of Richmond in the sum of Two thousand pounds current money, to which payment well and truly to be made we bind ourselves our heirs jointly and severally firmly by these presents; Sealed with our seals and dated this 2d. day of July 1788

THE CONDITION of this Obligation is such that whereas the above bound HARRY HETH hath been appointed by virtue of an Ordinance of the Common Hall for City of Richmond intitled, "An Ordinance to Amend and Reduce into one Ordinance the several Ordinances for Establishing a Revenue for the City of Richmond and for Regulating the Mode of Collection," COLLECTOR of Taxes for the said City to be collected for the year of our Lord one thousand seven hundred and eighty seven; Now if said HARRY HETH shall duly and faithfully execute the duties of his said Office according to the said Ordinance and shall well and truly demean himself therein. Then this Obligation to be void, else to remain of force and virtue

Sealed and Delivered in presence of

CLAI: WATKINS, as to Heth & Pryor   HARRY HETH
ADAM CRAIG as to Boyd & Reynolds   J. PRYOR
                                                     ROBT. BOYD
                                                     W. REYNOLDS

At a Monthly Court of Hustings held for the City of Richmond at the Courthouse on Monday the 28th of July 1788   This Bond having been duly executed and acknowledged by the Obligors, was this day returned to Court & ordered to be recorded
Teste ADAM CRAIG, C.C.

pp.   (On margin: HARRY HETH's Bond as Collector of the City Taxes for 1788)
220-   KNOW ALL MEN by these presents that we HARRY HETH, JOHN PRYOR, ROBERT
221   BOYD and WILLIAM REYNOLDS of the City of Richmond are held and firmly
           bound unto the Mayor, Aldermen and Commonalty of the City of Richmond in
the sum of Two thousand pounds current money to which payment well and truly to be made we bind ourselves our heirs jointly and severally firmly by these presents; Witness our hands and seals 2d. day of July one thousand seven hundred and Eighty eight and in the 12th year of the Commonwealth

THE CONDITION of the above Obligation is such that Whereas the above bound HARRY HETH hath been appointed by virtue of an Ordinance of the Common Hall for City of Richmond intitled, "An Ordinance to Amend and Reduce into one Ordinance the several Ordinances for Establishing a Revenue for the City of Richmond and for Regulating the Mode of Collection," COLLECTOR of the Taxes for said City to be collected for the present year one thouand seven hundred and eighty eight, Now if said HARRY HETH shall duly and faithfully execute the duties of his said Office according to the said Ordinance and shall well and truly demean himself therein, then the above Obligation to be void, otherwise to remain in full force and virtue

Sealed and Delivered in the presence of

CLAI: WATKINS as to Heth & Pryor   HARRY HETH
ADAM CRAIG as to Boyd & Reynolds   J. PRYOR
                                                     ROBT. BOYD
                                                     W. REYNOLDS

At a Monthly Court of Hustings for the City of Richmond held at the Courthouse on Monday the 28th of July 1788   This Bond having been duly executed and acknowledged by the Obligors was this day returned to Court & ordered to be recorded
Teste ADAM CRAIG, C.C.

pp.   (On margin: STOCKDELL & Ux. to ALEXANDER)
221-   The Commonwealth of Virginia to NATHANIEL WILKINSON, THOMAS PROSSER
222   and JOHN PENDLETON JR., Gent. Justices of the County of HENRICO, Greeting;
           Whereas JOHN STOCKDELL and ELIZABETH his Wife by their certain Indenture

of Trust bearing date the nineteenth day of March one thousand seven hundred and eighty seven have sold and conveyed unto WILLIAM ALEXANDER that part of a lot or Tenement of land lying in the City of Richmond with the houses and improvements thereon being the same occupied by said STOCKDELL, Also three half acre lotts or Tenements of land lying on SHOCKOE HILL in aforesaid City with the houses and improvements thereon being the same now occupied by DABNEY MILLER with the appurtenances thereunto belonging; And Whereas the said ELIZABETH cannot conveniently travel to our Court of Hustings for said City to make acknowledgment of the Conveyance. Therefore we do give unto you or any two or more of you power to receive the acknowledgment which said ELIABETH shall be willing to make before you (the Commission for the privy exa-mination of ELIZABETH, the Wife of JOHN STOCKDELL); Witness ADAM CRAIG Clerk of our said Court the 19th day of April 1788 in the 12th year of the Commonwealth   ADAM CRAIG, C. C.

HENRICO County Sc. Pursuant to the within Commission to us directed, we have this day examined ELIZABETH STOCKDELL, Wife of JOHN STOCKDELL, privily and apart from her said Husband (the return of the execution of the privy examination of ELIZABETH STOCK-DELL); Given under our hands and seals this 29th day of April 1788
                                   NATHL: WILKINSON
                                   THO: PROSSER
     At a Court of Hustings for the City of Richmond held at the Courthouse in the said City on Monday the 28th of July 1788   This Commission with the Certificate of the execution thereof endorsed was this day returned and ordered to be recorded
                         Teste ADAM CRAIG, C. C.

pp.   (On margin: THOMAS & Ux. to NICOLSON)
223-   THIS INDENTURE made this sixth day of July in the year of our Lord one thou-
224   sand seven hundred and eighty eight Between JACOB THOMAS and ANNE his
          Wife of one part and THOMAS NICOLSON of the other part; Witnesseth that in
consideration of the sum of Thirty pounds current money of Virginia in hand paid by said THOMAS NICOLSON to said JACOB THOMAS and ANNE his Wife, have bargained and sold unto THOMAS NICOLSON his heirs a certain piece of ground lying in City of Richmond, bounded, Beginning at the East corner of said THOMAS NICOLSONs Kitchen, thence along the Cross Street leading to the River twenty two feet and a half, thence a Westerly course sixty three feet eight inches, thence a Northernly course twenty two feet and a half, thence an Easterly course sixty three feet eight inches to the beginning; the said piece of ground being part of a lot known by the plan of said City by the number Twenty (20); To have and to hold the piece of ground with all its appurtenances to THOMAS NICOLSON his heirs and JACOB THOMAS and ANNE his Wife do by these presents warrant and forever defend to THOMAS NICOLSON a good and sufficient title in fee simple to said piece of ground against every person; In Witness whereof they have hereunto set their hands and affixed their seals the day and year above written
Signed Sealed & Delivered in the presence of
     GEO: NICOLSON,   JACOB THOMAS
     WILLIAM NICOLSON, CHAS: COPLAND   ANNE her mark + THOMAS
     At a Court of Hustings for the City of Richmond held at the Courthouse on Monday the 28th of July 1788   This Indenture was acknowledged by the within named JACOB THOMAS and MARY his Wife, parties thereto (the said MARY having been first privily examined as the Law directs) and is ordered to be recorded
                         Teste ADAM CRAIG, C. C.

pp.   (LOn margin: GALT to BUCHANAN)
224-   THIS INDENTURE made on the twenty first day of April in the year of Christ
226   one thousand seven hundred and eighty eight Between GABRIEL GALT of City of
         Richmond of one part and ALEXANDER BUCHANAN of the same place of other
part; Witnesseth that in consideration of Fifty nine pounds, Three shillings and Two
pence which GABRIEL GALT is justly indebted to NELSON HERON and CO., of the same
City, and honestly desires to secure and pay to them; And for the farther consideration
of the sum of five shillings like money to said GALT in hand paid by ALEXANDER
BUCHANAN, said GABRIEL GALT by these presents doth bargain sell and confirm to
ALEXANDER BUCHANAN his heirs a certain lott or piece of land in City aforesaid bounded; Beginning at the corner of the MASONS HALL and running Westerly on the same
Street with it fifty feet, then Southward on the Cross Street two hundred and twenty six
feet, then parrallel to the first line fifty feet and then parrallel to the Cross Street two
hundred and twenty six feet to the place of beginning, with all houses and other appurtenances belonging; and all services benefits and profits of said Lott houses and premises: To have and to hold the lot houses and other premises unto ALEXANDER
BUCHANAN his heirs and GABRIEL GALT doth hereby grant that he shall warrant and
forever defend the said lott houses and other premises unto said BUCHANAN his heirs
against every other person; UPON TRUST, nevertheless, the said BUCHANAN his heirs
shall (after the sixteenth day of October in the year of Christ one thousand seven hundred and eighty eight as soon as said BUCHANAN his heirs shall think proper or the said
GALT shall request, (which ever of these two circumstances shall first happen) sell for
the best price that can be gotten, after giving ten days public notice, the said Lott
Houses and premises and out of the money arising from such sale, discharge to ALEXAN-
DER BUCHANAN the sum of fifty nine pounds, Three shillings and Two pence with lawful interest from the sixteenth day of April one thousand seven hundred and eighty
eight until the same shall be fully discharged, and the expences attending the drawing
and recording this Indenture and the contingent charges or the sale and other necessary expences that shall attend the securing and obtaining the above mentioned money
and the said BUCHANAN his heirs shall pay or cause to be paid the overplus, if any
remain from such sale, to GABRIEL GALT his heirs or to his Order; In Witness whereof
the said GABRIEL GALT hath hereunto set his hand and seal on the day and year first
above written
Sealed and Delivered in the presence of
         HARRY HETH,   G. GALT
         MARKES VANDEWALL, JOHN PATMAN
   At a Court of Hustings for the City of Richmond held at the PUBLIC BUILDINGS in the
said City on Monday the 24th of November 1788, being Quarterly Court
This Indenture was proved by the Oaths of HARRY HETH, MARKES VANDEWALL and
JOHN PATMAN, the witnesses thereto, and ordered to be recorded
                       Teste ADAM CRAIG C. C.

pp.   (On margin: GRAVES & Ux. to NICOLSON)
226-   THIS INDENTURE made this second day of July in the year of our Lord one thou-
227   sand seven hundred and eighty eight Between FRANCIS GRAVES and MARTHA
         his Wife of City of Richmond of the one part and WILLIAM NICOLSON of the said
City of other part; Witnesseth that in consideration of the sum of Five shillings current
money of Virginia to them the said FRANCIS GRAVES and MARTHA his Wife in hand paid
by these presents do bargain sell and confirm to WILLIAM NICOLSON his heirs a certain
piece or part of a lot of ground lying in the City aforesaid and bounded; Beginning

seventy one feet from the East end of JOHN STOCKDELL's LONG HOUSE on the Street called and known by the name of CARYS STREET, And runing along the said Street sixty eight feet, from thence right angle thirty seven feet to the lot the said GRAVES bought of FOSTER WEBB JUNIOR, from thence along the line of the said lot sixty eight feet, from thence thirty seven feet to the beginning; the said piece of ground being part of the lot known by the plan of the City by the number (blank) To have and to hold the piece of ground with all its appurtenances to WILLIAM NICOLSON his heirs; And FRANCIS GRAVES and MARTHA his Wife do warrant the piece of ground with all appurtenances against the claim of every person to WILLIAM NICOLSON his heirs and shall for ever defend by these presents; In Witness whereof they the said FRANCIS GRAVES and MARTHA his Wife have hereunto set their hands and affixed their seals the day and year first above written
Signed Sealed & Delivered in presence of us
     EDWARD DAVIS,   FRANCIS GRAVES
     JULIUS CURLE, W. REYNOLDS   MARTHA GRAVES
  At a Court of Hustings for the City of Richmond held at the Courthouse in the said City on Monday the 28th of July 1788   This Indenture was proved by the Oaths of EDWARD DAVIS and JULIUS CURLE, witnesses thereto; And at another Court of Hustings for the said City held at the PUBLIC BUILDINGS on Monday the 24th of November following, the said Indenture was further proved by the Oath of WILLIAM REYNOLDS, the other witness thereto, and ordered to be recorded
                    Teste ADAM CRAIG, C.C.

pp   (On margin. NICHS. GAUTIER's Will)
228-   IN THE NAME OF GOD Amen. I NICHOLAS GAUTIER of the City of Richmond being
229   sick and weak in body tho of sound mind and memory do make this my Last Will
        and Testament in manner and form as follows: returning thanks for the many Blessings received, I recommend my Soul to God who gave it, my body to the Earth to be decently intered and all funeral charges and my just debts to be first paid, I then give and bequeath to my loving Wife, FRANCES GAUTIER, a Negro woman, Silvy, and her increase to her and her heirs for ever; Also, I give to my Wife, FRANCES GAUTIER, a sum of money due me by JOHN M. FUTCHERON for a certain tract of land purchased from me and that on the payment of the money, my Wife FRANCES GAUTIER, make to the said FUTCHERON his heirs a lawful conveyance of said tract of land to him & his heirs for ever;
  Item I leave the use and benefit of my whole Estate both real and personal in America to my loving Wife. FRANCES GAUTIER, that she may enjoy the benefits thereof without interruption and if by accident of fire or otherwise the houses be destroyed, I give to her, my loving Wife, full power to make sale of one half the lot purchased of WILLIAM HAY to build a house or houses on the other as she may see fit and at her death to be disposed of as follows: At the death of my loving Wife, my whole Estate mentioned above which lies in America, the Legacies excepted, I leave to be equally divided amongst my Brothers and Sisters, and if either of them shall have departed this life to his heir lawfully begotten of their body;
  Item. I leave to my Oldest Brother, JOHN B. GAUTIER, all my Estate in the Kingdom of FRANCE, for his use during life on condition he pays the passages of his two Sons to and from America out of the said Estate in FRANCE, and it is my Will and desire at his, my Oldest Brothers death, that the said Estate in FRANCE be divided amongst his Daughters equally and that the gift remain to them and their heirs for ever;
  I do ordain and appoint my loving Wife, FRANCES GAUTIER, the sole Executrix of this

my last Will and Testament, and as a proof of this being the real desire of my mind, I
have hereunto set my hand and affixed my Seal this twelve day of March in the year
1788
In presence of
    RICHARD CROUCH JUNIOR,   NICHS: GAUTIER
    JOHN BRANDER. W. FOUSHEE
  At a Quarterly Court of Hustings continued and held for the City of Richmond at the
PUBLIC BUILDINGS in the said City on Tuesday the 25th of November 1788
  This Will was presented in Court by FRANCES GAUTIER, the Executrix therein named,
and was proved by the Oaths of RICHARD CROUCH JR. and JOHN BRANDER, two of the
witnesses thereto, and ordered to be recorded. Whereupon the said FRANCES relin-
quished her right of Executorship on the Estate of her said deceas'd Husband in favour
of WILLIAM FOUSHEE, Gent., And on the motion of the said WILLIAM FOUSHEE, who made
Oath thereto, and together with DANIEL LAWRENCE HYLTON, his security, entered into
and acknowledged their Bond in the penalty of Five hundred pounds conditioned as the
Law directs; Administration is granted him on the said decedents Estate with his said
Will annexed in due form   Teste ADAM CRAIG C.C.

pp.   (On margin: ROPER to WATKINS)
230-   THIS INDENTURE made this Thirtieth day of December in the year of our Lord
231   one thousand seven hundred and Eighty eight Between JESSE ROPER of County of
    HENRICO and City of Richmond of one part and FRANCIS WATKINS of County of
PRINCE EDWARD of other part; Witnesseth that JESSE ROPER in consideration of the sum
of Five shillings to him in hand paid by FRANCIS WATKINS by these presents doth bargain sell and confirm unto FRANCIS WATKINS and his heirs a certain lot of land lying
on the South side of the Main Street of the City of Richmond in that part of the said City
formerly called SHOCKOE, and bounded, Beginning on the line of the Main Street at the
corner of the Store now occupied by EBENEZER MACNAIR,which is next to the Store now
occupied by Messrs. LYLE and MITCHELL, and running from thence up the said Main
Street forty feet, from thence running sixty feet at right angles with the said Main
Street, from thence running forty feet parrellel with the first line and from thence
running in a straight line to the beginning; with all houses ways and other appurtenances thereunto belonging: To have and to hold the lot or parcel of land with the
appurtenances thereunto belonging to FRANCIS WATKINS and his heirs free and clear
from all incumbrances and charges whatsoever and JESSE ROPER will for himself and
his heirs warrant and defend the lott with the appurtenances to FRANCIS WATKINS his
heirs for ever against the lawful claim or demand of any person; In Testimony whereof the said JESSE ROPER hath hereunto set his hand and affixed his seal the day and year
first above written
Signed Sealed and Delivered in the presence of
    JESSE EEY,   JESSE ROPER
    JOS: DARMSDATT
  At a Court of Hustings for the City of Richmond held at the Courthouse on Monday the
26th day of January 1789, being a Monthly Court   This Indenture was acknowledged
by JESSE ROPER, one of the parties thereto, and ordered to be recorded
      Teste ADAM CRAIG C.C.

pp.   (On margin: BYRD's Trustee to LYLE)
232-   THIS INDENTURE made this fourth day of September in the year of our Lord one
234   thousand seven hundred and eighty eight Between CHARLES CARTER Esquire

of SHIRLEY in County of CHARLES CITY, surviving Trustee of the Honourable WILLIAM BYRD Esquire now deceased, of one part and JAMES LYLE of County of CHESTERFIELD, Merchant, of other part; Witnesseth that CHARLES CARTER conformable to a Decree of the Worshipful Court of the County of HENRICO made on the sixth day of March last past, and in virtue of the power and authority vested in him by an Act of Assembly intituled "An Act to Secure to Persons who Derive Titles to Lots, Lands or Tenements under the Lottery or under a Deed of Trust of the late WILLIAM BYRD Esquire, a fee simple Estate therein," and for the sum of five shillings current money to him by JAMES LYLE in hand paid, said CHARLES CARTER, surviving Trustee as aforesaid by these presents doth bargain sell and confirm all that lot of land in the former Town of SHOCKOE, now part of the City of Richmond, which was distinguished in the Original Plan of said Town and is now known in the Plan and Asessment Roll of said City by the number (353), Three hundred and Fifty Three, containing or supposed to contain half an acre of ground and which was drawn as a Prize in the Lottery of WILLIAM BYRD Esquire annexed to the Ticket number (1932), Nineteen hundred and Thirty two, with all demand, legal and equitable, of the deceased WILLIAM BRYD's heirs and of said CHARLES CARTER as Trustee his heirs. To have and to hold the lot of land and all other the premises unto JAMES LYLE his heirs and CHARLES CARTER and his heirs the granted land and premises against all persons claiming under him unto JAMES LYLE his heirs shall by these presents warrant and for ever Defend; In Witness whereof the said parties have hereunto set their hands and seals the same day and year first in this Indenture written Signed Sealed and delivered in the presence of

THOMAS KEENE,   CHARS: CARTER
LEWIS PRICE, BENJAMIN RAWLINGS

Received Fourth Septr. 1788. from JAMES LYLE in the within Indenture named the sum of five shillings being the full consideration money for the Land and other premises thereby conveyed
Teste THOAS KEENE, LEWIS PRICE   CHARS. CARTER
At a Court of Hustings for the City of Richmond held at the Courthouse in the said City on Monday the Twenty sixth day of January 1789, being a Monthly Court;
This Indenture was proved by the Oaths of THOMAS KEENE, LEWIS PRICE and BENJAMIN RAWLINGS, the witnesses thereto, and together with the Receipt thereon endorsed which was also proved by the Oaths of the said THOMAS KEENE and LEWIS PRICE, the witnesses thereto are ordered to be recorded
Teste ADAM CRAIG, C. C.

pp.   (On margin: CLARKE to MINOR)
234-   THIS INDENTURE WITNESSETH that THOMAS CLARKE, Son of THOMAS CLARKE
235   deceased, doth put himself an Apprentice to DABNEY MINOR of County of HEN-
       RICO to learn the Art or Mystery of a Carpenter or House Joiner, and with him after the manner of an Apprentice to serve from the day of the date hereof during the term of Four years or until he shall arrive to the age of Twenty one years, during all which term the said Apprentice his said Master shall faithfully serve and in all things behave himself as a faithful Apprentice ought to do, And the said Master for his part engages to teach or cause to be taught the said Apprentice the Art or Mystery of a Carpenter or House Joiner, and find him sufficient clothes to work in during his Apprenticeship, also washing, lodging and diet, and to pay said Apprentice at the expiration of his apprenticeship the sum of Three pounds current money of Virginia and for the true performance of the above articles, the parties bind themselves each unto the other firmly by these presents; In Witness whereof the parties have hereunto set their

hands and seals this Fifteenth day of December one thousand seven hundred and eighty eight
In presence of (no witnesses recorded)   THOMAS CLARKE
                                                          DABNEY MINOR

   At a Court of Hustings for the City of Richmond held at the Courthouse of the said City on Monday the Twenty sixth of January 1789, being a Monthly Court,
This Indenture of Apprenticeship was with the consent and approbation of the Court executed and acknowledged by the parties thereto and ordered to be recorded
                           Teste ADAM CRAIG, C.C.

pp.   (On margin: BYRD's Trustee to WHITE)
235-   THIS INDENTURE made this Fourth day of September in the year of our Lord one
237   thousand seven hundred and eighty eight Between CHARLES CARTER of SHIRLEY
         Esquire, only surviving Trustee of the late WILLIAM BYRD Esquire, deceased, of
one part and SAMUEL WHITE of the County of CAMPBELL of the other part; Witnesseth
that as well in consideration of the sum of One shillings current money paid as of the
Lottery Ticket number (7462) in the Lottery of said WILLIAM BYRD Esquire, delivered
by SAMUEL WHITE to said CHARLES CARTER, said CHARLES in virute of and under the
powers to him granted by a certain Act of Assembly intituled "An Act to Secure to Persons who Derive Titles to Lots, Land or Tenements under the Lottery or under a Deed of
Trust of the late WILLIAM BYRD Esquire a fee simple therein," by these presents doth
bargain sell and confirm unto SAMUEL WHITE his heirs all that half acre lot of land in
the Town of MANCHESTER, known and distinguished in the plan of said Town as established previous to the drawing of the aforesaid Lottery by the number (82), Eighty two,
and which was drawn in said Lottery as a Prize appertaining to the aforesaid Ticket
number (7462) seven thousand four hundred and sixty two, with all rents issues and
profits thereof; To have and to hold the lot of land and premises unto SAMUEL WHITE his
heirs and CHARLES CARTER as aforesaid for himself and his heirs doth promise SAMUEL
WHITE his heirs that said CHARLES CARTER and his heirs the lot and premsies unto said
SAMUEL his heirs against every person claiming under him shall warrant and for ever
by these presents defend; In Witness whereof the said CHARLES CARTER, Trustee as
aforesaid, hath hereunto set his hand and seal the day and year first above written
Signed Sealed and Delivered in the presence of
         THOMAS KEENE,   CHARS. CARTER
         BENJAMIN RAWLINGS, LEWIS PRICE
   Received 4th September 1788 from SAMUEL WHITE in the within Indenture named, the
Lottery Ticket and money in the said Indenture mentioned, in full consideration for the
lot &c. thereby conveyed
Teste THOMAS KEENE,   CHARS. CARTER
         BENJAMIN RAWLINGS, LEWIS PRICE
   At a Court of Hustings for the City of Richmond held at the Courthouse of the said City
on Monday the Twenty sixth day of January 1788, being a Monthly Court;
This Indenture together with the Receipt thereon endorsed were proved by the Oaths of
THOMAS KEENE, BENJAMIN RAWLINGS and LEWIS PRICE, the witnesses thereto, and
ordered to be recorded   Teste ADAM CRAIG, C.C.

   (At this point in this Book, the numbers jump from page 237 to page 338. The missing page
numbers do not appear in the Index of this Book, and there is a note penned by someone at top of
page 338, "100 No. left out."

p.   (On margin: H. HETH's Bond as Secy. for 1789)

338   KNOW ALL MEN by these presents that we HARRY HETH, JOHN PRYOR, GEORGE NICOLSON and WILLIAM REYNOLDS of the City of Richmond are held and firmly bound unto the Mayor, Recorder, Aldermen and Common Council of the City of Richmond in the just and full sum of One thousand pounds current money of Virginia; to which payment well and truly to be made we bind ourselves our heirs firmly by these presents; Sealed with our seals and dated the Twenty sixth day of January 1789

THE CONDITION of the above Obligation is such that whereas the said HARRY HETH hath been appointed SERJEANT of the City of Richmond for one year from the date hereof, If therefore said HARRY HETH shall truly and faithfully execute the duties of his Office for the term of one year ensuing the date hereof, Then this Obligation to be void, else to remain in full force and virtue

Sealed & Delivered in the presence of

ADAM CRAIG   HARRY HETH
                               J. PRYOR
                               GEO: NICOLSON
                               W. REYNOLDS

At a Quarterly Court of Hustings for the City of Richmond held at the Courthouse on Monday the Twenty third of March 1789   This Bond was acknowledged in Court by the Obligors and ordered to be recorded

Teste ADAM CRAIG, C. C.

pp.   (On margin: NEW to KAY. Apprentice)

339-   THIS INDENTURE Witnesseth that BENJAMIN NEW of County of HENRICO and

340   State of Virginia by and with his own consent, by these presents with his own free will and accord, put himself Apprentice to JOSEPH KEY, Plaisterer, of the City of Richmond to learn his Art Trade and Mystery, and after the manner of an Apprentice to serve said JOSEPH KAY the term of Three years and Nine months from the day of the date hereof during the full term said Apprentice his said Master faithfully shall serve and in all things behave himself as a faithful Apprentice ought to do, and the said Master shall use the utmost of his endeavours to teach or cause to be taught or instructed, the said Apprentice in the Trade or Mystery of a Plaisterer, and procure or provide for him sufficient meat drink clothes washing and lodging, fitting for an Apprentice during the term of Three years and Nine months and for the true performance of all the agreements aforesaid, the parties bind themselves each unto the other firmly by these presents; In Witness whereof the said parties have interchangeably set their hands and seals hereunto dated the Twenty third day of March in the year of our Lord one thousand seven hundred and eighty nine and in the year of the Commonwealth the Thirteenth

Sealed and Delivered in the presence of

FRANCIS RATLIFFE,   BENJAMIN NEW
FORTUNATUS GREEN   JOSEPH KAY

At a Quarterly Court of Hustings for the City of Richmond held at the Courthouse on Monday the 23d. of March 1789   This Indenture of Apprenticeship was with the consent of the Court executed and acknowledged by the parties thereto and ordered to be recorded   Teste ADAM CRAIG C. C.

pp.   (On margin: BYRD's Trustee to WARREN)

341-   THIS INDENTURE made this 4th day of November in the year of our Lord one

342   thousand seven hundred and Eighty eight Between CHARLES CARTER, the only

surviving Trustee of the Honourable WILLIAM BYRD deceased of the one part and THO-
MAS WARREN of the other part; Witnesseth that CHARLES CARTER pursuant to the
power vested in him by Act of Assembly as the only surviving Trustee of WILLIAM
BYRD deceased and in consideration of a Lottery Ticket No. 2181, as well as of Five shillings current money of Virginia to him in hand paid by these presents doth bargain
sell and confirm unto THOMAS WARREN his heirs a certain half acre lot lying in City of
Richmond number Four hundred and Twenty Seven, drawn a Prize of the Ticket number Two thousand one hundred and eighty one; and known in the plan of said City in
figures by number 427 (Four hundred and twenty seven); To have and to hold the half
acre lot with all houses improvements and appurtenances belonging to THOMAS WAR-
REN his heirs; And CHARLES CARTER by virtue of the Trust in him reposed against all
persons claiming under him the half acre lot and its appurtenances to THOMAS WAR-
REN his heirs by these presents shall warrant and for ever defend; In Witness whereof
the said CHARLES CARTER the only surviving Trustee of WILLIAM BYRD deceased, hath
hereunto set his hand and affixed his seal the day and year above written
Signed Sealed and Delivered in presence of
      NICHOLAS VOSS,   CHARS. CARTER
      WILLIAM MINOR, FORTU: SYDNOR
      MANN SATTERWHITE JR.   JOSHA: HUMPHREYS
  At a Monthly Court of Hustings for the City of Richmond held at the Courthouse in the
said City on Monday the 27th day of April 1789   This Indenture was proved by the
Oaths of NICHOLAS VOSS, JOSHUA HUMPHREYS and FORTUNATUS SYDNOR, witnesses
thereto, and ordered to be recorded Teste ADAM CRAIG, C.C.

pp.   (On margin: SINGLETON & Ux. to HARRISON)
342-   THIS INDENTURE made this eighth day of January in the year of our Lord one
344   thousand seven hundred and Eighty nine Between ANTHONY SINGLETON and
      LUCY his Wife of City of Richmond of one part and BENJAMIN HARRISON JR. of
the same place of the other part; Witnesseth that said ANTHONY and LUCY his Wife in
consideration of the sum of Ten pounds current money in hand paid to them by said
BENJAMIN HARRISON, by these presents do bargain and sell unto said BENJAMIN HAR-
RISON his heirs two certain half acre lots situate in City of Richmond on the Main Street
and known in the plan of said City by the numbers Five hundred and Eighty Three and
Five hundred and Eighty Four, and also all the buildings and inclosures thereto belonging; To have and to hold the two half acre lots and all the premises with the appurtenances unto said BENJAMIN HARRISON his heirs and ANTHONY SINGLETON and LUCY
his Wife for themselves and their heirs the two half acre lots and premises against
every person to said BENJAMIN HARRISON his heirs shall warrant and for ever defend
by these presents; In Witness whereof the said ANTHONY SINGLETON and LUCY his Wife
have hereunto set their hands and affixed their seals the day and year above written
Sealed and Delivered in the presence of
This Eighth day of January one thousand seven
hundred and eighty nine HARRY HETH,   ANTHONY SINGLETON
      LEWIS BURWELL, MARY HARRISON,   LUCY SINGLETON
      BEN: HARRISON
  Richmond Eighth January 1789. Received of BENJAMIN HARRISON Ten pounds in full
for the purposes within mentioned
Test MARY HARRISON,   A. SINGLETON
      BENJAMIN HARRISON, HARRY HETH
  The Commonwealth of Virginia to NATHANIEL WILKINSON, TURNER SOUTHALL, MILES

SELDEN, JOHN HARVIE and JOHN PENDLETON, Gent., Justices of HENRICO County,
Greeting: Whereas (the Commission for the privy examination of LUCY, the Wife of ANTHONY
SINGLETON); Witness ADAM CRAIG, Clerk of the said Court the 12th day of February 1789
in the 13th year of the Commonwealth   ADAM CRAIG C.C.
  HENRICO County to wit, Pursuant to the written Commission, we have this day exa-
mined Mrs. LUCY SINGLETON, Wife of the within named ANTHONY SINGLETON, separate
and apart from her Husband (the return of the execution of the privy examination of LUCY
SINGLETON); Certified under our hands and seals the 9th day of March 17 eighty nine
                         JOHN HARVIE
                         JOHN PENDLETON
  At a Monthly Court of Hustings for the City of Richmond held at the Courthouse in the
said City on Monday the 27th of April 1789   This Indenture with the Receipt thereon
endorsed were acknowledged by ANTHONY SINGLETON, one of the parties thereto, and
together with the Commission annexed and the Certificate of the execution thereof, are
ordered to be recorded   Teste ADAM CRAIG, C.C.

pp.   (On margin: HARRISON to SINGLETON)
345-   THIS INDENTURE made this Eighth day of January in the year of our Lord one
346   thousand seven hundred and Eighty nine Between BENJAMIN HARRISON of City
         of Richmond of one part and ANTHONY SINGLETON of the same place of the other
part; Witnesseth that BENJAMIN HARRISON in consideration of the sum of Ten pounds
current money of Virginia in hand paid to him by ANTHONY SINGLETON by these presents do bargain and sell unto ANTHONY SINGLETON his heirs two certain half acre lotts
lying in City of Richmond on the Main Street and known in the plan of said City by the
numbers Five hundred and Eighty Three and Five hundred and Eighty Four, and also all
the buildings and inclosures thereon, and all rights and appurtenances belonging; To
have and to hold the two half acre lots and all the premises above mentioned with the
appurtenances unto ANTHONY SINGLETON his heirs, And BENJAMIN HARRISON for himself his heirs the said two half acre lots and premises with the appurtenances against
all persons to ANTHONY SINGLETON his heirs shall warrant and for ever defend by these
presents; In Witness whereof the said BENJAMIN HARRISON hath hereunto set his hand
and affixed his seal the day and year first above written
Sealed and Delivered in the presence of
This Eighth day of January one thousand seven
hundred and eighty nine. HARRY HETH,   BENJ: HARRISON
        MARY HARRISON, LEWIS BURWELL,
        BEN: HARRISON
  Richmond eighth day of January 1789. Received of ANTHONY SINGLETON Ten pounds
in full for the purposes within mentioned
Teste HARRY HETH,   BENJ: HARRISON
        MARY HARRISON, BEN: HARRISON
  At a Monthly Court of Hustings for the City of Richmond held at the Courthosue in the
said City on Monday the 27th of April 1789   This Indenture together with the Receipt
thereon endorsed was acknowledged by BENJAMIN HARRISON JUNIOR, one of the
parties thereto, and ordered to be recorded
                         Teste ADAM CRAIG, C.C.

pp   (On margin: EVANS's Exrx. to CAMPBELL)
346-   KNOW ALL MEN by these presents that I JANE CAMPBELL, Executrix of the Last
347   Will and Testament of NATHANIEL EVANS deceased, by these presents do make
         and appoint my Brother, WILLIAM CAMPBELL, of the County of BOTETOURT, my

true and lawful Attorney irrecovable for me and in my name and to my sue as Executrix aforesaid to ask demand sue for recover and receive all sums of money, debts and demands whatsoever which are now due or were owing unto the said NATHL: EVANS in his life time or which may hereafter become due by and from the Debtors of said NATHANIEL, to the Estate of the said NATHANIEL, and in default of payment thereof, to take all lawful ways and means as Executrix aforesaid or otherwise for the recovery thereof by Attachment, Arrest Distress or otherwise and sufficient discharges for the same and in my name as Executrix and do all lawful acts and things concerning the premises as fully in every respect as I myself might or could do if myself was personally present, And I do by these presents in consideration of the great trouble that my said Brother, WILLIAM CAMPBELL, must necessarily be at in collecting and settling the Debts belonging to the said Estate, oblige myself as Executrix to allow my Brother five p centum for collecting the Debts of said Estate besides his reasonable expences necessarily incurred about the said collection, hereby allowing and confirming all my Attorney shall in my name as Executrix lawfully do or cause to be in and about the premises by virtue of these presents; In Witness whereof I the said JANE CAMPBELL, as Executrix of the Last Will and Testament of NATHANIEL EVANS, deceased have this 23d. day of Octo: 1788 hereunto set my hand and affixed my seal
Signed Sealed and Acknowledged in the presence of us
        W: JOHNSON,   JANE CAMPBELL
        WM: DUVALL
    At a Monthly Court of Hustings for the City of Richmond held at the Courthouse in the said City on Monday the Twenty seventh of April 1789   This Power of Attorney was proved by the Oath of WILLIAM DUVALL, a witness thereto, and ordered to be recorded
                        Teste ADAM CRAIG, C. C.

pp.   (On margin: MAUZEY to BUCHANANs Exors. Original delivd. JNO: BUCHANAN
348-   this 25th March 1801. A. STEVENSON)
350   THIS INDENTURE made this fourth day of February in the year of our Lord one
         thousand seven hundred and Eighty nine Between PETER MAUZEY of City of
Richmond and County of HENRICO of one part and JOHN BUCHANAN and ALEXANDER BUCHANAN, Executors of JAMES BUCHANAN deceased, of the other part; Whereas PETER MAUZEY stands justly indebted unto the Estate of JAMES BUCHANAN the just and full quantity of Eleven thousand and fifty two pounds of Merchantable Crop Tobacco of the Upper Inspections on JAMES RIVER, and also the just and full sum of Twenty pounds current money of Virginia with interest on the Tobacco and money from the first day of April one thousand seven hundred and eighty three, which (though willing) he is at present unable to pay. NOW THIS INDENTURE Witnesseth that said PETER MAUZEY for securing the payment of the aforesaid quantity of Tobacco and sum of money with the interest to the Estate of JAMES BUCHANAN and in consideration of the sum of Five shillings by JOHN BUCHANAN and ALEXANDER BUCHANAN, Executors of JAMES BUCHANAN, to PETER MAUZEY in hand paid by these presents do bargain and sell unto JOHN BUCHANAN and ALEXANDER BUCHANAN, Executors of JAMES BUCHANAN deceased, their heirs two improved half acre lots lying in City of Richmond, one of the said Lots denominated in the plan of said City, No. 517 (Five hundred and seventeen); the other No. 518 (Five hundred and eighteen) with all buildings profits and appurtenances to said two lots belonging, and the rents and issues thereof; To have and to hold the premises with the appurtenances unto JOHN BUCHANAN and ALEXANDER BUCHANAN, Executors of JAMES BUCHANAN deceased, their heirs; and PETER MAUZEY doth grant for himself and his heirs the premises with the appurtenances unto JOHN BUCHANAN and ALEXANDER

BUCHANAN, Executors of JAMES BUCHANAN deceased, their heirs against the lawful claim of every person to warrant and for ever defend by these presents; PROVIDED always that these presents are upon this Condition, that if PETER MAUZEY his heirs do pay the aforesaid Quantity of Tobacco and the sum of money with lawful interest on the same on or before the first day of July next ensuing, Then these presents and every thing herein contained shall cease determine and become void; And it is agreed that until default shall be made that it shall be lawful for PETER MAUZEY to hold possess and enjoy the premises any thing herein to the contrary notwithstanding; In Witness whereof the parties to these presents have hereunto set their hands and seals subscribed and set, the day and year first above written

Sealed and Delivered in the presence of
Teste   GEORGE GAIRDNER,   JNO: BARRET,   PETER MAUZEY
        NELSON BERKLEY JUNIOR

At a Monthly Court of Hustings for the City of Richmond continued and held at the Courthouse on Tuesday the 28th of April 1789   This Indenture was proved by the Oaths of GEORGE GAIRDNER, JOHN BARRET and NELSON BERKELEY JR. the witnesses thereto, and ordered to be recorded   Teste ADAM CRAIG, C.C.

p.   (On margin: WM. COULTER's Bond as Constable)
350   KNOW ALL MEN by these presents that we WILLIAM COULTER, JAMES BISSET
        and JOHN BRYAN of the City of Richmond are held and firmly bound unto the
Mayor, Recorder, Aldermen and Common Council of City of Richmond in the just and full sum of One hundred and fifty pounds current money of Virginia to which payment well and truly to be made we bind ourselves our heirs firmly by these presents, Sealed with our seals and dated this 28th day of April 1789

THE CONDITION of the above Obligation is such that Whereas the said WILLIAM COULTER hath been appointed a CONSTABLE for the City of Richmond, If therefore the said WILLIAM COULTER shall truly and faithfully execute the duties of his said office, and shall also truly and faithfully collect and account for all monies which shall come to his hands in virtue of his Office as Constable, then this Obligation to be void, else to remain in full force and virtue

Sealed and Delivered in the presence of
        JOHN ROBINSON JUNIOR   WM. COULTER
                                         JAMES BISSET
                                         JOHN BRYAN

At a Monthly Court of Hustings for the City of Richmond continued & held at the Courthouse on Tuesday the 28th of April 1789   This Bond was (in open Court) executed and acknowledged by the Obligors and ordered to be recorded
                        Teste ADAM CRAIG, C.C.

pp.   (On margin: HOWARD to McCLOUD)
351-   THIS INDENTURE made this twenty fifth day of May Anno Domini one thousand
352   seven hundred and Eighty nine Between JOHN HOWARD of HANOVER County of
        one part and JOSEPH McCLOUD of HENRICO County of the other part; Witnesseth
that JOHN HOWARD in consideration that JOSEPH McCLOUD stands bound for him the said JOHN HOWARD and others in a Bond payable to JOHN DAVIS of County of (blank) on which a suit is now depending in the District Court of HENRICO which with the costs may amount to Forty pounds current money of Virginia, which may more fully appear by the Records of the said Court, And to indemnify said JOSEPH McCLOUD as security aforesaid, said JOHN HOWARD by these presents doth bargain and sell unto JOSEPH McCLOUD his

heirs all that Tenement whereon said HOWARD lately lived in City of Richmond and
which was purchased by said JOHN HOWARD of RICHARD ADAMS; To have and to hold
the said Tenement with all improvements thereon and appurtenances thereunto belonging to JOSEPH McCLOUD his heirs; PROVIDED nevertheless that if JOHN HOWARD his
heirs do not faithfully discharge and pay off the said Debt and Costs with interest
thereon within one month after said JOHN DAVIS obtains a Judgment in the said District Court on said Bond, That then said JOHN HOWARD doth by these presents impower
and authorize ADAM CRAIG of City of Richmond whom he appoints as Trustee to sell said
Tenement and its appurtenances for ready money having previously advertised the
same in one of the Virginia Gazettes for three weeks preceeding the time of such sale
and after paying the debt aforesaid and costs attending the sale, said Trustee to account
for the balance arising from said Sale to JOHN HOWARD, and JOHN HOWARD doth by
these presents authorize the Trustee to make conveyance of said Tenement to such pur-
chaser or purchasers of said Tenement, subject to the same conditions that JOHN
HOWARD is bound to fulfill in his engagements with RICHARD ADAMS; In Witness
whereof the said JOHN HOWARD and JOSEPH McCLOUD have hereunto set their hands and
seals on the day and year first above written
Signed Sealed and delivered in the presence of us
        (no witnesses recorded)   JOHN his mark ✝ HOWARD
    At a Quarterly Court of Hustings for the City of Richmond held at the Courthouse in the
said City on Monday the 25th of May 1789   This Indenture was acknowledged by JOHN
HOWARD, one of the parties thereto, and ordered to be recorded
                        Teste ADAM CRAIG, C.C.

pp.   (On margin: MARKES VANDEWALL's Bond as Vendue Master, No. 1)
352-   KNOW ALL MEN by these presents that we MARKES VANDEWALL of City of
353   Richmond and WILLIAM LEWIS and MILES SELDEN of County of HENRICO, are
         held and firmly bound unto the Mayor, Aldermen and Commonalty of said City of
Richmond in the just and full sum of Two thousand pounds, to which payment well and
truly to be made we bind ourselves our heirs firmly by these presents; Sealed with our
seals and dated this twenty fifth day of May one thousand seven hundred and eighty
nine
    THE CONDITION of the above Obligation is such that Whereas the above bound MARKES
VANDEWALL hath been appointed VENDUE MASTER of City of Richmond for the term of
Two years from the day of the date hereof; If therefore said MARKES VANDEWALL shall
duly and faithfully perform the duties of his said Office and shall duly and faithfully
observe the several regulations enjoined of him under his said Appointment by the
Ordinance of the Common Hall of the said City intituled, "An Ordinance for amending
and comprising into one Ordinance the several Ordinances respecting the appointment and duty of VENUE MASTERS," then the above Obligation to be void, otherwise to
remain in full force and virtue
Sealed and Delivered in the presence of
        The Court   MARKES VANDEWALL
                                               WM. LEWIS
                                               MILES SELDEN
    At a Quarterly Court of Hustings for the City of Richmond held at the Courthouse in the
said City on Monday the 25th of May 1789   This Bond was in open Court executed and
acknowledged by the Obligors and ordered to be recorded
                        Teste ADAM CRAIG, C.C.

p.   (On margin: COWLEY to Loudon. Delivered to Negro Loudon)
353   KNOW ALL MEN by these presents that I ABRAHAM COWLEY of County of HEN-
          RICO have emancipated and set free for ever a Negro man slave named Loudon,
about Forty seven years of age and I do hereby for myself my heirs relinquish and re-
nounce for ever all right or title which I have to said Negro man Loudon. In Testimony whereof I have hereunto subscribed my name and affixed my seal this Thirteenth day of May in the year of our Lord one thousand seven hundred and eighty nine
Sealed and Delivered in the presence of
          RICHARD BOWLER,   ABRM: COWLEY
          SAML: EGE
   At a Quarterly Court of Hustings for the City of Richmond held at the Courthouse in the
said City on Monday the 25th of May 1789   This Deed of Emancipation was acknowledged by ABRAHAM COWLEY, one of the parties thereto, & ordered to be recorded
                         Teste ADAM CRAIG, C.C.

pp.   (On margin: BEALL to McCLURG)
354-   THIS INDENTURE made the 19th day of December one thousand seven hundred
356   and eighty eight Between SAMUEL BEALL of the County of JAMES CITY of one
          part and JAMES McCLURG of the City of Richmond of other part; Witnesseth that
whereas SAMUEL BEALL stands justly indebted to the said JAMES McCLURG in the sum of
Six hundred and Fifty eight pounds, Eleven shillings in actual Gold and Silver as will
fully appear by said SAMUEL BEALL's Bond to said JAMES McCLURG, one bearing date
the 24th May 1784 for L. 200 interest paid up to May 24th 1788; a second Bond dated June
3d. 1784 for the like sum of L. 200 interest paid up to June 3d. 1788; a third bond for
L. 200..2..2 dated June 5th 1784 interest paid up to June 5th 1788; a fourth and last Bond
dated June 26th 1786 for L. 58...8...10, interest paid up to June 26th 1788.
   THIS INDENTURE Witnesseth that for securing the aforesaid sums due by Bonds as
before recited to the amount of Six hundred and fifty eight pounds, Eleven shillings, to
be paid in actual Gold and Silver and also interest arising thereon in the like coin, due
as aforesaid, said JAMES McCLURG his heirs from SAMUEL BEALL his heirs in consideration of the sum of Five shillings current money in hand paid by JAMES McCLURG said
SAMUEL BEALL by these presents doth bargain and sell unto JAMES McCLURG his heirs
two lots in the City of Richmond, late the property of EDMUND RANDOLPH Esquire,
whereon said RANDOLPH formerly lived, part of which is now in the occupation of JOHN
HOPKINS, as will more fully appear by a reference to said E. RANDOLPH's Deed of Conveyance to SAMUEL BEALL, bearing date the 18th day of December 1788, with all houses
profits and appurtenances to the same belonging; PROVIDED Always and these presents
are upon this Condition, that if SAMUEL BEALL his heirs shall pay or cause to be paid
unto JAMES McCLURG his heirs the sum of Six hundred and Fifty eight pounds, Eleven
shillings with the interest arising thereon which part to be paid in actual Gold and
Silver within six months from the date of these presents, then these presents shall become void and in case of default or non payment it shall be lawful for JAMES McCLURG
his heirs to enter upon the lot and houses and to hold the same or to make sale thereof
and to convey the same as his or their own property in fee simple for ever; In Witness
whereof the parties to these presents have hereunto set their hands and affixed their
seals the day and year first above written
Signed Sealed & delivered in the presence of us
          JOHN MAY, ED: CARRINGTON,   SAMUEL BEALL
          EDM: RANDOLPH, JAS: INNES,
          WILLIAM DUNCAN, SERAFINO FORMICOLA,
          FRANCIS RICAUD

At a Quarterly Court of Hustings for the City of Richmond held at the Courthouse in the said City on Monday the 25th of May 1789   This Indenture was proved by the Oaths of JAMES INNES Esqr., WILLIAM DUNCAN and SERAFINO FORMICIOLA, witnesses thereto, and ordered to be recorded.   Teste ADAM CRAIG, C. C.

pp.   (On margin: MARKES VANDEWALL's Bond as VENDUE MASTER for Commissions
356-   which may become due to the Corporation. No. 2.)
357   KNOW ALL MEN by these presents that we MARKES VANDEWALL of the City of
           Richmond and DANIEL VANDEWALL and GILLEY M. LEWIS of the County of HEN-
RICO are held and firmly bound unto the Mayor, Aldermen and Commonalty of the City of Richmond in the just and full sum of Five hundred pounds, to which payment well and truly to be made we bind ourselves jointly and severally firmly by these presents; Sealed with our seals and dated this twenty sixth day of May 1789
   THE CONDITION of the above Obligation is such that whereas the above bound MARKES VANDEWALL hath been appointed as VENDUE MASTER for the City of Richmond, If therefore said MARKES VANDEWALL shall duly and punctually account for and pay to the Chamberlayne of said City all Commissions which shall accrue and become due in virtue of his said appointment agreeably to the Ordinance of the Common Hall of the City of richmond intituled, "An Ordinance for amending and comprising into one Ordi- nance the several Ordinances respecting the appointment and duty of Vendue Masters," Then this above Obligation to be void, otherwise to remain in full force and virtue
Sealed and Delivered in the presence of
            The Court   MARKES VANDEWALL
                                                   DANIEL VANDEWALL
                                                   GILLEY M. LEWIS
   At a Quarterly Court of Hustings for the City of Richmond continued and held at the Courthouse in the said City on Monday the 26th of May 1789   This Bond was in open Court executed and acknowledged by the Obligors and ordered to be recorded
                        Teste ADAM CRAIG, C. C.

pp.   (On margin: RANDOLPH & Ux. to BEALL)
357-   THIS INDENTURE made this eighteenth day of December one thousand seven
359   hundred and eighty eight Between EDMUND RANDOLPH and ELIZABETH his Wife
           of County of YORK, of one part and SAMUEL BEALL of JAMES CITY County of
other part; Witnesseth that in consideration of Five shillings in hand paid said EDMUND RANDOLPH and ELIZABETH his Wife by these presents doth bargain sell and confirm unto SAMUEL BEALL his heirs the houses and lots in City of Richmond on SHOCKOE HILL whereon the said RANDOLPH formerly lived, part of which is now in the occupation of JOHN HOPKINS, which lots being two in number and the houses the said RANDOLPH sold to GEORGE NICHOLAS, who hath requested him to convey the same to the said BEALL in fee simple with all profits commodities and appurtenances to the same belonging; and the rents issues and profits thereof; To have and to hold the houses and lots with its appurtenances unto SAMUEL BEALL his heirs and EDMUND RANDOLPH and his heirs the premises unto SAMUEL BEALL and his heirs against the lawful claim of all persons will by these presents forever warrant & defend; In Witness whereof the parties to these presents have hereunto set their hands and affixed their seals the day and year first above written
Signed Sealed and delivered in the presence of
       JOHN MAY, H. BROOKE,.   EDM. RANDOLPH
       JAS: INNES, RICHARD ADAMS JR.
       CARTER BRAXTON JR.

The Consideration received by me from GEORGE NICHOLAS for the within mentioned
houses and lots was One thousand seven hundred pounds current money, warranting to
said NICHOLAS rent for the said lots one hundred & twenty pounds currency p annum
for three years
Witness H: BROOKE, JOHN MAY   EDM: RANDOLPH
   At a Quarterly Court of Hustings for the City of Richmond held at the Courthouse in the
said City on Monday the 25th of May 1789   This Indenture was proved by the Oath of
JAMES INNES Esqr., one of the witnesses thereto; And at a Court of Hustings for the said
City continued and held at the Courthosue on Tuesday following, This Indenture toge-
ther with a certain certificate thereunder written were acknowledged by EDMUND
RANDOLPH, a party thereto, and ordered to be recorded
                         Teste ADAM CRAIG, C.C.

pp.   (On margin: JOHNSTON to BUCHANAN. 1908 May 22, deld. to ADAM HARELL)
359-   THIS INDENTURE made this twentieth day of September in the year of our Lord
360   one thousand seven hundred and Eighty two Between WILLIAM JOHNSTON of
         County of HENRICO, Merchant and Marriner, of one part and JAMES BUCHANAN
of City of Richmond and County aforesaid, Merchant, of other part; Witnesseth that
WILLIAM JOHNSTON in consideration of the sum of Five hundred pounds current money
of Virginia to him in hand paid by JAMES BUCHANAN, by these presents doth bargain
and sell unto JAMES BUCHANAN his heirs one certain Tenement in the City of Richmond
including two half acre lots denoted in the plan of said City by the numbers Eighty
Seven and One hundred and One, Together with all houses gardens fences and all other
appurtenances to the same belonging; To have and to hold the said Tenement and the
two half acres of land and premises with the appurtenances unto JAMES BUCHANAN his
heirs and WILLIAM JOHNSTON for himself his heirs will warrant and defend the two
half acre lots and premises unto JAMES BUCHANAN his heirs against the lawful claims
of any person; In Witness whereof the said WILLIAM JOHNSTON hath hereunto set his
hand and seal the day and year first above mentioned
Signed Sealed and delivered in the presence of
         JOHN PENDLETON JR.   WM: JOHNSTON
         JOHN BARRET,   JNO: McKEAND
   Received 20th September 1782, From the within named JAMES BUCHANAN the sum of
five hundred pounds being the consideration in the within Deed mentioned. L. 500.0.0.
Teste JOHN BARRET   WM: JOHNSTON
   At a Quarterly Court of Hustings for the City of Richmond continued and held at the
Courthouse in the said City on Wednesday the 27th of May 1789   This Indenture was
proved by the Oaths of JOHN PENDLETON JR., JOHN BARRET and JOHN McKEAND, witnesses thereto, and together with the Receipt thereon endorsed which was also proved
by the Oath of said JOHN BARRET, the witness thereto, & ordered to be recorded
                         Teste ADAM CRAIG, C.C.

pp.   (On margin: BUCHANAN to HETH)
361-   THIS INDENTURE this twenty seventh day of May in the year of our Lord one
362   thousand seven hundred and eighty nine Between ALEXANDER BUCHANAN of
         the City of Richmond of one part and HARRY HETH of the same place of the other
part; Witnesseth that ALEXANDER BUCHANAN in consideration of the sum of One hundred and Twenty pounds current money of Virginia to him in hand paid by HARRY
HETH by these presents doth bargain sell and confirm unto HARRY HETH his heirs, one
certain Tenement in the City of Richmond containing two half acre lots of land dis-

tinguished in the plan of the said City by the numbers Eighty Seven and One hundred
and One; with all houses waters and other appurtenances thereunto belonging; which
two half acre lots of land were conveyed by WILLIAM JOHNSTON to JAMES BUCHANAN by
Indenture of Bargain and Sale bearing date the Twentieth day of September in the year
one thousand seven hundred and eighty two; and devised by JAMES BUCHANAN in his
Last Will and Testament to said ALEXANDER BUCHANAN and his heirs; To have and to
hold the two half acre lots of land with the appurtenances thereunto belonging to
HARRY HETH his heirs free from the claim or demand of any persons claiming under
said JAMES BUCHANAN and at the time of sealing and delivery of this Indenture free &
clear from all incumbrances or charges, In Testimony whereof the said ALEXANDER
BUCHANAN hath hereunto subscribed his name and affixed his seal the same day and
year first above written
Sealed Signed and delivered in presence of
            (no witnesses recorded)   ALEXR: BUCHANAN
    At a Quarterly Court of Hustings for the City of Richmond continued and held at the
Courthouse in the said City on Wednesday the 27th of May 1789   This Indenture was
acknowledged by ALEXANDER BUCHANAN, one of the parties thereto and ordered to be
recorded   Teste ADAM CRAIG C. C.

pp.   (On margin: BLADES to HEISLER and COOK)
362-   THIS INDENTURE WITNESSETH that CAMPBELL BLADES, Orphan of GEORGE
363   BLADES deceased, hath put himself and by these presents with the advice and
            consent of his Brother, WILLIAM BLADES, doth voluntarily and of his own free
will and accord put himself Apprentice to HESILER and COOK, Tin Plate Workers, in the
City of Richmond, to learn their Art Trade and Mystery and after the manner of an
Apprentice to serve the said HEISLER and COOK from the day of the date hereof during
the full term of five years five months and twenty nine days, and during all which
term the said Apprentice his said Masters faithfully shall serve and in all things behave himself as a faithful Apprentice ought to do during said term; And the said Masters shall use the utmost of their endeavours to teach or cause to be taught or instructed the said Apprentice in the Trade or Mystery of Tin Plate Work, and procure or
provide for him sufficient meat drink clothes washing and lodging fitting for an
Apprentice during the term of Five years five months and twenty nine days and also to
cause the said Apprentice to be taught to read, write and Cypher, and at the expiration
of his servitude to pay him the sum of Three pounds, Ten shillings, And for the true
performance of all the agreements aforesaid, the parties bind themselves each unto the
other firmly by these presents; In Witness whereof the parties have interchangeably
set their hands and seals hereunto dated the Twenty first day of June in the year of our
Lord one thousand seven hundred and eighty nine and in the thirteenth year of the
Commonwealth
Sealed and Delivered in the presence of
            (no witnesses recorded)   CAMPBELL his mark ✓ BLADES
                                                      HESELER & COOK
    At a Monthly Court of Hustings for the City of Richmond held at the Courthouse on
Monday the 22d. of July 1789   This Indenture was with the consent and approbation
of the Court executed and acknowledged by the parties and ordered to be recorded
                       Teste ADAM CRAIG C. C.

p.   (On margin: JOS: HARRELs Bond as Constable)
364   KNOW ALL MEN by these presents that we JOSEPH HARREL, GEORGE TODD, JOHN
        BURNES and CHARLES BOYLE of City of Richmond are held and firmly bound
unto the Mayor, Recorder, Aldermen and Common Council of said City of Richmond in
the just and full sum of One hundred and fifty pounds current money of Virginia to
which payment well and truly to be made we bind ourselves our heirs jointly and
severally firmly by these presents; Sealed with our seals and dated this 28th day of
April 1789
        THE CONDITION of the above Obligation is such that Whereas the said JOSEPH HARREL
hath been appointed a CONSTABLE for the City of Richmond; If therefore the said JO-
SEPH HARREL shall truly and faithfully execute the duties of his said Office and shall
also truly and faithfully collect and account for all monies which shall come to his
hands in virtue of his Office as Constable, Then this obligation to be void, else to remain
in full force and virtue
Sealed and Delivered in the presence of
        ADAM CRAIG as to J. H. & G. Todd   JOSEPH HARREL
        JOHN ROBINSON JUNR. as to Burnes & Boyle   GEORGE TODD
                                                    JNO: BURNES
                                                    CHARLES BOYLE

    At a Monthly Court of Hustings for the City of Richmond held at the Courthouse on
Monday the 22d. of June 1789   This Bond was proved by the Oaths of ADAM CRAIG as to
JOSEPH HARREL and GEORGE TODD, & by JOHN ROBINSON JUNR. as to JOHN BURNES and
CHARLES BOYLE and ordered to be recorded
                        Teste ADAM CRAIG, C.C.

p   (On margin: THOMPSON to DOVE)
365   KNOW ALL MEN by these presents that I JOHN THOMPSON of KING WILLIAM
        County in consideration of the sum of Twenty pounds current money of Virginia
to me in hand paid by JAMES DOVE of City of Richmond, Merchant, by these presents do
bargain sell and deliver over unto JAMES DOVE one Negro Boy named James: To have
and to hold the bargained premises unto JAMES DOVE his heirs and I said JOHN THOMP-
SON for myself my heirs shall warrant and forever defend against all persons by these
presents unto JAMES DOVE his heirs: In Witness whereof I hereunto set my hand and
affix my seal at Richmond aforesaid this 30th day of April 1789
Teste WILLIAM LIPSCOMB.   JOHN THOMPSON
       P. YOUNGHUSBAND
    At a Monthly Court of Hustings for the City of Richmond held at the Courthouse on
Monday the 27th of July 1789   This Bill of Sale was proved by the Oaths of WILLIAM
LIPSCOMB and PLEASANT YOUNGHUSBAND, the witnesses thereto, and ordered to be
recorded   Teste ADAM CRAIG C.C.

pp.   (On margin: WALLACE to JACKSON & Uc.)
365-   THIS INDENTURE WITNESSETH that ELIZABETH WALLACE with the consent and
366   approbation of her Mother, REBECCA WALLACE, hath put herself and by these
        presents doth voluntarily and of her own free will and accord, put herself Ap-
prentice to TOBY JACKSON and REBECCA his Wife to learn the Art, Trade & Mystery of a
Sempstress and after the manner of an Apprentice to serve the said TOBY JACKSON and
REBECCA his Wife from the day of the date hereof during the full term of Five years
during all which term the said Apprentice her said Master and Mistress faithfully shall
serve, and in all things behave herself as a faithful Apprentice ought to do, And the

said Master and Mistress shall use the utmost of their Endeavours to teach or cause to be
taught or instructed the said Apprentice in the Trade or Mystery of a Sempstrass and
procure and provide for her sufficient meat drink clothes washing and lodging fitting
for an Apprentice during the term of five years and to learn her to read and write and
Arithmetick as far as the Rule of Three, and at the expiration of her time of service to
be paid the fee of Three pounds Ten shillings and for the true performance of all the
agreements aforesaid, the parties bind themselves each to the other firmly by these
presents; In Witness whereof the said parties have interchangeably set their hands
and seals hereunto dated the Twenty seventh day of July in the year of our Lord one
thousand seven hundred and eighty nine
Sealed and Delivered in the presence of
        The Court   ELIZABETH her mark X WALLACE
                                               TOBY his mark ✝ JACKSON
                                               REBECCA her mark ✝ JACKSON

   At a Monthly Court of Hustings for the City of Richmond held at the Courthouse on
Monday the Twenty seventh of July 1789   This Indenture with the consent and approbation of the Court executed and acknowledged by the parties and ordered to be
recorded   Teste ADAM CRAIG C. C.

pp.   (On margin: PERKINS to DUGARD)
366-   THIS INDENTURE WITNESSETH that BEVERLEY PERKINS of the County of HENRI-
367   CO in the City of Richmond, aged Ten years, hath put himself and by these pre-
       doth voluntarily and of his own free will and accord put himself Apprentice to
ABRAHAM DUGARD in said County and City, to learn his Art Trade and Mystery, and
after the manner of an Apprentice to serve the said ABRAHAM DUGARD from the day of
the date hereof during the full term of Eleven years, during all which term the said Apprentice his Master faithfully shall serve and in all things behave himself as a faithful Apprentice ought to do, And the said Master shall use the utmost of his Endeavours
to teach or cause to be taught or instructed the said Apprentice in the Trade or Mystery
of a Taylor, reading, writing Arithmetick as far as the Rule of Three, and procure for
him sufficient meat drink clothes washing and lodging fitting for an Apprentice,
during the term of Eleven years, he said ABRAHAM DUGARD shall furnish the said
BEVERLEY PERKINS with a suit of clothes and Three pounds Ten shillings in Gold or
Silver, And for the true performance of all the agreements aforesaid, the parties bind
themselves each unto the other firmly by these presents; In Witness whereof the said
parties have interchangeably set their hands and seals hereunto Dated the Twenty
eighth day of April in the year of our Lord one tousand seven hundred and eighty nine
and in the thirteenth year of the Commonwealth
Sealed and Delivered in the presence of
        The Court   BEVERLEY his mark X PERKINS
                                               A. DUGARD

   At a Monthly Court of Hustings for the City of Richmond held at the Courthouse on
Monday the 27th of July 1789   This Indenture was with the consent and approbation
of the Court executed and acknowledged by the parties and ordered to be recorded
                          Teste ADAM CRAIG C. C.

pp.   (On margin: DUNSCOMB & Ux. to AUSTIN)
367-   THIS INDENTURE made the Eleventh day of April one thousand seven hundred
369   and eighty nine Between ANDREW DUNSCOMB and PHILADELPHIA his Wife of the
       City of Richmond of one part and CHAPMAN AUSTIN of County of HANOVER of

the other part; Witnesseth that ANDREW DUNSCOMB and PHILADELPHIA his Wife in consideration of the sum of Five hundred and Thirty one pounds current money to them in hand paid by CHAPMAN AUSTIN, by these presents doth bargain sell and confirm unto CHAPMAN AUSTIN his heirs a part of a lott of land situated in the City of Richmond on a Main Street that leads nearest to the Capitol and being a part of the lott number Four hundred and forty seven to adjoin the BRICK HOUSE of said DUNSCOMB and run forty one feet three inches on the said Street towards the Lott the property of DABNEY MILLER (which he leased to JOHN STOCKDELL and now in the possession of JAMES VAUGHAN) and seventy feet back from the said Street, Together with all privileges and appurtenances thereunto belonging; To have and to hold the part of a lott and premises with the appurtenances unto CHAPMAN AUSTIN his heirs; and ANDREW DUNSCOMB and PHILADELPHIA his Wife for themselves their heirs doth agree with CHAPMAN AUSTIN his heirs that he shall quietly hold the part of a lott and premises with the appurtenances free and clear from all incumbrance whatsoever, and said DUNSCOMB and PHILADELPHIA his Wife for themselves and their heirs shall warrant and for ever defend the part of a lott and premises with the appurtenances unto CHAPMAN AUSTIN his heirs from all persons that shall lay any claim thereunto; in Witness whereof the said ANDREW DUNSCOMB and PHILADELPHIA his Wife have hereunto set their hands and affixed their seals the day and year above written
Sealed and Delivered in presence of
    HUGH FRENCH,   SAMUEL DUVAL,   AW. DUNSCOMB
    FRANCIS RATLIFF, JESSE BOWLES,   PHILA: DUNSCOMB
    BENJA: OLIVER JR.,   WILLIAM MINOR
  The Commonwealth of Virginia to THOMAS B. ADAMS, DAVID LAMBERT and ROBERT BOYD, Gentlemen, Justices of the Court of Hustings for the City of Richmond, Greeting; Whereas (the Commission for the privy examination of PHILADELPHIA, the Wife of ANDREW DUNSCOMB); Witness ADAM CRAIG, Clerk of our said Court the 29th day of June 1789 in the 13th year of the Commonwealth   ADAM CRAIG, C.C.
  In Obedience to the within Commission to us directed, we have personally waited on the within named PHILADELPHIA DUNSCOMB, Wife of the within named ANDREW DUNSCOMB, and examined her privily and apart from the said ANDREW DUNSCOMB (the return of the execution of the privy examination of PHILADELPHIA DUNSCUMB); Certified under our hands and seals this 29th day of July 1789   T. B. ADAMS
                                               DAVD: LAMBERT
  At a Court of Hustings for the City of Richmond held at the Courthouse on Monday the 28th day of September 1789   This Indenture was proved by the Oaths of FRANCIS RAT-LIFFE, BENJAMIN OLIVER JR. and WILLIAM MINOR, witnesses thereto, and together with the Commission annexed and the Certificate of the execution thereof are ordered to be recorded   Teste ADAM CRAIG, C.C.

pp.   (On margin: MURRAY with CRAWFORD)
370-   ARTICLES of AGREEMENT made this thirtieth day of May one thousand seven
371   hundred and eighty nine Between SIMON MURRAY of City of Richmond of one
        part and JOHN CRAWFORD of said City of other part; Witnesseth that SIMON MUR-RAY hath demised granted and to Rent unto JOHN CRAWFORD a certain Tenement joining the corner of MARKET ALLEY in the said City, which now CHARLES BOYLE occupies (that is to say a part) and that the said SIMON MURRAY doth hereby covenant and agree for himself his heirs &c. that JOHN CRAWFORD his heirs shall occupy the demised Tenement for the term of two years and nine months from the above date from any molestation for the consideration of the sum of Twenty pounds in hand paid, whereby

the said SIMON MURRAY acknowledges to have received for to clear his Ground Rent
due to NICHOLAS SEABROOKE, And it is further agreed by JOHN CRAWFORD his heirs &c.
to pay Quarterly unto NICHOLAS SEABROOKE the Ground Rent that may be due from the
first day of taking possession of said Tenement; And it is further agreed that JOHN
CRAWFORD do pay unto NICHOLAS B. SEABROOKE five pounds quarterly supposing that
sum to be due for Ground Rent at the end of the year should it be more or less, And it is
further agreed by each party that if NICHOLAS B. SEABROOKE should refuse the Ground
Rent that is due from JOHN CRAWFORD, then JOHN CRAWFORD shall pay the said SIMON
MURRAY the money that is due for the Ground Rent; In Witness whereof each of the
parties have set their hands and seals this thirtieth day of May one thousand seven
hundred and eighty nine
Signed Sealed and Delivered in presence of
    JOHN V. KAUTZMAN,   SIMON MURRAY
    GEORGE TODD, WILLIAM TODD   JNO: CRAWFORD
At a Court of Hustings for the City of Richmond held at the Courthouse on Monday the
26th of October 1789   These Articles of Agreement were proved by the Oaths of GEORGE
TODD and WILLIAM TODD, witnesses thereto, and ordered to be recorded
              Teste ADAM CRAIG, C. C.

pp.   (On margin: QUARRIER & Wife to GRAY. Deld. GEO: GRAY Decr. 7, '99)
371-   THIS INDENTURE made this Twelfth day of November in the year of our Lord
378   one thousand seven hundred and eighty nine Between ALEXANDER QUARRIER of
        City of Richmond in the State of Virginia, Coach Maker, and ELIZABETH his Wife
of one part and GEORGE GRAY of the same City of other part; Witnesseth that in consideration of the sum of Five shillings current money of Virginia by GEORGE GRAY to
ALEXANDER QUARRIER and ELIZABETH his Wife in hand paid; and for the further consideration intent and purpose of efectually securing so far as may be the payment to
WILLIAM ALEXANDER of City of Richmond, Merchant, of the full sum of One thousand
four hundred and eighty five pounds current money which ALEXANDER QUARRIER now
justly owes to said WILLIAM ALEXANDER for articles of Merchandize imported by WIL-
LIAM ALEXANDER at the special instance and request of ALEXANDER QUARRIER and to
him now delivered, at such periods and with such interest as hereafter is mentioned, to
wit, the sum of three hundred and seventy one pounds five shillings on the first day of
April in the year one thousand seven hundred and Ninety with lawful interest from
that time, the sum of Four hundred and twenty six pounds eighteen shillings and nine
pence on the first day of April in the year one thousand seven hundred and Ninety one;
with lawful interest from that time, the sum of Four hundred and eight pounds seventeen shillings and six pence on the first day of April in the year one thousand seven
hundred and Ninety two with lawful interest from that period, and the sum of Three
hundred and eighty nine pounds sixteen shillings and three pence on the first day of
April in the year one thousand seven hundred and Ninety three with lawful interest
from that time. In case the payments shall not be punctually made, said ALEXANDER
QUARRIER and ELIZABETH his Wife do by these presents bargain and sell unto GEORGE
GRAY three lots of land in City of Richmond distinguished in the plan thereof by the
numbers Five hundred and seven (507), Five hundred and Twenty five (525), Five hundred and Twenty seven (527), each containing or supposed to contain half an acre,
being the same which are now in possession and occupation of said ALEXANDER QUAR-
RIER and which were heretofore purchased by him, to wit, the two former from WIL-
LIAM DUVAL and the latter from JOHN HARVIE Esqrs., with all houses dwelling houses,
kitchens, outhouses, coach houses workshops, warehouses, improvements and appurte-

nances belonging; To have and to hold the lots of land and all other the premises and appurtenances unto GEORGE GRAY his heirs, IN TRUST, and for the express uses herein after expressed, that is to say, First that in case ALEXANDER QUARRIER his heirs do fail to pay WILLIAM ALEXANDER or assigns the sum of Fourteen hundred and Eighty five pounds current money by instalments agreeable to the respective proportions and at the periods before expressed, and shall be deficient in the payment in whole or in part of any instalment for the space of six calender months beyond the day the instalment ought to have been paid, said GEORGE GRAY his heirs shall sell and dispose of the lots premises and appurtenances at Public Auction in City of Richmond for ready money or otherwise as WILLIAM ALEXANDER shall require, six weeks notice of such sale having been previously given in one or more of the Virginia Gazettes and out of the proceeds of such sale, after discharging thereout all expences accruing upon the execution of the trust, shall pay so far as such proceeds may be adequate thereto so much of the sum of One thousand four hundred and eighty five pounds with the interest thereon as may and shall at time of such sale be remaining unpaid; Secondly, that all excess in the proceeds to be paid to said QUARRIER his heirs, and Lastly ALEXR: QUARRIER his heirs producing a Receipt to GEORGE GRAY his heirs or other discharge of the aforesaid Debt and interest from WILLIAM ALEXANDER or assigns the aforesaid lots and premises being then unsold, said GEORGE GRAY his heirs will reconvey to ALEXANDER QUARRIER or to his heirs in fee simple by good and sufficient Deed or Deeds to be made out at his or their expence; In Witness whereof the parties to this Indenture have hereunto set their hands and affixed their seals the day and year first herein written
Signed Sealed and delivered in presence of
ANDW: RONALD, J. B. DANDRIDGE,   ALEXR: QUARRIER
RD. SMYTH, ROBT. ALEXANDER   ELIZABETH QUARRIER
                                         GEORGE GRAY

Received 12th November 1789 from GEORGE GRAY in this Indenture named the sum of five shillings being in full of the consideration money for the lots and other estate hereby granted   L. 0...5...0.
Witnesses ANDW: RONALD,   ALEXR: QUARRIER
J. B. DANDRIDGE

The Commonwealth of Virignia to DAVID LAMBERT, JOHN GUNN and SAMUEL McCRAW Gentlemen, Justices of the Court of Hustings for the City of Richmond, Greeting; Whereas (the Commission for the privy examination of ELIZABETH, the Wife of ALEXANDER QUARRIER); Witness ADAM CRAIG, Clerk of our said Court the 20th day of November 1789 in the 14th year of the Commonwealth   ADAM CRAIG, C.C.

Pursuant ot the within Commission to us directed, we have examined the within named ELIZABETH QUARRIER, Wife of the within named ALEXANDER QUARRIER, and she the said ELIZABETH freely relinquished her right of Dower in the land and premises within conveyed (the return of the execution of the privy examination of ELIZABETH QUARRIER); Given under our hands and seals this 21st day of November 1789, we the Subscribers having previously read the said Deed and explained the purport thereof to the said ELIZABETH
                SAML: McCRAW
                JOHN GUNN

At a Quarterly Court of Hustings for the City of Richmond held at the Courthosue the 25th day of November 1789   This Deed of Trust was acknowledged by ALEXANDER QUARRIER and GEORGE GRAY, parties thereto, and together with the Receipt thereon endorsed, which was also acknowledged by the said ALEXANDER QUARRIER and (blank) the Commission annexed and the Certificate of execution thereof, ordered to be recorded
                Teste ADAM CRAIG, C.C.

pp.   (On margin: DUVAL & Ux. to QUARRIER)
378-
379   THIS INDENTURE made this thirtieth day of June Anno Domini one thousand seven hundred and eighty nine Between WILLIAM DUVAL and ANNE his Wife of County of HENRICO of one part and ALEXANDER QUARRIER of City of Richmond of other part; Witnesseth that WILLIAM DUVAL and ANNE his Wife in consideration of the sum of (blank) to them in hand paid by ALEXANDER QUARRIER, by these presents do bargain sell and confirm unto ALEXANDER QUARRIER his heirs three certain half acre lots lying in City of Richmond and known in the plan of the City by the numbers 508, 325 & (blank), To have and to hold the two half acre lots with all its appurtenances thereunto belonging to ALEXANDER QUARRIER his heirs and WILLIAM DUVAL and ANNE his Wife the three lots with all its appurtenances thereunto belonging against themselves and their heirs and against the claim of any person to ALEXANDER QUARRIER his heirs by these presents shall warrant and for ever defend; In Witness whereof the said WILLIAM DUVAL and ANNE his Wife have hereunto set their hands and affixed their seals the day month and year above written
Signed Sealed and delivered in presence of

    T. POPE,   WILLIAM DUVAL
    ELIZA: DAVIS   ANNE DUVAL

At a Quarterly Court of Hustings for the City of Richmond held at the Courthouse on Monday the twenty third day of November 1789   This Indenture was acknowledged by WILLIAM DUVAL, one of the parties thereto, and ordered to be recorded
             Teste ADAM CRAIG, C. C.

pp.   (On margin: SEPNOR to MURCHIE)
379-
381   THIS INDENTURE made this twenty ninth day of August Anno Domini one thousand seven hundred and Eighty nine Between HENRY SEPNOR of City of Richmond of one part and JOHN MURCHIE of the Town of MANCHESTER in County of CHESTERFIELD of other part; Witnesseth that HENRY SEPNOR in consideration of One hundred and thirty pounds current money of Virginia to him in hand paid by JOHN MURCHIE, by these presents doth bargain and sell unto JOHN MURCHIE his heirs the following slaves, to wit, Molly, Ned, Scint, Hugh and Jone and their increase, with the consent and approbation of JOSEPH CORYELL certified by his being a party hereto; To have and to hold all the slaves with their increase to said JOHN MURCHIE his heirs PROVIDED NEVERTHELESS that if HENRY SEPNOR his heirs shall pay or cause to be paid unto JOHN MURCHIE his heirs the amount of Three Judgments which JOHN MURCHIE obtained as Assignee of JAMES CALLOWAY, against the said HENRY SEPNOR in the County Court of CHESTERFIELD, which three Judgments it is supposed may amount with the interest and costs to about One hundred and thirty pounds current money of Virginia, which may more certainly appear reference being had to the Records of said County Court, which payment HENRY SEPNOR obliges himself his heirs to make to JOHN MURCHIE with all interest and costs of said suits on or before the twenty fifth day of December Anno Domini one thousand seven hundred and eighty nine with the costs and charges of drawing & recording this Deed of Mortgage, then this Deed of Mortgage to be null and void, otherwise to remain in full force; In Witness whereof the said HENRY SEPNOR and JOSEPH CORYELL have hereunto set their hands and affixed their seals the day month and year first above written
Signed Sealed and delivered in the presence of

    WM: DUVAL,   ARTHUR STEWART,   HENRY SEPNOR
    JOHN CLARK

At a Quarterly Court of Hustings for the City of Richmond held at the Courthouse on
Tuesday the twenty fourth of November 1789   This Mortgage was proved by the Oaths
of WILLIAM DUVAL and ARTHUR STEWART, two of the witnesses thereto and ordered to
be recorded   Teste ADAM CRAIG, C.C.

pp.   (On margin: LAMBERT & Ux. to RONALD)
381-   THIS INDENTURE TRIPARTITE made this twenty fourth day of November in the
386   year of our Lord one thousand seven hundred and eighty nine Between DAVID
         LAMBERT of City of Richmond and SALLY his Wife of the first part; BENJAMIN
DUVAL of the same City of the second part; And ANDREW RONALD of the same City of the
third part; Witnesseth that whereas said BENJAMIN heretofore purchased from said
DAVID a certain piece of ground or part of two lots of land herein after described and
conveyed for the sum of Four hundred and fifty pounds current money of Virginia,
upon condition that said BENJAMIN should have no right to demand a legal Conveyance
for the same until the whole of the said purchase money with all interest accruing
thereon should be paid up and satisfied to said DAVID, And that the piece of ground with
all the improvements which might be made thereon should remain vested in the said
DAVID as a security to him for the payment of said purchase money and interest; since
the time of which agreement, the said BENJAMIN hath been in the actual possession of
said piece of ground and hath built and erected a Dwelling House with sundry out
houses and made other improvements thereon; And part of the purchase money, to wit,
the sum of Three hundred and thirteen pounds, one shilling, bearing interest from the
eighth day of August which was in the year one thousand seven hundred and eighty
eight for which a Judgment of that date was obtained by said DAVID against said BENJA-
MIN in the Court of HENRICO County; And Whereas said DAVID is at this time indebted to
a certain JOHN BOUSH and ROBERT BOUSH, Executors of SAMUEL BOUSH, and assignees of
WILLIAM PENNOCK in the sum of Two hundred & forty one pounds with interst thereon
from the tenth day of July in the year one thousand seven hundred and eighty seven &
also the sum of One pounds twelve shillings and ten pence half penny as by Judgment
of HENRICO County Court obtained against the said DAVID in the month of August last
may appear; And Whereas said BENJAMIN is altogether unable to discharge his debt
aforesaid to said DAVID except by a Sale of the piece of ground with the buildings and
improvements thereon without which said DAVID cannot dischage the Debt aforesaid to
said JOHN and ROBERT BOUSH, THIS INDENTURE THEREFORE Farther Witnesseth that in
consideration of the several sums of Five shillings and of Five shillings current money
to DAVID LAMBERT and his aforesaid Wife, and to BENJAMIN DUVAL in hand paid by
ANDREW RONALD for the purpose of securing said JOHN and ROBERT and to DAVID LAM-
BERT the speedy payment of the debts, said DAVID LAMBERT & Wife and said BENJAMIN
DUVAL do release and confirm unto ANDREW RONALD his heirs all that piece of ground
or part of two lots of land, situate on the North East side of the Main Street in the City of
Richmond which begins at the corner of JOSIASH ISAACS's Lot or piece of ground and
runs thence up along the said Street to ANNE EGE's lot, thence along ANNE EGE's lot to
the Middle Street, thence along the Middle Street thirty three feet to ISAIAH ISAACS's
thence along the line of said ISAACS to the beginning, they being part of the lots Thirty Three and Forty Seven as will appear by the plan of this City, with all houses outhouses, kitchens, cellars, yards, gardens and appurtenances belonging; To have and to
hold the granted piece of ground or part of two lots of land with all other the premises
and appurtenances to ANDREW RONALD his heirs, IN TRUST, and upon this special confidence that ANDREW RONALD his heirs shall as soon after the first day of May next (but
not before) as to him or them may seem proper and convenient, sell and dispose of the

piece of ground and other premsies and appurtenances herein before granted to the
highest bidder by Public Sale in the City of Richmond (such sale having been first
three times advertised in some one or more of the Richmond Newspapers) for ready
money or Tobacco, for Military Certificates or upon Credit as to said RONALD his heirs
shall appear best and most eligible or as JOHN and ROBERT BOUSH or the survivor of
them may advize and authorize without controul therein of said DAVID and BENJAMIN
and out of the proceeds of the sale (after defraying the charge of this Indenture and all
other costs and expences attending the execution of this Trust) so far as the same may
extend, shall in the first place pay to JOHN and ROBERT BOUSH the sum of Two hundred
and forty one pounds current money with interest thereon from the tenth day of July
one thousand seven hundred and eighty seven; also the sum of One pound, twelve shillings and ten pence half penny, these two sums being the amount due from said DAVID
LAMBERT to JOHN and ROBERT BOUSH and which when paid will discharge so much of
the debt as aforesaid which is due from BENJAMIN DUVAL to said DAVID; And the said
DAVID his heirs shall warrant and defend the granted land and premises against all
persons whomsoever to said ANDREW RONALD his heirs; In Witness whereof the parties
to these presents have hereunto set their hands & affixed their seals the day & year
first in this Indenture written
Signed Sealed and delivered in the presence of
    JACOB EGE,   DAVID LAMBERT
                                 SALLY LAMBERT
                                 BENJA: DUVAL

    Richmond 27th July 1789. We hereby acknowledge each for himself to have this day
received from ANDREW RONALD in the within Indenture named the sum of Five shillings being in full of the consideration money for the land thereby conveyed
                                 DAVID LAMBERT
                                 BENJ: DUVAL

    At a Quarterly Court of Hustings for the City of Richmond held at the Courthouse on
Tuesday the twenty fourth of November 1789   This Indenture together with the
Receipt thereon endorsed was acknowledged by DAVID LAMBERT and BENJAMIN DUVAL,
parties thereto, and ordered to be recorded
                Teste ADAM CRAIG C.C.

pp.   (On margin: McCRAW to MEANS)
386-   THIS INDENTURE made this nineteenth day of May in the year of our Lord one
387   thousand seven hundred and eighty nine Between SAMUEL McCRAW of City of
        Richmond of one part and ROBERT MEANS of the said City of other part; Witnes-
seth that SAMUEL McCRAW in consideration of the sum of Seven hundred and fifty
pounds in hand paid by ROBERT MEANS, by these presents doth bargain sell and confirm unto ROBERT MEANS his heirs a certain piece or parcel of ground containing One
hundred and Six feet in front and one hundred and sixty five back lying on the Main
Street on SHOCKOE HILL in the city of Richmond, and being part of a lot known in the
plan of said City by number Six hundred Sixty One, in figures (661), and being the same
which McCRAW purchased of JOSHUA MORRIS; To have and to hold the parcel of ground
with all buildings improvements and appurtenances thereunto belonging to ROBERT
MEANS his heirs; And SAMUEL McCRAW for himself his heirs doth covenant and agree
with ROBERT MEANS and his heirs that he will warrant and for ever defend the right
and title of the bargained and sold premises free from the lawful claim of all persons;
In Witness whereof the said SAMUEL McCRAW hath hereunto set his hand and affixed
his seal the day and year in this Indenture written

Signed Sealed and delivered in presence of
      EDM: THOMAS; JNO: STREET,   SAML; McCRAW
      W. MARSHALL JR. ROBERT B. VOSS
  It is understood that his Deed is meant to include the House now repairing by C. W.
STEPHENSON
Teste EDM: THOMAS,   SAML: McCRAW
    JNO: STREET, WM: PRICE
  At a Court of Hustings for the City of Richmond held at the Courthouse on Tuesday the
twenty fourth of November 1789   This Indenture together with the Memorandum
thereunto written was acknowledged by SAMUEL McCRAW one of the parties thereto,
and ordered to be recorded   Teste (no signature)

p.   (On margin: WARINGTON & KEENE to Abraham)
388   TO ALL TO WHOM these presents may concern, Know ye that we JAMES WARING-
       TON and THOMAS KEENE, Merchants of the City of Richmond, in consideration of
the sum of Forty pounds current money of Virginia to us in hand paid by Slave Abraham do by these presents Emancipate him, the said Abraham, commonly called and
known by the name of ABRAHAM SKIPWITH, and do as far as the Laws of Virginia will
admit, vest him with all the rights and privileges of a free born Citizen of the same,
clear from the claim of our heirs or any other person: And do by these presents warrant and for ever defend the freedom as aforesaid to the said ABRAHAM SKIPWITH. In
Witness whereof we have hereunto set our hands and seals this 28th day of December
one thousand seven hundred and eighty nine
Signed Sealed and delivered in the presence of
    (no witnesses recorded)   THOS: KEENE
                 for WARINGTON & KEENE
  At a Court of Hustings for the City of Richmond held at the Courthosue on Monday the
Twenty eighth day of December 1789   This Deed of Emancipation was acknowledged
by THOMAS KEENE one of the parties thereto and ordered to be recorded
             Teste ADAM CRAIG, C.C.

p.   (On margin: DRAKE to GOFF)
389   KNOW ALL MEN by these presents that I JOHN DRAKE being possessed of a
       Negro man named Moses, Now Know ye that I said JOHN DRAKE by these presents
do constitute and appoint Mr. PHILIP GOFF my true and lawful Attorney for me and in
my name to sell the said slave, Moses, to such person or persons as may bargain with
him for the said Negro, and also for me and in my name to make absolute sale and dispose of the said Negro man and give such Bill of Sale as may be required by the purcha-
ser. And I do hereby ratify and confirm the bargain and sale which shall be made by
my Attorney concerning the Negro man. In Witness whereof, I hereunto set my hand
and seal this thirty first of December one thousand seven hundred and eighty nine
Signed Sealed and delivered in presence of
    HENRY SEPNOR,   JNO: DRAG
    PETER LENEVE
  At a Monthly Court of Hustings for the City of Richmond held at the Courthosue on
Monday the twenty fifth day of January 1790   This Power of Attorney was proved by
the Oath of HENRY SEPNOR, one of the witnesses thereto, and ordered to be recorded
             Teste ADAM CRAIG C.C.

pp.   (On margin: HUGH PATTON's Will)
390-   I HUGH PATTON of the City of Richmond and Commonwealth of Virginia being
393   sick of Body but of sound mind, memory and understanding do make and pub-
        lish this my Last Will and Testament in manner and form following. First, my
will and desire is that immediately after my decease, an Inventory shall be taken of all
the Goods in the Store now under the Firm of PATTON and HOWARD, which Inventory
shall be taken according as they are charged in the Books, and my will and desire is
that C. P. HOWARD, my present Partner, shall enter into Bond with my Executors and
Executrix hereafter mentioned for the payment of all the Goods according to the
Appraisement equal to six several payments, to wit, the first payment to be made at the
expiration of six months, the second at the expiration of nine months, the third at the
expiration of twelve months, the fourth at the expiration of fifteen months, the fifth at
the expiration of eighteen months, and the sixth and last at the expiration of Twenty
four months; Also my will and desire is that an Inventory shall be taken of the Goods in
the Store now carried on in the name of THOMAS HOOPER, and for the said HOOPER to
enter into Bond with my Executors and Executrix in form and manner as with CHARLES
P. HOWARD as before directed;
  Second, My will and desire is that my said Executors and Executrix or the Survivors of
them shall sell at Public Auction for ready money in the City of PHILADELPHIA, my
House and Lots, lying in SPRING GARDEN in the State of PENSYLVANIA, at present in the
occupation of JOHN McMIN. Also, my will and desire is that my said Executors and Executrix shall not sell or dispose of any Public Securities of which I may die possessed
until all my other affairs are settled after my decease, and that they shall draw the interest that may accrue within the said term on all or any of the said Public Securites,
which interest money they may if they deem it beneficial for may Estate lay out in the
purchase of other Public Securites; And at the expiration of the time that may be necessary for the selling of my business, although I am satisfied that the Goods and Merchandize in the two Stores herein before mentioned together with my outstanding
debts are greatly more than sufficient to pay all my just Debts owing from me, yet from
a desire that no Creditor of mine shall remain unpaid, I do subject (in case of a
deficiency) the before mentioned Public Securites to the payment of my Debts at the
period before mentioned; Also my desire is that my Executors shall with all convenient
dispatch collect all debts due to me and whatever part of the debts shall remain uncol-
lected at the expiration of Two years and a half after my death, together with all Bonds
or Notes that may be taken payable to my Executors herein after mentioned, shall be by
them sold at Public Auction to the highest bidder for ready money, And after my just
debts are paid, my will is that the proceeds of all my Goods and Merchanidze shall be
divided in five equal parts, two fifths of which I give and bequeath unto my Son, HUGH
PATTON, and the remaining three fifths I give and bequeath in equal portions to my
Wife, ELIZABETH, my Daughter, AGNESS, and my Daughter, MARY. The proceeds of the
sale of all my Public Securites before mentioned with whatever interest money may be
drawn for the said Public Securities, and the proceeds of the Sale of my House and Lots
aforesaid with every other kind of property, my will is shall be divided in five equal
parts, two fifths I give to my Son, HUGH PATTON, and the remaining three fifths I give
and bequeath to my Wife, ELIZABETH, my Daughter, AGNESS, and my Daughter, MARY.
I give and bequeath to my Wife, ELIZABETH, all my household furniture and my Negro
man slave named Harrison, together with my horse, saddle and bridle. I give and bequeath to my Mother, MARY PATTON, twenty pounds Sterling money, but in case of her
death, it is to go to my Sister, MARGARET. I give and bequeath to AGNESS KAY, (my
Mother's Mother), twenty pounds Sterling money but in case of her death it is to be
divided between my Wife and Children as aforesaid;

I appoint my good and worthy Friends, ANDREW NOBLE and HUGH CARD of the Parish of MAUCHLIN and HUGH PATTON and JOHN THOMPSON of the Parish of LOUDEN in North Britain, Guardians to my three Children herein before mentioned during their minority. My will is that immediately after the expiration of two years and a half from the time of my death, that my Executors shall pay to the Guardians herein appointed to my Children, my said Childrens several portions herein alloted to the, which said several portions or Legacies to my said Children I desire shall be placed by their said Guardians in the BANK of SCOTLAND, and that my said three Children shall be maintained and educated with the interest arising therefrom until they shall respectively attain to lawful age or marry, at which time or times their several portions or Legacies shall be delivered to them.

And I do appoint by this my Last Will and Testament (wherein all others revoked) my dear Wife, ELIZABETH PATTON, my Executrix, and my Worthy Friends, WILLIAM MITCHELL and JAMES BROWN, my Executors.

Signed Sealed, published & declared by   Richmond, January the sixteenth
HUGH PATTON as his Last Will and   one thousand seven hundred and
Testament in presence of us   ninety
        CHARLES P. HOWARD, JAMES DOVE,   HUGH PATTON
        BARTLETT STILL, THO: HOOPER,
        CALLOM JONES

At a Monthly Court of Hustings for the City of Richmond held at the Courthouse on Monday the twenty second of February 1790. This Will was proved by the Oaths of JAMES DOVE, THOMAS HOOPER and CALLOM JONES, witnesses thereto, and ordered to be recorded. Whereupon ELIZABETH PATTON, the Executrix, and WILLIAM MITCHELL, an Executor named in the said Will, relinquished their right of Executorship under the said Will, the said Executrix by a Writing under her hand and seal which was proved by CALLOM JONES and CHARLES P. HOWARD, the witnesses thereto, And the said MITCHELL in person, And on the motion of JAMES BROWN, the other Executor named in the said Will, who made Oath thereto, and Together with WILLIAM MITCHELL, THOMAS KEENE and WILLIAM FENWICK, his securites, entered into and acknowledged their Bond in the penalty of Twenty thousand pounds conditioned as the Law directs, Certificate is granted them for obtaining a Probat thereof in due form
                Teste ADAM CRAIG, C.C.

pp.   (On margin: LIPSCOMB & Ux. to JORDAN)
393-   THIS INDENTURE TRIPARTITE made this twenty third day of January Anno
397   Domini one thousand seven hundred and Ninety, Between WILLIAM LIPSCOMB
        of the City of Richmond of one part and SARAH LIPSCOMB, his Wife of the City aforesaid of the second part, and NOBLE JORDAN of the County of HENRICO of the third part; Witnesseth that Whereas some unhappy differences have lately arisen betwixt the said WILLIAM LIPSCOMB and SARAH his Wife and they have mutually agreed to live seperate and apart from each other, And the said WILLIAM LIPSCOMB hath consented to convey in fee simple one moiety of his Estate, both real and personal, to the said NOBLE JORDAN in Trust for the said SARAH's support and benefit in lieu of any Dower that the said SARAH may or might be entitled to in case she should survive the said WILLIAM LIPSCOMB: NOW THIS INDENTURE Witnesseth that WILLIAM LIPSCOMB in pursuance of the aforesaid proposal and agreement and in consideration of the sum of Five shillings current money of Virginia to him in hand paid by NOBLE JORDAN on behalf of the said SARAH, as her Trustee, by these presents doth bargain and sell unto NOBLE JORDAN his heirs in Trust for the sole use and benefit of said SARAH, her heirs, one moiety of an

half acre lott number 52, Fifty Two, lying in City of Richmond with the Corner House
thereon wherein Mr. WYATT now lives, the said lott to be equally divided, leaving out
the other houses on said lott and bounded, Beginning at the North East side of the lot
and running nearly a Southwesterly course so as to divide it as nearly equal as may be,
and the following slaves, Horse, goods and chattels, household and kitchen furniture,
that is to say, a Negro fellow named Ben, and a Negro wench named Annica, one bay
Mare with one womans saddle and bridle with the furniture thereto belonging; one
riding chair with all the harness thereto belonging; four feather beds and their furniture complete, four bedsteads and bed cords, two tables, one dozen chairs, eighteen
plates, five dishes, one dozen spoons, one dozen knives and forks, three iron pots and all
other articles contained in a Schedule hereto annexed, and one moiety of Five hundred
pounds, which are due to him in Bonds, Bills, Notes and open Accounts, to be fairly and
justly divided, one moiety of which he doth assign and transfer to said NOBLE JORDAN
his heirs in Trust for the sole use and benefit of said SARAH her heirs; To have and to
hold one moiety of the said lott and house with its appurtenances, the said slaves with
their increase, and all the goods and chattels and one moiety of said debts to him the
said NOBLE JORDAN his heirs for said SARAH her heirs free from the claim and demand
of WILLIAM LIPSCOMB his heirs, And WILLIAM LIPSCOMB in pursuance of his proposal
and Agreement doth hereby for himself his heirs promise and agree to and with NOBLE
JORDAN, the said Trustee, and assignes, and doth also agree with said SARAH his Wife in
manner and form following, that is to say, that it shall and may be lawful to and for said
SARAH his Wife and that he said WILLIAM LIPSCOMB shall permit and suffer said
SARAH at all times from henceforth during her natural life to live seperate and apart
from him and to reside and be in such place and in such family and with such relations
friends and other persons and to follow and to carry on such trade and business as said
SARAH from time to time at her will and pleasure notwithstanding her present cover-
ture and as if she was a feme sole and unmarried shall think it, and that WILLIAM LIPS-
COMB shall not at any time sue her in any Court for living seperate and apart from him
or compel her to cohabit with him, trouble her for living seperate from him, nor shall
without the consent of said SARAH visit her or knowingly come into any House or place
where she shall or may dwell or be, nor claim any part of said lot slaves personal estate
good and chattels before mentioned; And if the said SARAH shall survive the said WIL-
LIAM LIPSCOMB that then it is agreed between WILLIAM LIPSCOMB and NOBLE JORDAN
that immediately after the said event that said SARAH her heirs shall be possessed of all
the Estate herein given by said WILLIAM absolutely free and dischrged from the Trust
aforesaid; And NOBLE JORDAN doth oblige himself his heirs that in consideration of the
provision herein before made by said WILLIAM to said SARAH, that said SARAH in case
she should outlive said WILLIAM her heirs shall not claim Dower out of the State of said
WILLIAM after his death and that she shall be utterly excluded therefrom unless said
WILLIAM should by Deed in his life time or by his Last Will and Testament give or devise his other Estate to her which is not comprized in this Deed; In Witness whereof
said WILLIAM LIPSCOMB, SARAH LIPSCOMB and NOBLE JORDAN have hereunto
respectively set their hands and affixed their seals the day month and year above
written
Signed Sealed and delivered in the presence of us
        WM: ROSE.   WM: DUVAL,   WILLIAM LIPSCOMB
        DAVID LAMBERT   SARAH LIPSCOMB
                                                   NOBLE JORDAN

    1790. January 23rd. Received of NOBLE JORDAN, Trustee for SARAH LIPSCOMB, the
within sum of Five shillings current money of Virginia, the consideration within
mentioned

Teste WM: ROSE, WM: DUVAL,   WILLIAM LIPSCOMB
         DAVID LAMBERT
(Schedule refered to in the within Deed and annexed)
One small Pine table, one Dressing Glass, one Tea Board and Waiter, two brass candle
stands, one tea spoon and one table spoon, Silver, one Water Pitcher, three Beer glasses,
two salt cellars, one pair of sugar tongs, one milk pot, one tea canaster, two pewter
dishes, two pewter basons, one safe, one pair of fire tongs and shovel, one Tea Kettle,
Chocolate Pot, one Queen's China Bowl, seven saucers and three cups.
    The above Schedule is not mentioned in the Indenture that is between WILLIAM and
SARAH LIPSCOMB. January 25th 1790   REUBEN GEORGE
    At a Monthly Court of Hustings for the City of Richmond held at the Courthouse on
Monday the twenty second of February 1790   This Deed of Trust with the Receipt
thereon endorsed were proved by the Oaths of WILLIAM ROSE, WILLIAM DUVAL and
DAVID LAMBERT, the witnesses thereto, together with the Schedule annexed, are
ordered to be recorded   Teste ADAM CRAIG C.C.

pp.   (On margin: GRAVES & Ux. to DUVAL)
398-   THIS INDENTURE made this twenty sixth day of November Anno Domini one
399   thousand seven hundred and eighty nine Between FRANCIS GRAVES and
        MARTHA his Wife of City of Richmond of one part and WILLIAM DUVAL of Coun-
ty aforesaid of other part; Witnesseth that FRANCIS GRAVES and MARTHA his Wife in
consideration of the sum of Twelve thousand five hundred and fifty nine pounds in
Military Commutaion Certificates to them in hand paid, by these presents do bargain
and sell unto WILLIAM DUVAL his heirs the following Tenements and Houses lying in
City of Richmond, that is to say, the Tenement with a large corner House thereon at the
corner of the Main Street beginning at DOCTOR WILLIAM FOUSHEE's Tenement on the
Main Street, thence South fourteen degrees West fifty five feet on DOCTOR FOUCHEE's
line, thence South seventy four and one half degrees East forty eight feet on a line that
was formerly HENRY BANKS's to the Cross Street leading from MAYO's BRIDGE by
ALEXANDER DONALD's House, thence along the said Cross Street North eighteen degrees
East thirty three and one half degrees East to the Main Street, thence up the Main Street
fifty four and one quarter feet to the beginning. Also the BRICK STORE HOUSES at
present occupied by SAMUEL PAINE and JOHN & THOMAS GILLIATT, extending up the
Main Street forty three feet to an Alley, thence along the Alley to a Lane or Street
leading from the Cross Street to THOMAS SOWELL's to the Capitol, including the BRICK
LUMBER HOUSE and Kitchen at presence occupied by the said PAINE and GILLIATTs, including all said FRANCIS GRAVES's ground or tenements between the said Lane leading
to said Capitol and the said Main Street that the said GRAVES has any right to or interest
in either in Law or in Equity, and also the Tenement and Houses thereon, which said
GRAVES purchased of the Commonwealth known by Number Fifteen lying one hundred
and forty feet on an Alley beginning at the lower line of lots number twelve and thirteen and running along the said line seventy one and one half feet, thence at nearly a
paralel line with said Alley so as to leave eighty two feet on the Street running down to
the River and up to its intersection with said Alley as by reference to a plan signed by
the Commissioners and recorded in HENRICO COURT will fully appear; To have and to
hold the lots, houses and Alleys with all appurtenances thereunto belonging unto WIL-
LIAM DUVAL his heirs; In Witness whereof they the said FRANCIS GRAVES and MARTHA
his Wife have hereunto set their hands and affixed their seals the day month and year
first above written

Signed sealed and delivered in presence of us
SAML. BELL. SAMUEL DUVAL,   FRANCIS GRAVES
T. POPE. SAML: DUVAL JUNR.

At a Monthly Court of Hustings for the City of Richmond held at the Courthouse on
Monday the twenty second of February 1790   This Indenture was acknowledged by
FRANCIS GRAVES, one of the parties thereto, and ordered to be recorded
Teste ADAM CRAIG, C. C.

pp.   (On margin: LYONS to NICE)
400-   THIS INDENTURE Witnesseth that DIXON LYONS, Orphan of JOHN LYONS deceased,
401   hath put himself and by these presents doth voluntarily and of his own free
        will and accord put himself Apprentice to WILLIAM NICE (Hatter) to learn his
Art, Trade and Mystery, and after the manner of an Apprentice to serve the said WIL-
LIAM NICE from the day of the day hereof for and during the term of seven years or
until he shall arrive to the age of Twenty one years; during all which term said Apprentice his said Master faithfully shall serve and in all things behave himself as a
faithful Apprentice ought to do; And said MARTIN shall use his utmost endeavours to
teach or cause to be taught or instructed the said Apprentice in the Trade or Mystery of
a Hatter, and to cause said Apprentice to be taught reading and writing and Arithmatic
as far as the Rule of Three, And also at the expiration of his Apprenticeship to pay him
the sum of three pounds ten shillings and procure or provide for him sufficient meat,
drink, clothes, washing and lodging fitting for an Apprentice during the term of Seven
years; or until he he shall arrive to the age of Twenty one; And for the true performance of all the covenants and agreements aforesaid, the parties bind themselves each
unto the other firmly by these presents; In Witness whereof the said parties have
interchangeably set their hands and seals thereunto dated the Twenty second day of
February in the year of our Lord one thousand seven hundred and ninety and in the
fourteenth year of the Commonwealth
Sealed and Delivered in the presence of
        The Court   DIXON his mark X LYONS
                                               WILLIAM NICE

    At a Monthly Court of Hustings for the City of Richmond held at the Courthouse on
Monday the 22d. of February 1790   This Indenture was with the consent and approbation of the Court executed and acknowledged by the parties and ordered to be
recorded   Teste ADAM CRAIG, C. C.

pp.   (On margin: AZEL GALT's Bond as Serjt. for 1790)
401-   KNOW ALL MEN by these presents that we AZEL GALT, JOHN ROPER and WIL-
402   LIAM BURTON are held and firmly bound unto the Mayor, Recorder, Aldermen
        and Common Council of the City of Richmond in the just and full sum of Two
thousand pounds current money of Virginia, to which payment well and truly to be
made we bind ourselves our joint and several heirs firmly by these presents; Sealed
with our seals and dated this Twenty third day of February one thousand seven hundred
and ninety
THE CONDITION of the above Obligation is such that whereas the said AZEL GALT hath
been appointed SERJEANT of the City of Richmond for one year from the date hereof
anf from thence until a new appointment of a Serjeant for the said City be made; If
therefore said AZEL GALT shall truly and faithfully execute the duties of his said Office
for the term aforesaid, Then this Obligation to be void, else to remain in full force and
virtue

Sealed and Selivered in the presence of
`   The Court

                                    AZEL GALT
                                    JOHN ROPER
                                    WM: BURTON

    At a Monthly Court of Hustings for the City of Richmond continued and held at the
Courthouse on Tuesday the 23d. of February 1790   This Bond was executed and acknowledged by the Obligors and ordered to be recorded
                    Teste ADAM CRAIG, C.C.

pp.   (On margin: BURTON & Ux. to ANDERSON)
402-   THIS INDENTURE made this sixth day of October in the year of our Lord one
404   thousand seven hundred and eighty nine, Between WILLIAM BURTON of County
        of HENRICO and MARY his Wife of one part and DAVID ANDERSON of the Town of
PETERSBURG, Merchant, of other part: Witnesseth that WILLIAM BURTON and MARY his
Wife in consideration of the sum of Three hundred pounds current money of Virginia
to them by DAVID ANDERSON in hand paid, do by these presents bargain and sell unto
DAVID ANDERSON his heirs a certain piece of ground in the City of Richmond near to
SHOCKOE WAREHOUSES, being a part of the piece of ground which hertofore was sold
and conveyed by three of the Commissioners appointed by the Act of Assembly for
selling certain Public Lands in and near the City of Richmond, to WILLIAM BURTON, as
by their Deed bearing date the first day of September in the year one thouand seven
hundred and eighty six duly recorded in the Court of the County of HENRICO may
appear, which piece of ground hereby meant to be granted begins at the North and
West corner of WILLIAM DUVAL's lot and runs on the line of JAMES LYLE, North 70 1/2
degrees East seventy feet to an Alley seven feet, thence down said Alley ninety feet or
to where it intersects with a Street thirty three feet wide and runs thence with said
Street South 19 degrees West thirty feet, thence North 84 degrees East forty feet, thence
South 19 degrees West forty feet to a Stake in DUVAL's line, and thence with his line to
the place begun at; with all houses stores warehouses granaries pailings inclosures
improvements and appurtenances to said piece of ground belonging; and the rents
issues and profits thereof, To have and to hold the granted premises & appurtenances
unto DAVID ANDERSON his heirs, And WILLIAM BURTON for himself his heirs doth
covenants with DAVID ANDERSON his heirs that he will for ever warrant and defend;
In Witness whereof the said WILLIAM and MARY have hereunto set their hands and
seals the day and year first in this Indenture written
Signed Sealed and Delivered in presence of
        JOHN WATSON   WILLIAM BURTON
        SAMUEL CLARK, HILLOSBY H. OWEN   MARY BURTON
  Received 6th October 1789 from DAVID ANDERSON in the preceeding Indenture named,
the sum of Three hundred pounds being the full consideration for the piece of ground
and other the premises thereby L. 300.
Teste SAMUEL CLARK,   WILLIAM BURTON
        JNO: WATSON
    At a Quarterly Court of Hustings for the City of Richmond held at the Courthouse on
Monday the twenty second day of March 1790   This Indenture together with the
Receipt thereon endorsed was acknowledged by WILLIAM BURTON, one of the parties
thereto, and ordered to be recorded
                    Teste ADAM CRAIG, C.C.

pp.   (On margin: VALENTINE to RICHARDSON's &c.)
405-   THIS INDENTURE made the fifth day of July in the year of our Lord one thou-
407   sand seven hundred and eighty seven Between JACOB VALENTINE of County of
           PRINCESS ANNE and State of Virginia, Yeoman, of one part and WILLIAM and
GEORGE RICHARDSON of the State aforesaid, Jewelers, and REUBEN GEORGE of the State
aforesaid, Carpenter, of the other part; Witnesseth that JACOB VALENTINE in consideration of the sum of Five shillings to him in hand paid by WILLIAM and GEORGE
RICHARDSON and REUBEN GEORGE, by these presents doth bargain sell and to farm lett
unto WILLIAM and GEORGE RICHARDSON and REUBEN GEORGE their heirs a part of a lott
of ground in the City of Richmond distinguished in the plan of the said City by the
number Three hundred and Thirty Three & contained within the following bounds, to
wit, Beginning at the Eastern corner of a House now building by BARRET PRICE, thence
running & binding on the Main Street Eastward twenty five feet, thence Southward
seventy three feet, thence Westward twenty five feet, thence running Northward
seventy three feet to the first Station; To have and to hold the part of a lot of land with
all appurtenances thereunto belonging unto WILLIAM and GEORGE RICHARDSON and
REUBEN GEORGE their heirs during the term of Eleven years from the Fifth day of
September next, paying annually therefor the sum of One shilling current money of
Virginia: And WILLIAM and GEORGE RICHARDSON and REUBEN GEORGE for themselves
their heirs doth agree with JACOB VALENTINE his heirs to build a house of Wood twenty
five feet by twenty eight, two Storys high with a Cellar of the size of the House to be
compleated with Doors and Window Shutters below, the whole to be compleated in a
plain but workman like manner and painted on the outside as well as within; And WIL-
LIAM and GEORGE RICHARDSON and REUBEN GEORGE their heirs &c. will at the expiration of said term of Eleven years leave and relinquish all claim to said House unto JACOB
VALENTINE his heirs &c., or the person who shall at that time be the Proprietor of the
said part of a lot of land; and JACOB VALENTINE for himself his heirs doth likewise agree
to warrant that WILLIAM and GEORGE RICHARDSON and REUBEN GEORGE their heirs &c.
shall at all times during the term peaceably hold the premises against the lawful claim
of any person; In Witness whereof the parties have interchangeably set their hands
and affixed their seals the day and year first above written
Signed Sealed and delivered in presence of
         WM. G. HUBBARD,   JACOB VALENTINE
         WILLIAM NORVELL JUNR.   WM: & GEO: RICHARDSON
         GEO: BRIDGES   REUBEN GEORGE
    At a Quarterly Court of Hustings for the City of Richmond held at the Courthouse on
Tuesday the 23d. day of March 1790   This Lease was acknowledged by JACOB VALEN-
TINE, WILLIAM & GEORGE RICHARDSON & REUBEN GEORGE, the parties thereto and
ordered to be recorded   Teste ADAM CRAIG, C. C.

pp.   (On margin: RICHARDSONs &c. to GRAY)
407-   THIS AGREEMENT made this twelfth day of March in the year of our Lord one
410   thousand seven hundred and Ninety, Between WILLIAM RICHARDSON, GEORGE
           RICHARDSON and REUBEN GEORGE of one part and GEORGE GRAY of other part;
Witnesseth that Whereas by Indenture bearing date the fifth day of July one thousand
seven hundred and Eighty seven made and executed by and between a certain JACOB
VALENTINE of one part and the aforesaid WILLIAM and GEORGE RICHARDSON and REU-
BEN GEORGE of the other part; said JACOB VALENTINE did grant demise and let unto WIL-
LIAM and GEORGE RICHARDSON and REUBEN GEORGE a certain part of a lot of ground in
the City of Richmond distinguished in the plan of said City by the number (333), Three

hundred and Thirty Three, which piece of ground is thus described in said Indenture (the description of the lot repeated as in the foregoing Indenture); To have and to hold the piece of ground to WILLIAM and GEORGE RICHARDSON and REUBEN GEORGE during the term of Eleven years from the fifth day of September thence next ensuing; subject to rent and conditions in the said Indenture expressed; AND WHEREAS said WILLIAM and GEORGE RICHARDSON and REUBEN GEORGE afterwards entered upon the aforesaid demised premises and made certain improvements and built a house thereon conformable to the stipulations in the aforesaid Indenture contained, which House standing on the Main Street is sub-divided into two distinct shops or tenements, one of which is at this time in the actual possession of said WILLIAM & GEORGE RICHARDSON and the other in the possession of said GEORGE GRAY, they said WILLIAM RICHARDSON and GEORGE RICHARDSON in consideration of the sum of One hundred and fifty pounds current money to them by GEORGE GRAY paid, and REUBEN GEORGE in consideration of One shilling like money to him by GEORGE GRAY also paid, do hereby bargain sell set over and to farm let for the rest of the term unexpired unto GEORGE GRAY and to his assigns all that part of the aforesaid piece of ground which lies within the following boundaries, to wit, Beginning at the Eastern cordner of the House built by BARRET PRICE, thence running on the Main Street eleven feet and thence back seventy three feet, thence Westwardly eleven feet and thence to the beginning; with such part of the aforesaid House as is situate thereon and which is the upper or Westermost of the aforesaid Shops, now in the possession of GEORGE GRAY, and all other buildings and improvements thereon; To have and to hold the same to GEORGE GRAY and his assigns from the day preceeding immediately the date hereof until the expiration of aforesaid term of Eleven years from the original commencement thereof; In Witness whereof the said WILLIAM RICHARDSON, GEORGE RICHARDSON & REUBEN GEORGE have hereunto set their hands and seals the same day and year first herein written

Signed Sealed and delivered in the presence of

WILLIAM MOSBY,	WM: RICHARDSON
SAMUEL WILLIAMSON,	GEO: RICHARDSON
T. B. DANDRIDGE	REUBEN GEORGE

Received of GEORGE GRAY one shilling at the time of signing the within

WILLIAM MOSBY,	REUBEN GEORGE
SAMUEL WILLIAMSON, T. B. DANDRIDGE	

Received of GEORGE GRAY one hundred and fifty pounds Virginia at the time of signing the same

WILLIAM MOSBY,	WM: & GEO: RICHARDSON
SAMUEL WILLIAMSON, T. B. DANDRIDGE	

At a Quarterly Court of Hustings for the City of Richmond held at the Courthouse on Wednesday the 24th day of March 1790   This Lease together with the Receipts thereon endorsed were acknowledged by WILLIAM RICHARDSON and REUBEN GEORGE, parties thereto, and ordered to be recorded

Teste ADAM CRAIG, C. C.

pp.   (On margin: HUGH PATTON's Appraisement)
411-   APPRAISEMENT of the slaves and personal Estate of HUGH PATTON as presented
421   to us on the 8th day of March 1790.   One Negro man named Harrison, (L. 50...0)
1 Chest of Souchong Tea No. 5, 104 lbs. (L. 10...0...8); 1 Ditto No. 12 105 lbs. (L. 10...3...0); 1 Ditton No. 3. 100 lbs. (L. 9...11...4); 1 Ditto No. 4. 105 lbs. (L. 10...3...0); 1 Ditto Green ditto No. 11. 85 lbs. (L.20...2...0); 1 Ditto, Ditto, No. 12, 87 lbs. (L. 20...14...0); 1 Ditto, Ditto No. 21 89 lbs. (L. 21...6...0); a parcel of Bone Tumery, 1 ps. Velveret Cord;

(4 more pieces); 1 ps. yd. wide Southwallet, (another piece); 1 ps. white Corduroy, 3 ps. Persian Cord. (another peice); 3 ps. Irish Linen; 13 warming pans, 1 pair scales, 54 gross small metal buttons, 20 gross large ditto, 7 gross bone & horn ditto, 14 made up sets China; 143 bags D. head buttons, 1 ps. black Persian; (another piece) 42 D. shoe thread in a damaged.10 ps. painted Muslin, 15 ps. 4/4 Jaconett Muslin; 1 ps. striped ditto; 10 Muslin shalls damaged; (7 more) 41 ditto with borders; 269 hair brushes, 192 pair Candlesticks brass & Queens metal; 73 strips bordering,11 ps. Chintz bordering; 5 ps. Calico; 6 ps. ditto 14 yds. each; 16 ps. printed Linens, 7 doz. printed Shawls, 9 doz. & 7 linen ditto, 28 doz. Childrens handkerchiefs, 1 gown pattern, 7 1/4 yards printed Merseills, 2 ps. green Persian, 1 ps. white mode, 30 squares,130 Elastick Hat bands, 8 Gro: hooks & eyes, 15 pr. button looping; 2 gross Collar makers needles, 4 gross binding, 4 1/4 D. bobbing, 23 doz. & 11 pair shoe buckles, 39 ps. Ribbon in remnants, parcel of Faste, 1 doz. hats of various qualities; 1 ps. striped worsted, 2 1/4 yds. snuff coloured cloth, 4 yds. 7/8 cloth, 1 yd. drab ditto; 6 yds. mixed 7/8 damaged cloth, 3/4 yards Samon colo. cloth; 3/4 sewing silk, 3 ps. figured marley, 3 ps. black gauze, 1 ps. white do; 4 ps. needle worked lawn, 2 ps. striped lawn, 2 ps. ditto checked, 25 bottles westerns snuff, 4 bottles ditto broke, 37 Canisters Dutch snuff; 6 pair stays, 54 Straw hats, 97 chip ditto; 2 doz; pocket looking glasses, 6 pencils & cases, 9 doz. fans, 3 doz & 7 pair mens gloves; 22 doz. watch seals, 13 ps. gartering is 1 gross; 5 doz. breakfast plates is 60; sundry other ps. Delphware; 8 embroidered waistcoat patterns, 5 doz. Kilmarknock caps, 2 D. 11 oz. ball twist, 5 3/4 D. mohair, 5 pair mens silk gloves, 5 doz. worsted mitts, 4 1/2 D. silk & twist, 1 doz. pair boots some damaged; 11 pair shoes; 87 doz. Gimblets and Spikes gimblets, 8 Guns, 1 Carpet, 1 ps. red figured damask, 1 ps. Brown ditto, 2 doz. drawer locks but a small pr. keys; Awl hafts 64 doz., 1 Vol.Fothergill Medical & Philoso: works; Buchans Family Physician, Mairs Arithmatic, The Young Mans Best Companion, Traders Assistant, Thompsons Table of Interest; Enticks Dictionary, 2 leather trunks, 1 chest painted, 1 waistcoat pattern &c., 2 pair scales, 8 hogsheads Madeira Wine, 2 pipes ditto; 2 ditto ditto; 2 chests Bohea Tea: 1 Wheat fan;

Furniture: 1 press bedstead, 2 beds and furniture; 6 Walnut Chairs with leather bottoms, 1 doz. yellow Windsor chairs, 1 small square Walnut Table; 1 Fender, Shovel and tongs, 1 Bed, Bedstead 7 furniture, Mahogany Bedstead; 13 grates, 1 bedstead;, leather trunk, 1 4 foot walnut Table, 2 small trunks, 1 Bureau, 1 pair Mahogany tables, 1 Sopha and furniture, 1 pair pistols, 6 window curtains, cotton check, 1 looking glass; 1 small ditto, 4 pair blankets & 2 coverlids, 2 coverlids; 1 four foot Walnut table; 6 Mahogany chair green bottoms, 2 Gilt looking glasses, 1 bed and furniture, 1 Tea Board, 24 oz. Silver table spoons, 2 1/2 oz. Tea Spoons and Sugar Tongs; 1 set blue China, 1 Castor, parcel glass and Crockery ware; 1 Carron Grate &c., 1 blue Table; 4 Windsor Chairs, 1 mans saddle & bridle, 2 Dutch Ovens & 3 small pots, 1 water pitcher, 1 copper tea kettle; 1 frying pan, Ladle & flesh forks, pr. lorns & crane; 3 pair brass candlesticks, 1 washing Tub, 5 Diaper Table cloths, 2 barrels Snuff (a consignment), 1 Iron chest, 1 pair scales and weights, 1 pair weights and scale at THO: HOOPERs, 1 Horse, 1 single chair and harness (old), 5 Tin canisters large & powder Canister, 1 Carpet, 1 copper Kettle

(The foregoing is totalled at L. 1310...0...7.)

Public Securities. Pensylvania Loan Office Securities.
HUGH PATTON, 1371...16...10; THOMAS LEIPER 1200...0...0; HUGH PATTON 988...4...8; THOMAS EVINS 729...12..4; MOORE FAUNTLEROY 726...0...0; THOMAS CRAIG 588...7..6; COX and FRAZER, 525...0...0; ARTHUR St .CLAIR 411...1...7; CHARLES YOUNG 359...17...10; DANIEL BROADHEAD 277...6...5; ABSALOM BAIRD 207...17...0; HUGH PATTON 260...12...6; JOHN COX 208...6...0; DANIEL BROADHEAD 281...5...0; SAMUEL WILCOX 225...0...0; THOMAS LEIPER 225...0...0; JAMES & WILLIAM GIBBS 112...10...0; THOMAS FRANKLIN 55..7...3;

Ditto 34...12...6; HUGH PATTON 37...10...0; PHILIP ALBERT 29...2...11; THOMAS CRAIG 19...12..7; JOHN HARRINGTON 12...10...0; BARBARA ALBERT 2...6...1.

Total: 8888...19...10, Deduct 1/5 to reduce to V. Currency 4777...15...11.

(Five Unliquidated Continental Loan Office Certificates are listed to total $5000.00. Followed by what is termed Final Settlements): An Order drawn by THOMAS PALMER on JAMES NOURSE for 83 55/90 dollars final settlements October 21st 1789;

Military and Loan Office Certificates on the State of Virginia.
JOHN WILKINSON 22...1...1; ABNER CRUMP 100...0...0; REUBEN GEORGE 25...8...11; JAMES MUNRO 20...0...0; PETER DAVIS 91...1...4; MAN CLEMENTS 50...0...0. To total 309...1...4. (all noted "Interestdrawn to 1st Jany. 1789").

VIRGINIA Military Certificates. MARTHA CARR 4...7...0; ACHILLES JARRAT 4...0...0; BARTLETT ANDERSON 4...9...6 1/2; WILLIAM CLOPTON 4...10...0; JAMES WHITE 4...7...6; ELIZABETH HOOPER 3...5...0; DAVID ALVIS 3...10...6; MARY FOWLER 3...0...0; DAVID MIMMS JR. 3...15...0; MARY MILLS 3...14...9; ANDW. CASLIM 3...10...0; JESSE FOSTER 0...18...8; ELIZA: CHARMANS 26...0...0; WILLIAM CUACER 50...0...0; MER: SHELTON 50...0...0; ROBERT LAWSON 50...0...0; THOMAS AUSTIN 25...0...0; NELSON ANDERSON JR. 40...0...0; BARRETT WHITE 20...0...0; DOCTR. JOHN SHORE 26...28... 8 1/2; THOMAS BOWLING 21...17...6; PETER LEGRAND 30...0...0; JOHN AUSTIN 20...0...0; STEPHEN SAUN-DERS 18...13...6; JOHN HOPKINS 14...5...0; WILLIAM MACON 9...13...0; BARRET WHITE 9...9...3; DAVID MIMMS 9...0...0; STEPHEN SAUNDERS 10...12...8; NICHS: B. SEABROOKE 12...10...0; JUDY COLBS 11...5...10; JOHN STREET 11...6...10 1/2; GEORGE BOWLES 13...0...0; WILLIAM MACON 10...0...0; DAVID COCKRAN 8...14...1; DAVID WHITLOCK 6...15...0; FARGUS MANN 6...5...3; SOLOMON DAVIS 6...11...1L; LYDIA BROOK 7...3...9; JOSEPH SHELTON 6...3...6; DAVID MIMMS 7...3...0; SHERROD PARISH 6...5...0; CORNS. PEACE 6...15...0. FORTIONUS CRUTCHFIELD 5...17...4 1/2; BARRET WHITE 5...10...4; JOHN BEATRE 4...10...0.

PENSYLVANIA Militia. EDWARD BEATRE 1...2...0.

(The total shown for this appraisement: (L. 4443. 18...7).

In Obedience to an Order of the Worshipfuill Court of Huslings for the City of Rich-mond dated February 1790. We the Subscribers being first sworn have appraised the slaves and personal Estate of HUGH PATTON deced., in current money as presented to us amounting to Four thousand four hundred and Forty three pounds, eighteen shillings and seven pence currency. Given under our hands this 23d. day of March 1790

ROBERT POLLARD
ALEXR: MONTGOMERY
GEORGE GRAY

Returned into the Court of Huslings for the City of Richmond the 23d day of March 1790 and ordered to be recorded.

Teste ADAM CRAIG, C. C.

pp.   (On margin: LACY to WARREN)
421-   THIS INDENTURE TRIPARTITE made the tenth day of October one thousand
425   seven hundred and eighty nine Between EDMUND LACY of City of Richmond of
         first part; ISHAM GODDIN of the same City of the second part, And THOMAS
WARREN of the third part; Witnesseth that whereas EDMUND LACY is justly indebted to said ISHAM GODDIN in the sum of Four hundred and seventeen pounds and ten pence Military Certificates granted by the Auditors of Publick Accounts for the State to Offi-cers and Soldiers on Continental and State Establishments for which he hath granted two Promissory Notes, one for Sixty five pounds dated the ninth day of April one thou-sand seven hundred and eighty nine, the other for three hundred and fifty two pounds

and ten pence dated the eighth day of May one thousand seven hundred and eighty nine to said ISHAM GODDIN and Whereas said EDMUND LACY for the better securing the payment of said sum of Four hundred and seventeen pounds and ten pence of Military Certificates granted by the Auditors of Publick Accounts for the State to Officers and Soldiers on Continental Establishment hath agreed to convey unto THOMAS WARREN seven Negroes and their increase, to wit, Ben, Frank, Silvia, Nan, Squire, Louisa and Ned, in Trust in consideration of the premises on the part of said ISHAM GODDIN and also in consideration of the sum of Five shillings to me in hand paid by THOMAS WARREN, by these presents doth bargain sell and confirm unto THOMAS WARREN his heirs the above named Negroes; To have and to hold the said Negroes and their increase unto THOMAS WARREN his heirs upon this especial Trust and Confidence and to and for use intent and purpose following and for no other purpose; that is to say, for the raising of Four hundred and seventeen pounds and Ten pence Military Certificates granted by the Auditors of Public Accounts for this State to Officers and Soldiers in Continental or State Establishments with interest at the period of time mentioned, to wit, the twenty fifth day of December next ensuing this date and in case of default or delay in payment of said sum that then it shall be lawful for THOMAS WARREN his heirs to sell for ready money at Publick Auction the aforesaid Negroes to rasie the sum of money due and payable together with the Interest become due thereon such sale made in the City of Richmond; In Witness whereof the parties aforesaid have hereto set their hands and seals interchangeably the day month and year above written

In presence of us RICHD. BOWLER,   EDMUND LACY
  JOHN V. KAUTZMAN,   ISHAM GODDIN
  WM: MANN   ARTHUR MANN   T: WARREN

 At a Court of Hustings for the City of Richmond held at the Courthouse on Monday the 24th of May 1790   This Indenture was proved by the Oaths of RICHARD BOWLER, JOHN V. KAUTZMAN and WILLIAM MANN, witnesses thereto, and ordered to be recorded
       Teste ADAM CRAIG, C. C.

pp (On margin: CAWTHERN to HEISLER & COOK)
425- THIS INDENTURE Witnesseth that SAMUEL COCKRAN of City of Richmond by and
427 with his own consent and with the consent of RICHARD POWERS, his Guardian,
    hath put himself and by these presents by and with the advice of RICHARD POWERS his Guardian doth voluntarily and of his own free will and accord put himself Apprentice to HISELER and COOK, Tin Plate Workers, of the City of Richmond to learn his Art, Trade and Mystery, and after the manner of an Apprentice to serve the said HISELOR and COOK the term of eight years and seven months, during all which term the said Apprentice his said Master faithfully shall serve and in all things behave himself as a faithful Apprentice ought to do; And the said Master shall use the utmost of his Endeavours to teach or cause to be taught or instructed the said Apprentice in the Trade or Mystery of a Tin Plate Worker, and said HISELOR and COOK oblige themselves to teach or cause to be taught the said Apprentice to read and write and pay him three pounds ten shillings for his Freedom Dues and procure or provide him sufficient meat drink clothes washing and lodging fitting for an Apprentice during the term of eight years and seven months, And for the true performance of all the covenants and agreements aforesaid, the parties bind themselves each unto the other firmly by these presents; In Witness whereof the said parties have interchangeably set their hands and seals hereunto, Dated the twenty eighth day of June in the year of our Lord one thousand seven hundred and Ninety and in the 14th year of the Commonwealth

Sealed and Delivered in the presence of
(no witnesses recorded)

SAML: CAUTHERN
RICHARD POWERS
HISELER & COOK

At a Monthly Court of Hustings for the City of Richmond held at the Courthouse on Monday the twenty sixth of June 1790   This Indenture was with the consent & approbation of the Court executed and acknowledged by the parties thereto and ordered to be recorded   Teste ADAM CRAIG, C. C.

pp.   (On margin: COMMS; Sale of P. Lands to BARRET)
428-   THIS INDENTURE made this Twenty seventh day of April in the year of our
430   Lord one thousand seven hundred and eighty nine Between NATHANIEL WIL-
          KINSON, MILES SELDEN JR., JOHN HARVIE, THOMAS PROSSER and WILLIAM
FOUSHEE, Commissioners appointed by an Act of Assembly intituled, "An Act Directing the Sale of the Public Lands and other Property in or near the City of Richmond." Witnesseth that the Commissioners in conformity with the terms of said Act and in consideration of the sum of Seven hundred and twenty seven pounds, Fifteen shillings specie, the payment whereof has been secured as by the said Act is prescribed, by these presents do bargain and sell unto JOHN BARRET of the City of Richmond a lot of ground lying in said City on the West side of SHOCKOE CREEK and on the Main Street, beginning at a Stone near the upper corner of JAMES BUCHANAN's STORE and running up the Main Street forty one feet to the lower corner of the twelve feet Alley laid of for Public use by us as Commissioners, thence along the line of said Public Alley for one hundred and thirty one feet, thence by a line running South 53 1/2 E. down and paralel to the Main Street thirty four and a half feet and thence one hundred and thirty two feet to the Stone begun at on the Main Street, and which lot or peice of ground is marked and known by the number One (No. 1) in that plan of said Commissioners which states the partial sale of FRENCH & CRAWFORDs Tenement and which said Plan is recorded in the County Court of HENRICO which land under the Operation of an Act of Assembly intituled "An Act Concerning Escheats and Forfeitures from British Subjects," was escheated to the Commonwealth of Virginia as being the proper Estate of FRENCH & CRAWFORD, as British Subjects, as by inquest of Office remaining of Record in the General Court will appear: Together with all houses and improvements thereon and the rents issues and profits thereof; To have and to hold the piece of ground with all houses and improvements thereon to JOHN BARRET his heirs; In Witness whereof we have hereunto set our hands and affixed our seals this Twenty seventh day of April one thousand seven hundred and eighty nine as above written

Teste WM: ROSE as to N. W.   NATHL. WILKINSON
      WM: MARSHALL as to N. W.   JOHN HARVIE
      JACOB EGE as to N. W.   W. FOUSHEE
      JOSEPH HARREL as to N. W.

At a Monthly Court of Hustings for the City of Richmond held at the Courthouse in the said City on Monday the 27th of April 1789   This Indenture was acknowledged by JOHN HARVIE and WILLIAM FOUSHEE, two of the Commissioners therein named;

And at a Monthly Court of Hustings for the said City held at the Courthouse the 26th of July 1790.   This Indenture was proved by the Oaths of WILLIAM ROSE, JACOB EGE and JOSEPH HARREL, witnesses thereto as to NATHANIEL WILKINSON, another of the said Commissioners, and is ordered to be recorded

                     Taste ADAM CRAIG, C. C.

pp.   (On margin: DUGARD to Rachel)
430-   TO ALL TO WHOM these presents may concern, Know ye that I ABRAHAM
431   DUGARD of the City of Richmond in consideration of the sum of Five shillings in
         hand paid by my slave, Rachel (aged about twenty five or twenty six years and
commonly called & known by the name of RACHEL WOOD) have and do by these presents
emancipate her the said RACHEL WOOD and her three Children, Jack, Sal & Jem (aged
about six, four and two years) and do as far as the Laws of Virginia vest her and them
with all the rights and privileges of free born Citizens of the same, clear from the claim
of me my heirs or any other person do by these presents warrant and forever defend
the Freedom as aforesaid to said RACHEL WOOD and her three Children, Jack, Sal & Jem:
In Witness whereof I have hereunto set my hand & seal this twenty sixth day of July
one thousand seven hundred and Ninety
Signed Sealed and delivered in the presence of
       ISAAC N. CARDOZO,   A. DUGARD
       JOHN BURTON, JOHN LAWSON
At a Monthly Court of Hustings for the City of Richmond held at the Courthouse on
Monday the 26th of July 1790   This Deed of Emancipation was proved by the Oaths of
JOHN BURTON and JOHN LAWSON, witnesses thereto, and ordered to be recorded
                    Teste ADAM CRAIG, C.C.

pp.   (On margin: LYLE &c. to DONALD)
431-   THIS INDENTURE made the thirteenth day of May Anno Domini one thousand
432   seven hundred and eighty nine by and with the consent of JOHN STOCKDELL,
         testified by his signing and sealing this Indenture, between JAMES LYLE, Mer-
chant of the City of Richmond, of one part and ALEXANDER DONALD, Merchant, of the
City of Richmond of the other part: Witnesseth that JAMES LYLE in consideration of the
sum of Three hundred and Forty eight pounds current money of Virginia to him in
hand paid by ALEXANDER DONALD, by these presents doth bargain sell and confirm
unto ALEXANDER DONALD a certain lot of ground lying in City of Richmond on the
South side of the Main Street whereon WRIGHT SOUTHGATE now lives and bounded: Beginning near the House of JOHN MAYO Esquire, thence up said Main Street twenty six
feet to the corner of the BRICK HOUSE lately built by said STOCKDELL, including the
same, thence leaving the Main Street Southernly at a right angle with the said Main
Street about one hundred feet, that is to say, as far Southerly as the South end of Mr.
WILLIAM MITCHELL's LUMBER HOUSE, thence twenty six feet an Easterly course parallel
with the Main Street, thence at a right angle with the Main Street, leaving and giving
twenty six feet front on the Main Street to the beginning, being the same piece of
ground heretofore purchased by JOHN STOCKDELL from JAMES LYLE and which said
JOHN hath now directed to be conveyed to said ALEXANDER DONALD: To have and to hold
the lot or piece of ground as above described with all edifices thereon with every of its
appurtenances thereunto belonging to ALEXANDER DONALD his heirs and JAMES LYLE
the lot of ground with appurtenances against the claim of all persons to ALEXANDER
DONALS his heirs shall warrant and for ever defend by these presents: In Witness
whereof the said JAMES LYLE and said JOHN STOCKDELL hath in Testification of his
consent hereunto set their hands and affixed their seals the day month and year above
written
Signed Sealed and delivered in the presence of us
       I.M. STOCKDELL   JAMES LYLE
       JOHN BROWN, JAMES CAROTHON   JNO: STOCKDELL

At a Monthly Court of Hustings for the City of Richmond held at the Courthouse on
Monday the 26th of July 1790   This Indenture was acknowledged by JAMES LYLE and
JOHN STOCKDELL, parties thereto, and ordered to be recorded
                                    Teste ADAM CRAIG, C. C.

pp.   (On margin: GRAVES and Ux. to DONALD)
433-   THIS INDENTURE made this ninth day of March one thousand seven hundred
434   and ninety Between FRANCIS GRAVES & MARTHA his Wife of City of Richmond
         of one part and ALEXANDER DONALD of other part; Witnesseth that FRANCIS
GRAVES in consideration of the sum of forty five pounds specie by said ALEXANDER
DONALD to him in hand paid, by these presents doth bargain and sell unto ALEXANDER
DONALD his heirs a certain piece of ground lying in City of Richmond and on a twenty
one feet Alley and measuring thirty two feet on the said Alley beginning at the West
corner of Messrs WARINGTON & KEENE's BRICK KITCHEN and running up the said
twenty one feet Alley to the corner of THOMAS WALKERs House, and running along the
side of the said House until it strikes the ground of HENRY BANKS and runs along the
said BANKS's lot until it strikes the lot of ground the said ALEXANDER DONALD purchased
of JOHN STOCKDELL, thence along the said lot to WARINGTON & KEENE's Tenement,
thence along the said Tenement to the place begun at, all of which piece of ground is
part of Lot No. 11 as will fully appear by reference to a plat and Survey signed by the
Commissioners appointed to sell confiscated property in and about the City of Richmond and recorded in HENRICO Court: To have and to hold the piece of ground with
appurtenances to ALEXANDER DONALD his heirs and FRANCIS GRAVES & MARTHA his
Wife for themselves and their heirs doth agree with ALEXANDER DONALD that they will
warrant and defend the Title of the piece of ground to ALEXANDER DONALD and his
heirs for ever against the claim of every person; In Witness whereof the said FRANCIS
GRAVES and MARTHA hath hereunto set their hands and affixed their seals the day and
year first written
Signed Sealed and Delivered in the presence of
        SAMUEL COUCH,   FRANCIS GRAVES
        JAMES BENNETT, ROBT. BROADDUS   MARTHA GRAVES
   March 9th 1790. Received of (blank) forty five pounds specie which sum is in full for
the within mentioned piece of ground   L. 45..0..0.
        SAMUEL COUCH,   FRAS: GRAVES
        JAMES BENNETT, ROBERT BROADDUS
   At a Monthly Court of Hustings for the City of Richmond held at the Courthouse on
Monday the 26th of July 1790.   This Indenture was acknowledged by FRANCIS GRAVES
one of the parties thereto, and together with the Receipt thereon endorsed, which was
also acknowledged by the said FRANCIS GRAVES, are ordered to be recorded
                                    Teste ADAM CRAIG, C. C.

pp.   (On margin: GRAVES to COUCH)
434-   THIS INDENTURE made this tenth day of February one thousand seven hundred
436   and ninety Between FRANCIS GRAVES of City of Richmond of one part and
         SAMUEL COUCH of GOOCHLAND County of other part; Witnesseth that FRANCIS
GRAVES in consideration of the sum of Five shillings Virginia current money to him in
hand paid, by these presents doth bargain and sell unto SAMUEL COUCH his heirs a certain tract of land lying and being in the County of HENRICO and containing Two hundred and fifty acres, be the same more or less, and being the whole of the land which
FRANCIS GRAVES purchased of WILLIAM REYNOLDS, which will appear by reference

to said REYNOLDS Deed to said GRAVES, also all that lot of gRound lying in City of Richmond on CARY's STREET and bounded by the lot of WILLIAM NICOLSON and Lot No. 16
sold by the Commissioners directed to sell Public Lands in & about the City of Richmond
to said FRANCIS GRAVES, also the seven following Negroes, vizt., Daniel & Venus his
Wife & Selah a girl 12 years old & Anna 16 years old with her Child, Doll, at the breast &
Barnett 15 years old by Trade a Barber, also Charles 28 years old; To have and to hold all
the land lot and slaves with all appurtenances to SAMUEL COUCH his heirs UPON this
Express Condition, nevertheless, that if FRANCIS GRAVES his heirs shall indemnify and
keep harmless SAMUEL COUCH his heirs from the claim or demand of JOHN GROVES
which said SAMUEL COUCH is bound in a Bond as said FRANCIS GRAVES security for
faithful keeping the PRISON BOUNDS until legally discharged, and doth moreover pay
and satisfy his two Bonds to me the said COUCH one for One hundred and fifty two
pounds 8/ specie, and dated 22nd. day of May 1789; And another for one hundred and
seventy four pounds Military Certificates with Interest due thereon from and after first
day of January 1788 as will apepar by said Bonds. NOW IF FRANCIS GRAVES faithfully
keeps and observes the aforesaid PRISON BOUNDS so that I can in no way be made liable
for said JOHN GROVES Debt and pays and satisfies the Bonds as before mentioned with all
interest as aforesaid, then this Mortgage shall be null and void, otherwise to remain in
full force and virtue. In Witness whereof the said FRANCIS GRAVES & SAMUEL COUCH
hath set their hands and affixed their seals the day and year first and above written
Signed Sealed & delivd: in presence of
        REUBEN GEORGE as to Graves   FRANCIS GRAVES
        WM. YOUNG JR.,   SAMUEL COUCH
        JNO: STOCKDELL, WM. McKIM
  Feby. 10th 1790. Received of SAMUEL COUCH Five shillings specie, that being the full
consideration money for the within bargain & sale
Test JNO: STOCKDELL   FRANCIS GRAVES
  At a Monthly Court of Hustings for the City of Richmond held at the Courthouse on
Monday the 26th of July 1790   This Mortgage was proved by the Oaths of REUBEN
GEORGE, JOHN STOCKDELL & WILLIAM YOUNG JR., witnesses thereto, and together with
the Receipt thereon endorsed which was also proved by the Oath of the said JOHN
STOCKDELL, the witness to the same, ordered to be recorded
                 Teste ADAM CRAIG C.C.

(RICHMOND CITY Hustings Deeds No. 1, 1782-1792, continues to page 620. To complete this
Hustings Court Deed book, it will be continued in another Antient Press publication beginning in
the year 1790 on page 436 of Deed Book, 1782-1792).

ADAMS. Mallory 58, 59; Richard (Councilman
-1), (Gent. Justice -47), 54, 58, (Colo. -60), 73,
92; Richard Junr. 94; Thomas 60; Thomas B.
(Gent. Justice -99).

ALBERT. Barbara 115; Philip 115.

ALEXANDER. Robert 101; William 66, 67, 81,
100, 101.

ALISON. Francis 48, 50.

ALLEGRE. Mrs. 21.

ALLEN. Robert 44.

ALVIS. David 115.

AMBLER. Jacquelin (Alderman -1), 12, 15.

ANDERSON. Bartlett 115; David (of Town of
Petersburg-111); George 32, 39; Henry 27;
James 19; Nelson Junr. 115.

ARCHIBALD. Samuel 23.

ARMISTEAD. William 77.

AUSTIN. Chapman (of Hanover Co. -98), 99;
John 115; Moses 24; Thomas 115.

BAIRD. Absalom 114.

BANKS. Alexander 20; Cuthbert 17;
Henry 16, 17, 109, 119; Hunter & Co. -16.

BARKER. William 4.

BARR. Richard (Shoemaker -1).

BARRETT. John 91, 93, 117.

BARROW. William 10.

BASKERVILL. George H. 62.

BAXTER. Daniel 76.

BAYNE/BAINE. Robert 2, 9, 10.

BEALE. John 17, 72; Samuel (of Williamsburg
-52), 53, (of James City Co. -93), 94.

BECKLEY. John (Alderman -1), 24, 32, 39,
(Esqr.-44), 45, 49, 72.

BELL. Samuel 110.

BENNETT. James (of Westham -61), 62, 119.

BERKELEY. Nelson Junior 91.

BETTIS. Ben (Freed Mulatto -38).

BISSETT. James 27, 28, 91.

BLADES. Campbell (Orphan of George -96);
George (deced.-96); William 96.

BLAIR. Anne. 57; Archibald 56, 57.

BLAKEY. Smith 18, 36, 77.

BLANKENSHIP. Jane 66; Stephen 66.

BOOKER. Richard 20; William 55.

BOUSH. John 103, 04; Robert 103, 104;
Samuel (deced.-103).

BOWLER. Richard 74, 93, 111.

BOWLES. George 115; Jesse 99.

BOWLING. Thomas 115.

BOYD. Andrew (Reverend, deced.-15);
John 15, 72; Robert 15, 16, (Gent. Justice -23),
24, 54, 64, 79, 80, 99; Walter 15, 16;
William (Reverend, Minister in County of Wigtown in North Britain -15), 16.

BOYLE. Charles 97, 99.

BRANDER. John 84.

BRAXTON. Carter (of King William Co. -2),
Carter Junr. 94.

BRICE/BRYCE. Archibald (of Goochland Co. -6),
7, 13, 14; Mary (of Goochland Co. -6), 7, 13, 14.

BRIDGES. George 112.

BROADDUS. Robert 119.

BROADHEAD. Daniel 114.

BROADNAX. William (deced.-32).

BROOK(E). H. 94, 95; John 27, 49; Lydia 115.

BROWN. Benjamin 71, 72; James 107;
John 118; Joseph (Inventory -59); Robert 3.

BRUMELL. William (of London -51, 52).

BRYAN. Benjamin 27; John (Will of -27, 28);
John (Son of John) 27, 62, 91; Mary 27;
Obedience 27; Priscilla 27; Sarah 27;
Simkin 27; Wilson 27.

BUCHANAN. Alexander 4-6, 12, 42, 45, 82, 90,
91, 95, 96; James (Councilman -1), 4-6, 9, 10,
12, 21, 22, 29, 35, 45, (deced.-90), 91,
(Mercht.-95), 117; John 90.

BURGER. William 19.

BURNES. John 97.

BURTON. Frances Ann 23, 24; John 23, 26, 58,
118; Mary 111; William 16, 110, 111.

BURWELL. Lewis 88, 89.

BYRD. Lottery 44; William (Esqr.) 3, 6;
William (Esqr., deced.-3), 5, 12, 24, 25, 28, 42,
(of Westover, deced.-43), 46, 71, 72, 74, 86, 78,
79, 85, 86, 88.

CALLOWAY. James 102.

CAMPBELL. Jane (Executrix of Nathaniel Evans
-89), 90; John 11; William (of Botetourt Co.
-89), 90.

CARD. Hugh 107.

CAROTHAN. James 118.

CARR. Martha. 115.

CARRINGTON. Edward 93.

CARROLL. Edward 43, 64, 65.

CARSON. Elizabeth 17, 18; William (Will of
17, 18); William (Nephew of William -17).

CARTER. Ann 32; Charles 6; Charles (Esqr.
of Shirley in Charles City Co.,   (contd.)

EDDY. George (Merchant in Philadelphia -74), 75, 76; Thomas (Merchant in Fredericksburg -74), 75, 76.

EGE. Ann 26, 103; Dorothy 26; Jacob 26, 117; Samuel 26, 93.

EGGLESTON. John (of Chesterfield Co, -56), 57; Marion (Blair) 56.

ELLIOTT. Thomas 25, 62.

ELSON. Marcus 4.

ESKRIGGE. George 72.

EVANS/EVINS. Nathaniel (deced.-89), 90; Thomas 114.

FALVEY. Michael 9, 10.

FAUNTLEROY. Moore 114.

FELLOWSHIP FIRE COMPANY. Members listed 72.

FENWICK. William 107.

FIELD. John (Merchant of Philadelphia -74, 75-77.

FITZWHYLSONN. -55.

FORMICOLA. Serafino 33, 34, 57, 58, 93, 94.

FOSTER. Jesse 115; Seth 30.

FOUNTAINE. James Maury (Reverend of Gloucester Co.-12).

FOUSHEE. William (Mayor -1); 9, 10, 35, 67, 68, 71, 72, 84 (Doctor -109), 117.

FOWLER. Mary 115.

FRANKLIN. Elijah 23; Thomas 75, 114.

FRENCH. Hugh 99.

FRY. Christopher 79.

FUTCHERON. John M. 83.

GAIRDNER. George 91.

GALT. Azel (Serjeant -110), 111; Gabriel 8, (Gent. Justice -23), 24, 26, 58, 83; William 72.

GAUTIER. Frances 83, 84; John B. 83. Nicholas (Will of -83, 84.

GEDDY. William 60, 75.

GEOGHAGIN. Anthony 8, 11, 12, 32, 70.

GEORGE. Reuben 109, (Carpenter -112), 113, 115, 120.

GIBBS. James 114; William 114.

GILBERT. Robert 21, 30.

GILES. William 60.

GILLIAM. John 16.

GILLIATT. John 109; Thomas 109.

GLYNN. John 70.

GODDIN. Isham 115, 116.

GOFF. Philip 105.

GRAHAM. John 29, 30, 36.

GRAVES. Francis 15, 42, 43, 63, 64, 71, 72, 83, 83, 109, 110, 119; Martha 64, 82, 83, 109, 119, 120.

GRAY. George 67, 100, 101, 112, 113, 115.

GREAT BRITAIN/NORTH BRITAIN. London 2, 51-53; Louden Co. 107; Wigtown Co. -15.

GREEN. Fortunatus 68, 87.

GREENHOW. Lotts of 47.

GREGORY. Roger Junr. 51.

GROVES. John 55, 77, 120.

GUNN. John 22, 23, 26, 28, 72, 73, (Gent. Justice -101).

HAGUE. John 23.

HALL. Edward (of Edgecombe Co., in North Carolina -19).

HARREL. Joseph (Constable -97), 117.

HARRINGTON. John 115.

HARRISON. Benjamin 88, 89; Benjamin (of Berkeley in Charles City Co., Esqr. -3, 28). Benjamin (of Berkeley, Esqr., deced. -3); Benjamin Junr. 44, 72, 88; Mary 88, 89.

HARVIE. John (Gent. Justice -47), 48, 55, 56, 67, 71, 89, 100, 117.

HASLETT. William 72.

HAY. Charles 24, 43, 60; Elizabeth 34, (Betty -35); John (deced.-34), 35; William (Recorder -1), 19, 34, 35, 43, 44, (Gent. Justice -67), 68, 72, 83.

HERON. James 71, 72; Nathaniel 2; Nelson & Company 43, 71, 82.

HESILER & COOK. Ten Plate Workers 96, 116, 117.

HETH. Hary 22, (Serjeant -72, 73), 79, 80, 82, 87-89, 93.

HICKS. John 72.

HIGBEE. Joseph 72, (Merchant -74), 75, 76.

HOLLINGSWORTH. Stephen 72, 75.

HOLLOWAY. David 21, 27; Nathaniel 21.

HOLT. John Hunter (Will of -76).

HOOPER. Elizabeth 115; Thomas 106, 107.

HOPE. George 30.

HOPKINS. Charles (Merchant-46), 47, 72; John 93, 94, 115.

HOWARD. Charles P. 106, 107; John (of Hanover Co.-91), 92.

HUBBARD. William G. 112.

HUMANS. Charles 75.

HUMPHREYS. Joshua 33, 88.
HUNTER. James 7; James Junr. (Alderman-1).
HUNTER, BANKS & CO. -71.
HYLTON. Daniel Lawrence 84;
  Ralph 67, 68.

INNES. James (Esqr. -93), 94, 95.
IRELAND. Dublin 11; Kingdom of 10, 45.
IRVIN(G). Charles 9, 10.
ISAACS. Isaiah (Merchant-14), 18, 29, 103;
  Josiash 103.

JACKSON. Rebecca 98; Toby 65, 97, 98.
JAMES. Francis 47, 56; Francis J. 72.
JARRAT. Achilles. 115.
JEFFERSON. Thomas (Esqr. -77).
JOHNSON. Lain J. 64, 65, 75, 76; Thomas P.
  (Ports), 72, (Mercht.-74), 75-77; W. 90.
JOHNSTON. William (of Kingdom of Ireland)
  10, 11, 45; William (deced -77); William
  (Merchant & Mariner -95), 96.
JONES. Callom 107.
JORDAN. Fleming 2; Noble 107, 108;
  Pleasant 23, 24.

KAUTZMAN. John V. 59, 100, 116.
KAY. Agness 106.
KEENE. Thomas 72, 85, 86, (Mercht.-105),
  107.
KEMP. James 30.
KEOUN. Thomas 11.
KER. John 72.
KEY. Jesse 84; Joseph (Plaisterer-87).
KING. Robert Junr. 2.
KINGSTON. James (Esqr. -11).

LACY. Edmund 113, 116.
LAMBERT. David 19, 26, 28, 72, (Gent. Jus-
  tice -99), 101, 103, 104, 108, 109;
  Sally 103, 104.
LAWSON. John 118; Robert 113.
LE CANUT. Charles 20.
LEGRAND. Peter 113.
LEIPER. Thomas 114.
LENEVE. Peter 105.
LEWIS. Benjamin 62, 65, 66; Charles 41, 48,
  56; Gilly 23, 26, 72, 73, 94; William 92.
LIGGON. John 21.
LIPSCOMB. Sarah 107-109; William 58, 59,
  107-109.

LIVINGSTON. John 69.
LOCKHART. Patrick 6.
LOTT. Abraham 72, (Mercht.-74), 75, 76.
LOTT, HIGBEE & CO. -43, 74, 76.
LOVE. Alexander (Mercht. -2).
LUDEMAN. Catharina Juliana 22; Christina
  Sophia 22; William (Will of -22),
  (Inventory -28).
LYLE(S). James 20, 11, (Mercht. -118), 119;
  Nancy 22.
LYNE. James (of Chesterfield Co.-85); John 29.
LYONS. Dixon (Orphan of John -110);
  John (deced.-110); Peter (of Hanover Co. -4),
  (Esqr. -5).

McCLANE. James (deced., Inventory -23).
McCLOUD. Joseph 91, 92; William (deced.,
  Inventory -62).
McCLUNG. James 93.
McCOLL. John 62.
McCONNELL. Will: 16.
McCRAW. Samuel 72, 78, 79, (Gent. Justice -101)
  104, 105.
McKEAN. Thomas (Chief Justice of Pennsylvania
  Supreme Court -75).
McKEAND. John (Councilman-1), 4-7, 9, 10, 12,
  13, 45, 62, 65, 66, 95.
McKECHNIE. William 69.
McKIM. William 120.
McMILLAN. Alexander 76.
McMIN. John (of Philadelphia -106).
McROBERTS. Alexander (Mercht.-61), 62, (Gent.
  Justice -64), 65, 66, 72.

MACARTNEY. Robert 59.
MACGILL. Nathaniel 71, 72.
MACNAIR. Ebenezeir 19, 72, 84; Dolly 19;
  John 19; Ralph (late of Orange Co., in North
  Carolina, Attorney; Will of -19).
MACOMB. James 72, 75.
MACON. William 115.
MANN. Arthur 116; Fargus 115;
  Henry (Cabinet Maker -63); William 116.
MARKHAM. Bernard 6.
MARSHALL. Charles 47, 56; J. 72; James 56;
  John 15, (Gent. Justice -47), 56; William 117;
  W. Junr. 105.
MATTHEWS. George 6; Sampson 6.
MAUZEY. Elizabeth 27; John Simmoner 27;
  Mary (Bryan) 27; Peter 27, 90, 91.

PLEASANTS. Isaac Webster (of Goochland Co. -34), 41, 42; James Junr. 42; Jane (of Goochland Co. -41), 42; Samuel (Mercht. of Philadelphia -74), 75-77; Thomas W. 42;
PLUMMER. William S. 72.
POINDEXTER. Robert 30.
POLLARD. Robert 115.
POPE. T: 102, 110.
POWER(S). Jack (Esqr. of London, -2); Richard 116, 117.
PRICE. Barrett 44, 112, 113; Elisha 44; James 44; John W. 29, 30, 42; Lewis 44, 85, 86; William 103.
PROSSER. Thomas 55, 71, (Gent. Justice -80), 81, 117.
PRYOR. John 67, 68, 72, 73, 79, 80, 87.
PUGGETT. John 43.

QUARRIER. Alexander 72, (Coach Maker -100), 101, 102; Elizabeth 100, 101.
QUIGG. James 49.

RALEY. John 60.
RANDOLPH. Edmund (Esqr.-93), (of York Co. -94), 95; Elizabeth (of York Co. -94); Harrison 57, 58; Peyton 6.
RATLIFF. Francis 36, 87, 99.
RAWLINGS. Benjamin 44, 85, 86; Robert 7, 8, 72; Sarah 7, 8.
REID. James 19.
REILLY. John 32; Philip & Co. 9, 10.
REYNOLDS. William 72, 73, 79, 80, 83, 87, 119.
RICAUD. Francis 93.
RICHARDSON. George (Serjeant -1), 8, 13, 66, (Jeweler -112), 113; Peggy 22; William 1, 13, 22, 24, 38, 72, (Jeweler -112), 113.
ROBERTS. Alexander W. 22, 23.
ROBINSON. John (Esqr., deced.-5); John Junior 91, 97.
RONALD. Andrew 3, 6, 7, 13, 25, 72, 101, 103.
ROPER. Jesse 24, 84; John 26, 110, 111.
ROSE. Archibald 39; William 108, 109, 117.
ROSS. David & Co. 34.
ROUNTREE. Berry 4.
ROWLAND. Kitty 22; Zachariah 1.
RUSSELL. Hannah 48; John 37, 46, 48; William 69; William & Co. 36, 37, 40, 49, 50.
RUTHERFORD. Thomas 72.

SADLER. Henry (Mercht. -10), 45; Henry (Mercht. in New York -45).
SAMPSON. Stephen (Gent., of Goochland Co.-13), 14.
SATTERWHITE. Mann Junr. 88.
SAUNDERS. Stephen 115.
SCOTT. Ann 38, 39; Thomas 45, 46, 59, 69.
SEABROOKE. Nicholas B. 100.
SELDEN. Miles (Gent. Justice -89), 92; Miles Junr. 515, 71, 117; Nathaniel 29, 30, 42.
SEPNOR. Henry (of Chesterfield Co.-73), 74, 102, 105.
SHELTON. Joseph 115.
SHERER/SCHERER. Hannah 3, 4, 54; Nicolas 38; Samuel (Councilman -1), 3, 4, 8, 11, 12, 54, 55.
SHERMER. William (of England) 51-53.
SHORE. John (Doctor -115).
SIMS. John 62.
SINCLAIR. Alexander (of Town of Staunton, Mercht. -7, 8).
SINGLETON. Anthony 88, 89; Lucy 88, 89.
SKIPWITH. Abraham (Freed Negro -105); Fulwar 43, 51; Sir Peyton 60.
SMITH/SMYTH. John 18; Margaret (of Chesterfield Co. -73), 74; Richard 101.
SOUTHALL. James 36, 74; Turner (Coll: -35), (Gent. Justice -88).
SOUTHGATE. Wright 118.
SOWELL. Thomas 58, 59, 109.
SPENCE. Andrew 75.
ST. CLAIR. Arthur 114.
STEVENSHON/STEPHENSON. A: 90; C.W. 105.
STEWART. Arthur 102, 103; John 2, (Vendue Master -11), 22, 23, 26, 28; Sally 22.
STILL. Bartlett 49, 107; Bassett 30.
STOCKDELL/STOCKDALE. Elizabeth 66, 67, 80, 81; John 35-37, 42, 43, 61, 63, 66, 67, 73, 74, 80, 81, 99, 118-120; Long House of 83; Simon M. 67.
STONE. John 57.
STORRS. Gervas 46; Joshua (deced.-48); Susanna (Widow -48), 49.
STOVALL. Littleberry 49.
STREET. John 105, 115.
STREETS: Cary 43, 83, 120; Market Alley 99.
STROBIA/STRUBEA. John 54, 55.
SYDNOR. Fortunatus 88.

Heritage Books by Ruth and Sam Sparacio:

Abstracts of Account Books of Edward Dixon, Merchant of Port Royal, Virginia, Volume I: 1743–1747

Abstracts of Account Books of Edward Dixon, Merchant of Port Royal, Virginia, Volume II

Albemarle County, Virginia Deed and Will Book Abstracts, 1748–1752

Albemarle County, Virginia Deed Book Abstracts, 1758–1761

Albemarle County, Virginia Deed Book Abstracts, 1761–1764

Albemarle County, Virginia Deed Book Abstracts, 1764–1768

Albemarle County, Virginia Deed Book Abstracts, 1768–1770

Albemarle County, Virginia Deed Book Abstracts, 1771–1772

Albemarle County, Virginia Deed Book Abstracts, 1772–1776

Albemarle County, Virginia Deed Book Abstracts, 1776–1778

Albemarle County, Virginia Deed Book Abstracts, 1778–1780

Albemarle County, Virginia Deed Book Abstracts, 1780–1783

Albemarle County, Virginia Deed Book Abstracts, 1783–1785

Albemarle County, Virginia Deed Book Abstracts, 1785–1787

Albemarle County, Virginia Deed Book Abstracts, 1787–1790

Albemarle County, Virginia Deed Book Abstracts, 1790–1791

Albemarle County, Virginia Deed Book Abstracts, 1791–1793

Albemarle County, Virginia Deed Book Abstracts, 1793–1794

Albemarle County, Virginia Deed Book Abstracts, 1794–1795

Albemarle County, Virginia Deed Book Abstracts, 1795–1796

Albemarle County, Virginia Deed Book Abstracts, 1796–1797

Albemarle County, Virginia Will Book Abstracts: 1752–1756 and 1775–1783

Albemarle County, Virginia Will Book: 2, 1752–1764

Albemarle County, Virginia Wills, 1764–1775

Albemarle County, Virginia Will Book: 3, 1785–1798

Augusta County, Virginia Land Tax Books, 1782–1788

Augusta County, Virginia Land Tax Books, 1788–1790

Amherst County, Virginia Land Tax Books, 1789–1791

Caroline County, Virginia Appeals and Land Causes, 1787–1794

Caroline County, Virginia Appeals and Land Causes, 1795–1800

Caroline County, Virginia Committee of Safety and Early Surveys, 1729–1762 and 1774–1775

Caroline County, Virginia Guardian Bonds 1806–1821

Caroline County, Virginia Land Tax Book Alterations, 1782–1789

Caroline County, Virginia Land Tax Book Alterations, 1789–1792

Caroline County, Virginia Land Tax Book Alterations, 1792–1795

Caroline County, Virginia Land Tax Book Alterations, 1795–1798

Caroline County, Virginia Order Book Abstracts, 1765

Caroline County, Virginia Order Book Abstracts, 1767–1768

Caroline County, Virginia Order Book Abstracts, 1768–1770

Caroline County, Virginia Order Book Abstracts, 1770–1771

Caroline County, Virginia Order Book, 1764

Caroline County, Virginia Order Book, 1765–1767

Caroline County, Virginia Order Book, 1771–1772

Caroline County, Virginia Order Book, 1772–1773

Caroline County, Virginia Order Book, 1773

Caroline County, Virginia Order Book, 1773–1774

Caroline County, Virginia Order Book, 1774–1778

Caroline County, Virginia Order Book, 1778–1781

Caroline County, Virginia Order Book, 1781–1783

Caroline County, Virginia Order Book, 1783–1784

Caroline County, Virginia Order Book, 1784–1785

Caroline County, Virginia Order Book, 1785–1786

Caroline County, Virginia Order Book, 1786–1787

Caroline County, Virginia Order Book, 1787, Part 1

Caroline County, Virginia Order Book, 1787, Part 2

Caroline County, Virginia Order Book, 1787–1788

Caroline County, Virginia Order Book, 1788

Culpeper County, Virginia Deed Book Abstracts, 1769–1773

Culpeper County, Virginia Deed Book Abstracts, 1778–1779

Culpeper County, Virginia Deed Book Abstracts, 1781–1783

Culpeper County, Virginia Deed Book Abstracts, 1785–1786

Culpeper County, Virginia Deed Book Abstracts, 1788–1789

Culpeper County, Virginia Deed Book Abstracts, 1791–1792

Culpeper County, Virginia Deed Book Abstracts, 1795–1796

Culpeper County, Virginia Land Tax Book, 1782–1786

Culpeper County, Virginia Land Tax Book, 1787–1789

Culpeper County, Virginia Minute Book, 1763–1764

Digest of Family Relationships, 1650–1692, from Virginia County Court Records

Digest of Family Relationships, 1720–1750, from Virginia County Court Records

Digest of Family Relationships, 1750–1763, from Virginia County Court Records

Digest of Family Relationships, 1764–1775, from Virginia County Court Records

Essex County, Virginia Deed and Will Abstracts, 1695–1697

Essex County, Virginia Deed and Will Abstracts, 1697–1699

Essex County, Virginia Deed and Will Abstracts, 1699–1701

Essex County, Virginia Deed and Will Abstracts, 1701–1703

Essex County, Virginia Deed and Will Abstracts, 1745–1749

Essex County, Virginia Deed and Will Book, 1692–1693

Essex County, Virginia Deed and Will Book, 1693–1694

Essex County, Virginia Deed and Will Book, 1694–1695

Essex County, Virginia Deed and Will Book, 1695–1697

Essex County, Virginia Deed and Will Book, 1697–1699

Essex County, Virginia Deed and Will Book, 1701–1704

Essex County, Virginia Deed and Will Book, 1745–1749

Essex County, Virginia Deed, 1753–1754 and Will Book 1750

Essex County, Virginia Deed Abstracts, 1721–1724

Essex County, Virginia Deed Book, 1724–1728

Essex County, Virginia Deed Book, 1728–1733

Essex County, Virginia Deed Book, 1733–1738

Essex County, Virginia Deed Book, 1738–1742

Essex County, Virginia Deed Book, 1742–1745

Essex County, Virginia Deed Book, 1749–1751

Essex County, Virginia Deed Book, 1751–1753

Essex County, Virginia Land Trials Abstracts, 1711–1716 and 1715–1741

Essex County, Virginia Order Book Abstracts, 1695–1699

Prince William County, Virginia Deed Book Abstracts, 1791–1794

Prince William County, Virginia Deed Book Abstracts, 1794–1796

Prince William County, Virginia Deed Book Abstracts, 1796–1798

Prince William County, Virginia Deed Book Abstracts, 1798–1799

Prince William County, Virginia District Court Orders, 1793 (Part 1)

Prince William County, Virginia Land Causes Abstracts, 1789–1790

Prince William County, Virginia Land Causes Abstracts, 1790–1793

Prince William County, Virginia Order Book Abstracts, 1752–1753

Prince William County, Virginia Order Book Abstracts, 1753–1757

Prince William County, Virginia Order Book 1762

Prince William County, Virginia Order Book, 1762–1763

Prince William County, Virginia District Court Orders, 1793 (Part 2)

(Old) Rappahannock County, Virginia Deed Book Abstracts, 1682–1686

(Old) Rappahannock County, Virginia Deed and Will Book Abstracts:
  1656–1662   1662–1665   1663–1668   1665–1677
  1668–1670   1670–1672   1672–1673/4   1673/4–1676
  1677–1678/9   1678/9–1682   1682–1686   1686–1688
  1688–1692

(Old) Rappahannock County, Virginia Order Book Abstracts, 1683–1685

(Old) Rappahannock County, Virginia Order Book Abstracts, 1685–1687

(Old) Rappahannock County, Virginia Order Book Abstracts, 1687–1689

(Old) Rappahannock County, Virginia Order Book Abstracts, 1689–1692

(Old) Rappahannock County, Virginia Will Book Abstracts, 1682–1687

Richmond City, Virginia Hustings Deed Book, 1782–1790

Richmond City, Virginia Hustings Deed Book, 1790–1794

Richmond County, Virginia Account Book Abstracts, 1724–1751

Richmond County, Virginia Account Book Abstracts, 1751–1783

Richmond County, Virginia Deed Book Abstracts, 1692–1695

Richmond County, Virginia Deed Book Abstracts, 1695–1701

Richmond County, Virginia Deed Book Abstracts, 1701–1704

Richmond County, Virginia Deed Book Abstracts, 1705–1708

Richmond County, Virginia Deed Book Abstracts, 1708–1711

Richmond County, Virginia Deed Book Abstracts, 1711–1714

Richmond County, Virginia Deed Book Abstracts, 1715–1718

Richmond County, Virginia Deed Book Abstracts, 1718–1719

Richmond County, Virginia Deed Book Abstracts, 1719–1721

Richmond County, Virginia Deed Book Abstracts, 1721–1725

Richmond County, Virginia Order Book Abstracts, 1692–1694

Richmond County, Virginia Order Book Abstracts, 1694–1697

Richmond County, Virginia Order Book Abstracts, 1697–1699

Richmond County, Virginia Order Book Abstracts, 1699–1701

Richmond County, Virginia Order Book Abstracts, 1702–1704

Richmond County, Virginia Order Book Abstracts, 1704–1705

Richmond County, Virginia Order Book Abstracts, 1705–1706

Richmond County, Virginia Order Book Abstracts, 1707–1708

Richmond County, Virginia Order Book Abstracts, 1708–1709

Richmond County, Virginia Order Book Abstracts, 1709–1710

Richmond County, Virginia Order Book Abstracts, 1710–1711

Richmond County, Virginia Order Book Abstracts, 1711–1713

Richmond County, Virginia Order Book Abstracts, 1714–1715

Richmond County, Virginia Order Book Abstracts, 1715–1716

Richmond County, Virginia Order Book Abstracts, 1716–1717

Richmond County, Virginia Order Book Abstracts, 1717–1718

Richmond County, Virginia Order Book Abstracts, 1718–1719

Richmond County, Virginia Order Book Abstracts, 1719–1721

Richmond County, Virginia Order Book Abstracts, 1721–1725

Richmond County, Virginia Order Book Abstracts, 1737–1738

Richmond County, Virginia Order Book Abstracts, 1738–1740

Spotsylvania County, Virginia Deed Book, 1722–1725

Spotsylvania County, Virginia Deed Book, 1725–1728

Spotsylvania County, Virginia Deed Book, 1728–1729

Spotsylvania County, Virginia Deed Book, 1729–1730

Spotsylvania County, Virginia Deed Book: 1730–1731

Spotsylvania County, Virginia Order Book Abstracts:
  1724–1730 (Part II) and *1724–1730 Part III)*

Spotsylvania County, Virginia Order Book Abstracts, 1730–1732

Spotsylvania County, Virginia Order Book Abstracts, 1732–1734

Spotsylvania County, Virginia Order Book Abstracts, 1734–1735

Spotsylvania County, Virginia Order Book Abstracts, 1742–1744

Spotsylvania County, Virginia Order Book Abstracts, 1744–1746

Spotsylvania County, Virginia Order Book Abstracts, 1749–1751

Stafford County, Virginia Deed and Will Book, 1686–1689

Stafford County, Virginia Deed and Will Book, 1689–1693

Stafford County, Virginia Deed and Will Book, 1699–1709

Stafford County, Virginia Deed and Will Book, 1780–1786, and Scheme Book Orders, 1790–1793

Stafford County, Virginia Deed and Will Abstracts, 1810–1813

Stafford County, Virginia Deed and Will Abstracts, 1825–1826

Stafford County, Virginia Deed and Will Book Abstracts, 1785–1786 and 1809–1810

Stafford County, Virginia Deed Book, 1722–1728 and 1755–1765

Stafford County, Virginia Land Tax Books, 1782–1792

Stafford County, Virginia Order Book, 1664–1668 and 1689–1690

Stafford County, Virginia Order Book, 1691–1692

Stafford County, Virginia Order Book, 1692–1693

Stafford County, Virginia Will Book, 1729–1748

Stafford County, Virginia Will Book, 1748–1767

Westmoreland County, Virginia Deed and Will Abstracts, 1723–1726

Westmoreland County, Virginia Deed and Will Abstracts, 1726–1729

Westmoreland County, Virginia Deed and Will Abstracts, 1729–1732

Westmoreland County, Virginia Deed and Will Abstracts, 1732–1734

Westmoreland County, Virginia Deed and Will Abstracts, 1734–1736

Westmoreland County, Virginia Deed and Will Abstracts, 1736–1740

Westmoreland County, Virginia Deed and Will Abstracts, 1740–1742

Westmoreland County, Virginia Deed and Will Abstracts, 1742–1745

Westmoreland County, Virginia Deed and Will Abstracts, 1745–1747

Westmoreland County, Virginia Deed and Will Abstracts, 1747–1748

Westmoreland County, Virginia Deed and Will Abstracts, 1749–1751

Westmoreland County, Virginia Deed and Will Abstracts, 1751–1754

Westmoreland County, Virginia Deed and Will Abstracts, 1754–1756

Westmoreland County, Virginia Order Book, 1705–1707

Westmoreland County, Virginia Order Book, 1707–1709

Westmoreland County, Virginia Order Book, 1709–1712

Westmoreland County, Virginia Order Book, 1712–1714

Westmoreland County, Virginia Order Book, 1714–1716

Westmoreland County, Virginia Order Book, 1716–1718

Westmoreland County, Virginia Order Book, 1718–1721